Working with Female Offenders

Working with Female Offenders

A Gender-Sensitive Approach

KATHERINE VAN WORMER

WILEY

John Wiley & Sons, Inc.

Copyright © 2010 by John Wiley & Sons, Inc. All rights reserved.

Published by John Wiley & Sons, Inc., Hoboken, New Jersey.

Published simultaneously in Canada.

Library of Congress Cataloging-in-Publication Data:
Van Wormer, Katherine S.
   Working with female offenders : a gender-sensitive approach / Katherine van Wormer.
      p.   cm.
   Includes bibliographical references and index.
   ISBN 978-0-470-58153-7 (pbk. : acid-free paper)
   1. Women prisoners—United States.   2. Women prisoners—Counseling of—
United States.   3. Female offenders—United States.   I. Title.
   HV8738.V38   2010
   365'.660820973—dc22

                                                                                    2009038774

Printed in the United States of America

10 9 8 7 6 5 4 3 2 1

CONTENTS

PREFACE

In the summer of 1974 I was given free rein at Alabama's Julia Tutwiler Prison for Women to do research for my dissertation on gender role behavior within a unisexual environment. My primary aim was to study intimacy among women, the prison families they form, and masculine roles that some of the inmates adopt. My hidden agenda, though, unknown to the administrators or my dissertation committee, was to work toward prison reform. If conditions were sufficiently bad, my plan was to seize the opportunity to later make those conditions public.

I achieved the first goal at the Julia Tutwiler Prison—I learned about the close-knit relationships and gender role behavior in an all-female environment, but there was no need to pursue the second. The physical environment left much to be desired: 30 women were crammed into each cell and forced to endure the Alabama heat without much ventilation or air conditioning. Yet the social environment was, for the most part, as good as could be expected. The people who worked there, except the one male officer, were kind and attentive to the women's needs. The warden was innovative and nurturing toward her charges. The stories I heard from staff and inmates during those hot summer afternoons behind bars were alternately harrowing and moving; the most memorable were downright funny. The theme of the humor was getting one over on the authorities or some of the sexual antics taking place. But beyond the humor loomed the personal tragedies borne of poverty and abuse that had brought so many of the women to this wretched place. In the end, my dissertation was just another dull quantitative thesis. But the memory of my sojourn with the women of Julia Tutwiler Prison has stayed with me forever.

At the time of my prison research, some of the women who did well were being transferred into community residential centers. And progressive programs, such as university courses for credit, were offered to staff and inmates in the evening. Many of us—prison reformers and correctional staff—thought without voicing it that prison reform was right around the corner. Who among us then would have had even an inkling that in the next quarter century or so, after years of "zero tolerance" for drug use and crime, that conditions at

Julia Tutwiler (as elsewhere) would grow infinitely worse? Who would have believed that the population in the same old facility would triple in size? Or that a death row would be built there? Or that men would fill most of the staff positions? Who would have believed life sentences being handed down for conspiracy to sell drugs? Who would have thought that over 30 years later I would be writing the book that I did not feel I needed to write then?

That experience is only one incentive for writing this book. The other concerns a gap in the literature on innovative programming for female offenders. The material on correctional counseling is vast but not widely dispersed, while the material on correctional counseling with females is seriously limited. There is a need to synthesize and organize what is known about gender-specific programming from journal articles and workshops so that it is available in a readable form in one source. I experienced this need first as an instructor of criminal justice preparing students to enter the field of corrections and more recently as I taught counseling skills as a professor of social work. Now I have a chance to write the book to fill a gap in the literatures of both counseling and criminal justice.

From a gender-sensitive, feminist perspective, this book explores the special needs of girls and women within a system designed by men for male offenders. This book is timely in light of promising developments that are taking place at every level of the criminal justice system, the trend toward meaningful treatment and away from mandatory prison terms for drug offenders (see Greene and Pranis, 2006).

ORGANIZING FRAMEWORK AND RATIONALE

This volume is organized around this question: How can the criminal justice system be reshaped and reconceptualized to address the needs of offenders who are often themselves victims of abuse (early childhood and otherwise)? The focus of this book is on girls and women. In the belief that interventions that benefit women (e.g., parenting training and stress management) can also benefit men, I urge others to pursue the task of adapting the motivational techniques and restorative strategies presented in this book to the often-overlooked needs of boys and men who have gotten into trouble with the law.

An underlying assumption of this book is that the current male-oriented processes and predominant criminal thinking/behavioral therapies are flawed in themselves and not appropriate to the populations on which they are used. A related assumption with which few would disagree is that today's heavy reliance on incarceration takes a toll on the family and community and does little to promote rehabilitation. Relevant to female offenders, an alternative approach is needed, one that corresponds to what we know about female growth and development and about the mental and substance use disorders so prevalent among members of this population.

This book is geared not for professional counselors alone but also for persons who work or plan to work in some capacity—as correctional officers, counselors, lawyers—with female offenders and who desire to learn about evidence-based, gentler approaches for work with girls and women in trouble with the law. Probation officers, who increasingly are expected to engage in case management, should find the treatment guidelines of some use as well. *Working with Female Offenders* thus can serve as a professional handbook, as a textbook, or as supplemental reading in a variety of college courses related to corrections and to women's issues. Criminal justice students can benefit by learning the hands-on skills—anger management, motivational interviewing, conflict resolution, listening skills, for example—and social work students can benefit from a familiarity with the setting and preparation for work with involuntary clients.

Working with Female Offenders has as its major purpose to offer a gender-based framework that incorporates elements of motivational enhancement from psychology, a strengths perspective from social work, and restorative justice from criminal justice, a framework that can be tailored to the study of women involved at various levels of the criminal justice system. These concepts are rapidly gaining momentum within the criminal justice circles (especially in probation and other community corrections work), but they are not articulated in an integrated fashion for a wider criminal justice audience. This book aims to fill the gap in the literature of both the helping professions and criminal justice. Although counseling and social work provide the direct skills and knowledge, criminal justice provides the field, the milieu, within which these methods are to be applied. To help prepare people for work in the field of corrections, chapters are devoted to the nature of female crime and to the institutional settings in which much of the female-specific programming is designed to take place.

Despite the fact that most people who seek counseling are female, there are practically no comprehensive guidebooks available to help mental health practitioners understand the unique physical, emotional, and sociocultural issues affecting women. This book joins the very few recent books in existence on counseling techniques designed especially for women, such as Kopala and Keitel's (2003) *Handbook of Counseling Women* and Sanville's (2003) *Therapies with Women in Transition*. If books on gender-specific therapy and treatment are rare, manuals on counseling female offenders are rarer still. *Counseling Women in Prison* by Jocelyn Pollock (1998) and *Assessment and Treatment of Women Offenders* by Kelley Blanchette and Shelley Brown (2003) are notable exceptions and welcome additions to the literature. A major contribution to the literature is the publication offered by the National Institute of Corrections developed by Bloom, Owen, and Covington (2003), which describes the background characteristics of women offenders, presents the rationale for gender-responsive treatment, and offers specific guidelines for using gender-responsive strategies.

According to a recent report from the National Institute of Justice, today's criminal justice workers are expected to do much more than client referral; they are expected to utilize case management techniques to help their clients get integrated into the community (law-abiding community). Criminal justice practitioners and students, therefore, can benefit by gaining familiarity with basic counseling skills, such as anger management, conflict resolution, and listening skills, and practitioners trained in counseling and social work can benefit from gaining familiarity with the setting and preparation for work with involuntary clients.

A second major objective of this book is to critically examine relevant correctional policies and practices, including the treatment of girls in the juvenile justice system and the different treatment modalities that are being used today, the relevance of restorative justice to female crime victims, and the treatment of women in prison in the context of human rights issues.

A CAUTIOUS OPTIMISM

I write this book in a spirit of guarded optimism. My optimism stems largely from the conscious realization of the obvious: The pendulum has swung so far in one direction—to the punitive right—that there is no other way for it to go but downward toward the other side. Alternative interventions such as drug courts for first-time drug offenders are cropping up everywhere, bolstered by federal and state funding. At the same time, there is a new impetus toward treatment, especially for persons placed on probation. For parolees, there is considerable funding for reentry into society. In Iowa, for example, the numbers of persons under correctional supervision have risen far faster than the capacity to contain them. Offender substance abuse treatment is in big demand. Meanwhile, the victims' assistance movement continues to gain strength and momentum across the country, creating more opportunities for practitioners to work with victims and their families. Recent initiatives are taking place to promote healing of victims and their families through victim-offender conferencing.

FEATURES OF THE BOOK

Based on the knowledge provided in this book, readers should acquire an understanding of the dynamics of female gang delinquency and adult violent and nonviolent criminality, a global perspective on crime and punishment and treatment innovations, and an understanding of the pathways to crime across the life course. From a practice standpoint, readers of this volume will become familiar with innovative programs from across the United States, Canada, and Britain, such as those designed for new mothers and their infants in prison and effective gender-based programs for girls in detention.

This book offers these features:

- A detailed rationale for the use of a gender-sensitive framework for counseling female offenders on matters specific to their gender, such as sexual trauma and battering
- Practical guidelines for case management interventions, teaching skills of communication, assertiveness, and anger and stress management for female offender populations
- A focus on the pathway to addiction problems among girls and treatment to help them reduce the harm to themselves and others
- Illustrations from firsthand narratives by women who have been there
- Attention to international human rights issues and inclusion of documentation from international organizations such as Human Rights Watch
- Boxed readings on such topics as mothers who have killed their children, prison homosexuality, drug smuggling, and AIDS in prison
- Up-to-date statistics on criminal activity and imprisonment from such sources as the Bureau of Justice Statistics and Statistics Canada

Unique to this book compared to others in the field is:

- The inclusion of a chapter on the theoretical foundation for a gender-specific approach
- A biopsychosocial approach to female crime and delinquency
- Linking the antifeminist backlash in society to punishment of women in trouble with the law
- Inclusion of the latest scientific information on biological factors (e.g., brain research) in criminal behavior
- A critique of the criminal thinking/behavioral model that is widely used in criminal justice and substance abuse treatment circles in comparison with a gendered, strengths-based approach
- Outlining the techniques of motivational enhancement for female offenders

Because there is much we can learn from other countries, we explore innovative victim/offender programs in Canada, New Zealand, Britain, as well as the United States; become familiar with victim/assistance programs; survey the techniques of the strengths/empowerment approach for work with women clients in many capacities; and study the rudiments of substance abuse counseling for helping female offenders with addictions problems. Statistical documentation is provided whenever possible concerning the nature of female crime and victimization and the effectiveness of programs geared toward offender/victim populations.

ORGANIZATION OF THE BOOK

Working with Female Offenders is divided into four sections of one to four chapters each.

The journey we will be taking in the book follows Carol Gilligan's scheme for personal growth and development; the progression is from pathways to delinquency and crime, to work on issues of relationship and self-concept, to the healing that is integral to restorative justice strategies.

After an overview, Part I focuses on the principles of gender-sensitive counseling. Chapter 1 makes the case for gendered female offender treatment. Informed by the theoretical framework of Gilligan's relational theory, the chapter makes the case for a gender-specific approach for meeting the needs of female offenders. Arguments for a gender-specific approach are based on biological and developmental research that pinpoints male-female differences. The second part of the chapter introduces relevant concepts that will serve to guide the remaining chapters of the book.

Part II has as its major concern pathways to crime for juvenile and adult female offenders. Chapters 2 and 3 are concerned with the nature of girls' offending and women's involvement in crime. The pathways to crime (e.g., via addiction, criminal connections often through their partner) are described, as are gender-sensitive programs for girls, including restorative justice innovations.

Part III takes us into the parameters of the women's prison with attention to challenges of working in a total institutional setting. In order to provide empirical documentation of the unique needs of women inmates, I conducted a mail survey of 82 federal and state prison facilities in the United States that incarcerate women. The results are presented in Chapter 4. Other topics discussed in this chapter are boundary issues between staff and inmate, mental health care needs, and inmate-to-inmate relationships. Human rights standards are discussed in terms of professional treatment and pitfalls.

The two chapters of Part IV are devoted to specific skills for empowerment and addiction counseling. Chapter 6 develops a five-stage gender-sensitive empowerment model to address the needs of women on probation, parole, and in detention. The focus is on establishing a working relationship with involuntary clients, developing a language of strengths, and enhancing motivation for treatment. Chapter 7 concludes the book with a detailed discussion of feeling work with an emphasis on recovery from past victimization and trauma. That there is no clear dichotomy between victim and offender is a major underlying assumption of this chapter and this book. Over half of the women in prison are victims of early childhood sexual and/or physical abuse. The link to crime might have come via substance abuse or self-destructive relationships with abusive criminal men. Healing is a major theme. Because of the incredibly heavy occurrence of substance abuse in female involvement in crime and victimization, addictions treatment content is integrated throughout the text. Counseling approaches directed toward helping victims reclaim their lives as survivors are provided. My knowledge and special interest in the healing powers of restorative justice strategies inform these two treatment chapters as well as discussions of work with juvenile offenders. *Working with Female Offenders* offers these features:

- Presentation of a strengths/empowerment/restorative framework for counseling women in crisis
- Attention to the impact of the feminist movement and antifeminist backlash with regard to legal issues of special relevance to women as women
- Delineation of the basic precepts of restorative justice for holding offenders directly accountable to their victims
- The offering of practical guidelines for teaching skills of anger management, communication, and stress management from a gender-specific perspective
- The sharing of narratives from personal interviews with female offenders and correctional counselors
- Documentation of the claim that the war on drugs is a war on women of color
- Special attention to such controversial topics as prison homosexuality, AIDS in prison, girls in the gang, and women on death row
- Up-to-date statistics on crime and punishment from government resources such as the Bureau of Justice Statistics, the Office of Juvenile Justice and Delinquency Prevention, and Statistics Canada
- Infusion of content on strengths-based, motivational enhancement, and attention to evidence-based research on treatment intervention protocols

Central to *Working with Female Offenders* is the argument that on both the policy and practice levels, the time is ripe for change, for a radical restructuring of our court and correctional systems, for a focus more on accountability of the offender to the community and victim, and for a deemphasis on punishment and revenge in favor of helping people turn their lives around. The need for restructuring is evidenced in high recidivism rates within the system that are perhaps related to the denial of the salience of gender roles, power imbalances, and other social constructs that are at the root of many problems affecting women's criminal behavior. Women face unique challenges and have needs that call for counseling strategies tailored to fit gender-specific challenges. With regard to gender-sensitive treatment, we should never underestimate the power of an approach based on strengths and possibility rather than on the probability of failure. A philosophy based on hope and optimism may not change all or even most people. But, in the final analysis, it is the only thing that will effect change. The belief that people can and do change is a guiding theme of this work. The challenge to embark on such a change effort is a big one.

So let us begin ...

ACKNOWLEDGMENTS

I want to extend appreciation to the women in prison and administrators of correctional institutions who contributed personal statements and narratives for this book. Special gratitude is owed to Rachel Livsey, Senior Editor for social work and counseling, for believing in this project from the start and who guided it through fruition. I also want to recognize the contributions of my MSW graduate assistants, Renée Barbu, who provided not only clerical assistance but also took the initiative to obtain personal comments and interviews from across the correctional system, and Margaret Martinez, whose help in the final stage of the proofreading was invaluable. The University of Northern Iowa deserves thanks for providing me with a Graduate College Summer Grant that helped provide a block of time for the pursuit of this project.

ABOUT THE AUTHOR

Katherine Stuart van Wormer is a native of New Orleans. She was active in two civil rights movements: one in Chapel Hill, North Carolina, and the other in Belfast, Northern Ireland. After teaching English for three years in Northern Ireland, van Wormer got a PhD in sociology from the University of Georgia; her dissertation was on the gender role behavior at the women's prison in Alabama. In 1983, van Wormer returned to graduate school to get an MSSW from the University of Tennessee-Nashville. Van Wormer worked as a substance abuse counselor in Washington State and Norway for four years. The author of 14 books, van Wormer most recently has authored or coauthored *Woman and the Criminal Justice System* (Allyn & Bacon); *Death by Domestic Violence: Preventing the Murders and the Murder-Suicides* (Praeger); *Human Behavior and the Social Environment, Micro Level* and *Macro Level* (two-volume set, Oxford University Press); *Addiction Treatment: A Strengths Perspective* (Cengage); and *Restorative Justice Across the East and the West* (Casa Verde), all published from 2007 to 2009. Katherine van Wormer has taught extensively in academic departments of sociology, criminal justice, and social work. The framework adapted for the current book is at the intersection of these three fields.

Part I

GENDER-SENSITIVE VERSUS GENDER-NEUTRAL

Chapter 1

A GENDERED APPROACH

In emphasizing voice, I have tried to work against the dangers I see in the current tendency to reduce psychology to biology or to culture, to see people as either genetically determined or socially engineered and thus without the capacity for voice or resistance.

— **Carol Gilligan** (2009, January)

Women comprise a minority of those in the criminal justice system, just 6.9% of the prison population and 12.9% of the jail population (West & Sabol, 2009). Women make up 23% of persons on probation, and 12% of those on parole (Bureau of Justice Statistics, 2009b). Their rate of increase has been about twice that of the increase of males in confinement. Nevertheless, women are still a small minority of the total incarcerated population, and they are receiving treatment in a system run by men and designed for men.

According to government statistics, girls were 15% of juvenile offenders in residential placement (Snyder and Sickmund, 2006). Females in detention make up 14% of those who were charged with delinquent offenses and 40% of those in placement for status offenses (e.g., running away). Probably due to changes in law enforcement patterns in making arrests for domestic violence situations (as explained in the report), the female arrest rate has increased since 1994 while the male rate has declined.

Although gender-specific programming is coming into its own within juvenile institutions, at the adult level, traditional approaches abound. Within the adult corrections, a focus on equality that is equated with sameness lingers— this misunderstanding of the true spirit of equality often results in identical treatment models for men and women. We might do better to speak of equity or fairness rather than equality in the treatment accorded to diverse populations. An emphasis on equity rather than equality would entail a consideration of differences. From an equity principle, when people are in like circumstances, they should be treated alike, but when their circumstances are different, then equity and fairness may require differential treatment. This is what we learn from Rawls (1971), author of the definitive document on justice.

The reason that a gendered approach is crucial to the treatment of females within the criminal justice system is because girls are different from boys — physiologically, psychologically, and socially, and in more or less the same way, women are different from men.

In her argument for juvenile reform, Francine T. Sherman (2005) summarizes male-female differences:

> Adolescent girls who are in the justice system differ from boys developmentally in their focus on relationships; their internalized responses to trauma in the form of depression, self-mutilation, and substance use; and their externalized responses to trauma in the form of aggression. In addition, the pathways girls take into the justice system differ from those of their male counterparts in the prevalence and type of trauma, family loss, and separation they experience....
>
> Girls are more likely than boys to be detained for minor offenses and technical violations and are more likely than boys to be returned to detention for technical violations. Running away and domestic violence, both common in the lives of girls, tend to result in their detention and system involvement. All of these differences demand particular attention in criminal justice reform. (p. 16)

The fact that female offenders are seen as less of a security risk than male offenders opens the door to the possibility of a more flexible approach, one that is even community rather than institutional centered. Consider the next contrasting vignettes from the popular press. The first shows the personal dimension of our one-size-fits-all sentencing structure. The second confirms the value of suiting the punishment to the individual.

CONTRASTING CASE HISTORIES

One of the real-life stories told by organizers at the third annual Mothers in Prison, Children in Crisis rally was that of Sally Smith (Wirpsa, 1998). The rally was part of a national campaign advocating alternative programs for women convicted of drug-related violations. Among the facts presented were these: Women are the fastest-growing population in prisons and jails; the majority had been sentenced for nonviolent crimes; and two-thirds of female inmates are mothers of dependent children. One such woman, caught up in the current draconian anti-drug laws is Sally Smith.

Sally had lived every moment in absolute terror of her husband. Sometimes she was beaten with a baseball bat and furniture and hospitalized; other times she was locked in a closet until her visible wounds healed. Her abuser was a drug dealer. When caught, he was able to reduce his sentence by implicating his wife as a conspirator. This is how Sally Smith came to be sentenced to life without parole under Michigan's mandatory minimum sentencing laws (Families Against Mandatory Minimums, 1997). This is not an isolated case, as any visit to a women's prison will confirm.

Sherri Lechner's story, highlighted in *Ozarks Magazine* by Ross (2006) is more uplifting, and typical of cases that are referred to a drug court. Drug court is a fairly recent development that provides close supervision and intensive treatment in lieu of imprisonment. A native of the Ozarks, Sherri had the miserable childhood typical of most addicts. Neglected for the most part by her father, Sherri was taken by him to live in Texas because her mother was going to prison there on a drug charge. In the six years she spent in Texas, she was molested multiple times by a relative and a family friend and was introduced to alcohol, cocaine, and methamphetamines at about age 10, also by a family member.

After failing the eighth grade, Sherri returned to Springfield, Missouri, where she lived with her brother, Mike, in a neighborhood known for drug activity, called "the Holler" on the west side of town. Her mother came and went, often "on the run."

Within a year, at age 15, Sherri became pregnant. She did not use during her pregnancy. After the birth of her daughter, her drug use escalated from smoking meth crystals to daily intravenous use. She sent her child to live with a friend because, she said, her drug life and relationship with a man were more important.

In trouble for drug possession and related crimes, Sherri prayed to become pregnant again so she could get off drugs. Her prayers were answered. Then to avoid going to prison, she agreed to go through Judge Calvin Holden's drug court. It took two and a half years, but she finally graduated from the rigorous program in 2002. Sherri occasionally tells her story at graduation for the drug court class. She now works as a substance abuse technician at the same treatment center where she had once been a patient. She is working toward her

GED. She married her boyfriend after he was released from prison, where he earned his GED and read the Bible. He works as a truck mechanic and began classes at Ozark Technical Community College last fall, working toward a degree in social work.

In the stories of these two women, one can find the interconnection between social policy and women's victimization, in the first instance, and between social policy and women's salvation, in the second. These examples, moreover, provide a stark contrast between progressive and standard sentencing practices, a contrast that relates to differing correctional philosophies. Sherri was given her life back including career planning and she did not lose custody of her children; Sally, however, became one of the many hidden victims of the nation's crackdown on drug use. Nor was she helped by falling in the clutches of the gender-neutral laws that prescribe equality of punishment for women linked with male criminals, the circumstances notwithstanding.

Another theme that transcends these vignettes is the fact that when mothers are sent away to prison, the stage is set for a pattern of shame and victimization that often passes through the generations. But if preventive measures are taken, as happened in Sherri's case, this pattern can be arrested. A second theme that emerges here is the role of a drug-using boyfriend in a woman's life, setting in motion a downward spiral into lawbreaking and punishment.

In this book, we examine such programs with a focus on their implications for female victims of crime and the offenders. The task of this chapter is to make a convincing case for specialized programming for girls and women who are in the correctional system. The subject of this chapter is therefore gender, with a focus on the female. Our starting point is an overview of research on the biology of gender and gender differences relevant to female offending. A consideration of right-brain/left-brain differences that relate to gender also is provided. We also explore how these differences are played out in behavior, both in the classroom and in pathways to crime.

We examine also the basic principles on which the programming is based, principles that go under the rubric of restorative justice. This chapter discusses the concepts that underlie this form of justice and build on them to formulate a paradigm that links progressive thinking in social work, the strengths approach, to its counterpart in criminal justice, the restorative justice model.

BIOLOGICAL FACTORS

A biological approach accepts that there are fundamental differences between male and female and that these differences interact with cultural norms to influence differences in male/female criminality. Traditional and liberal (as opposed to radical) feminists who stress gender equality tend to disparage biological research, as Pollock (1999) suggests, because the theories hark back to the days when women were told they must fill their natural role as "mother of the species" and work in the home. The focus on sex differences in brain function, and especially such books that lack empirical rigor, such as *The Female Brain* by Louann Brizendine (2007), have been widely criticized by other scientists. In a recent *Newsweek* article highlighting Brizendine's book, neuropsychiatrist Nancy Andreasen asserts that nurture plays such a huge role in human behavior that focusing on biology is next to meaningless. "Whatever measurable differences exist in the brain," says Andreasen, "are used to oppress and suppress women" (2006, p. 46). Belknap (2007) agrees: "Central to the patriarchal ideology," she suggests, "is the belief that women's nature is biologically, not culturally determined" (p. 10). Historically, the focus on biological differences favored the male and held women to domestic pursuits and service jobs, and thus kept them out of the power structure.

As for myself, between science and ideology, I prefer to go with science. And scientific research tells us that much of what constitutes an individual's personality is genetically and biologically determined. I do agree with Bloom, Owen, and Covington (2003) that separating biological effects from the social and cultural effects is problematic. In any case, following Belknap, we can draw a distinction between *sex* and *gender*; sex is biologically determined and gender is societally based. *The Shorter Oxford Dictionary* (2007) indicates that both terms refer to male and female differences but that gender refers to cultural attributes.

Unlike liberal feminists, who are apt to stress equality and sameness of the genders, equal pay for equal work and the like, and to refute any claims of difference that could be used to hold women down, some radical feminists have been more willing to appreciate, even to celebrate, the differences. From this perspective, biological differences, far from being denied, can be seen as favoring the female of the species (Goodkind, 2005; van Wormer, 2007). Many such women-centered theorists, according to Robbins et al. (2006), celebrate the power in "women's ways of knowing" and "the woman's voice." This acknowledgment of difference is consistent with a scientifically based imperative to explore sex differences that manifest themselves in every system of body and brain (Gur, Gunning-Dixon, Bilker, & Gur, 2002). This position is interesting because it harks back to the Mother Goose nursery rhyme, popular in the early nineteenth century, that begins "What are little boys made of?" In any case, feminists of the liberal school, such as Goodkind (2005), find such a focus on difference objectionable because it fails to take into account variation within and between genders. She warns against "essential-izing" gender role differences and "portraying them as inherent and even bio-logically determined" (p. 59).

The position of this book is that in search of knowledge about human behavior, a holistic, biopsychosocial approach is essential. A holistic approach, such as that favored here, states that gender role difference is not a case of nature *versus* nurture but of *both* nature and nurture.

The basic biological factors that impinge on gender differences in crimi-nality are informed by research on physiology and neurology. In making the case for gender-sensitive programming in corrections, a logical starting point is a review of some of the scientific literature on sex differences.

Research Based on Animal Studies

Evolutionists such as Wrangham and Petersen (1996) offer a challenge to tradi-tional feminist cultural determinism. Their conclusions are bolstered by ape studies in which male chimpanzees compete aggressively for rank and domi-nance (to be the alpha male) while male predators attack the weak, and female chimps often bond with the predators. Is the frequency of male violence a mere artifact of physical strength? they ask. For answers, they look to human society.

Examining data drawn from global crime statistics on same-gender murder (to eliminate the factor of male strength), Wrangham and Peterson found the statistics to be amazingly consistent. In all societies except for Denmark, the probability that a same-gender murder has been committed by a man, not a woman, ranges from 92% to 100%. In Denmark, all the female-on-female murders were cases of infanticide. We need to remove our inhibitions based on feminist politics, these researchers argue. We need to study violence such as murder and rape as biological phenomena. The origins of male violence, as Wrangham and Peterson conclude, are found in the social lives of chimpan-zees and other apes, our closest living nonhuman relatives. Because some of the great apes, specifically the bonobos, are considerably less aggressive, more research is needed on this matter. Although evolutionists like Wrangham and Peterson may tend to exaggerate aggressive tendencies in males, others draw on the link between testosterone and aggression in humans and nonhuman animals to explain the male propensity for physical aggression (Palmer, 2008).

Brain Research

The advent of human brain-imaging techniques such as positron emission tomography and functional magnetic resonance imaging has heightened awareness of sex differences by revealing sex influences on brain functions for which the sex of participants was previously assumed to matter little, if at all. But these differences do matter, as neuroscientist Cahill (2006) asserts, and they are observed in gender differences in human behavior.

Brain research tells us what ideology cannot: that a sizable portion of human behavior is neurological. Women's brains are smaller than men's, but they have a higher processing quality. The region at the base of the brain that includes the amygdala is involved in emotional arousal and excitement is about the same size in men and women. But women have a significantly higher volume in the orbital frontal cortex than men do. This suggests, according to Gur et al. (2002), that when anger is aroused, women are better equipped than men to exercise self-control.

In his summary of recent neurological research, Cahill (2006) concludes that there are sex influences at all levels of the nervous system, from genes to behavior. Such research has shown sex differences in many areas of brain and behavior, including emotion, memory, vision, hearing, facial expressions, pain perception, navigation, neurotransmitter levels, stress hormone action on the brain, and diseases, including addiction. Recent animal research has increasingly documented new, often surprising, sex influences on the brain.

The picture of brain organization that emerges from Cahill's perspective is of two complex mosaics—one male and one female. Investigators are increasingly realizing that they can no longer assume that essentially identical processes occur in men and women, notes Cahill, nor that identical therapies will produce identical results.

Right-Brain/Left-Brain Research

Our brain consists of two separate structures—a right brain and a left brain—linked by a row of fibers. In most people, the left side specializes in speech, language, and logical reasoning (a fact that has been known for years due to the impact of strokes on this or the other side of the brain). The right hemisphere specializes in reading emotional cues (Cabeza, 2002). Much has been made of the differences in the kind of consciousness and in the functioning of the right and left hemispheres of the brain (Saleebey, 2001). The left brain is equated with reasoning while the right brain has been presumed, almost contemptuously, to be more primitive than the left, feminine as opposed to masculine.

Andreasen (2001) indicates that the right hemisphere can be considered a companion language region, as we know from direct functional imaging observations. She cautions us therefore against too much simplification in

breaking the brain into component parts. We almost never do only one mental activity at a time. Advances in neuroscience have taught us to what extent
the brain is a system; no single region can perform any mental or physical
function without coactivation and cooperation from multiple other regions.
"The human brain," notes Andreasen, "is like a large orchestra playing a great
symphony" (p. 85).

Scientific research throughout the 1990s revealed significant differences
in male and female learning styles and that these differences were related
in part to brain structure. Shaywitz and Shaywitz (1995), for example,
demonstrated through brain scanning that when listening to someone
speak, men used the left side of their brains. Women, in contrast, used
both sides of their brains to process the same information. The female
brain, in other words, was found to be more decentralized. More recent
studies, such as that by Cela-Conde et al. (2009) of Spain, asked males and
females to examine photographs of natural landscapes. When they looked
at a scene they deemed beautiful, both men and women had greater electrical activity in one region near the top of the brain. In women, this acti-
vation occurred in both halves of the brain, but in men it was restricted to
the right hemisphere.

Women, as Saleebey (2001) indicates, seem to be more hemispherically
egalitarian than men. We see this in the impact of strokes, which are more
clearly identifiable—right and left—in men than in women. Compared to
men, women have more pathways between the right and left brains and
between the right brain and body. *The New Feminine Brain* by brain scientist
Mona Lisa Schulz (2005) applauds this difference as a unique female strength.
This hyperconnectivity between the sides of the brain, Schulz suggests,
enables women to make right-brain emotional hunches and to talk about
them with left-brain language.

Several independent studies suggest that, for gay men, cognitive performance on measures that typically elicit sex differences is shifted in a
"female-like" direction (Rahman & Wilson, 2003). Klar (2004), in his investigation of brain hemispheres in male homosexuals, found differences that
relate to left- and right-handedness and suggest a biological/genetic factor
in sexual orientation. Research on the causes of transgenderism is pointing
increasing to early brain development in the womb (van Wormer, 2007).
There are thus many situations in which a child's brain may say he/she is
female while the genitalia are those of the male. Learning about the nature
of transgenderism—and we still have a lot to learn—reinforces other
research concerning the innateness of gender identity as male and female.
The particular forms that such differences take, however (e.g., whether one

wears dresses or polishes one's toenails), are socially constructed and vary by society.

PSYCHOLOGY OF GENDER

During the prepuberty period, girls mature much faster than boys. More boys than girls have best friends at school while the quality of their friendships is different—girls' friendships have a higher level of intimacy, exchange of confidences, and caring (Newman & Newman, 2008). There is no doubt that the male/female physical differences are as pronounced as ever at this stage of development and that these differences coincide with psychological differences.

Studies of adolescent girls indicate that from the 7th to 10th grades, they regress in self-confidence and intellectual development (Pipher, 1994). Obsessions with body image and efforts to appeal to the opposite gender take center stage. Given the salience of pressures toward role conformity, especially in high school, girls who are gender nonconforming have an especially difficult time.

Traditional theories of moral development equated maturity with the growth of independence and detachment from the primary relationships of childhood. In a radical break with the Freudian school, Jean Baker Miller (1976), a psychoanalyst by training, authored the groundbreaking book *Toward a New Psychology of Women*. Miller argued that girls and women developed their sense of self through intimate relationships with others. Inspired by Miller's work and by her research on adolescent girls, psychologist Carol Gilligan further conceptualized gender differences in growth and development. Her now-classic study *In a Different Voice* (1982) revealed the key factors that went into young women's decision making (whether to have an abortion). Her findings effectively showed that the dominant theories of moral development were irrelevant to the life course of young women. Far from growing in the direction of social autonomy, young women were seen to develop their sense of self through intimate relationships with family and friends. Caring and connectedness were the transcending themes in their lives.

Gilligan's methodology consisted of listening to women's voices. From her interviews with 29 young women facing a decision on whether to end a pregnancy, she filtered out these three progressive stages of moral development: (1) orientation to personal survival, (2) goodness viewed as self-sacrifice, and (3) the morality of postconventional or nonviolent responsibility. At the most advanced level of maturity, women have learned to tend to their own interests as well as to the interests of others. Gilligan concluded that women, unlike men, hesitate to prioritize justice in making decisions in that their decisions take into account the complexities of personal relationships.

A model can be considered useful and to possess power if it can explain both deviant or norm-breaking and normative behavior. In my view, Gilligan's model meets this test. Thus we can reverse her theory to explain its opposite—a failure in moral development can lead into criminal or other lawbreaking activity. This behavior can relate to the pursuit of selfish goals, such as stealing from another. Or the failure could represent involvement in a dysfunctional relationship or a surrender of the self to an addictive substance or behavior. Significantly, Gilligan (1979) referred to this paradox of interconnectedness in an early paper: "Women's moral weakness, manifest in an apparent diffusion and confusion of judgment, is thus inseparable from women's moral strength, an overriding concern with relationships and responsibilities" (p. 77).

In studies on problems facing adolescent girls, renewed attention was paid to Gilligan's (1982) thesis that the way girls think, interact, and develop is psychologically distinctive from the male based model. Due to the growing awareness by educators of the disparities in the treatment of boys and girls in the coed classroom, and in the juvenile justice system, programs were designed as non-coeducational, with the needs of females specifically in mind.

In the 1990s, a great deal of attention was paid to girls' psychological needs. The publication of works such as the American Association of University Women's (AAUW) (1995) study *How Schools Shortchange Girls* and Mary Pipher's (1994) *Reviving Ophelia* was accompanied by a wave of media accounts and follow-up studies questioning the premise that gender equality exists in U.S. schools. Evidence was provided in such studies as these to show that boys get the bulk of educational resources and are called on in class more frequently by teachers.

Why, asked Pipher (1994), are more American girls falling prey to depression, eating disorders, addictions, and suicide attempts than ever before? The answer, she found, is our look-obsessed, media-saturated society, a culture that stifles girls' creative spirit and natural impulses. Girls generally have a free spirit, she argued, until they reach puberty around age 11 or 12; then their confidence and energy drop precipitously.

Gilligan's model was tested in an academic paper that examined judicial rulings on the basis of gender. Martin, Epstein, and Boyd (2007) found that gender does make a difference in the rulings consistent with Gilligan's model. The key finding of the study was that when a woman was present on a judicial panel, male judges were significantly influenced in how they decided the cases investigated—gender discrimination cases. The fact of male and female differences in approaches to ethical decision making was widely discussed when President Obama was choosing a nominee for the U.S. Supreme Court. Arguments concerning the importance of having women on the bench were built on the "different voice" theory of Carol Gilligan as well as on empirical research from the legal literature (Lithwick, 2009). A distinction was drawn between a male's emphasis on autonomy and an ethics of rights and justice in resolving a case and women's subscribing to an ethics of care with an emphasis on the social impact of a decision.

In short, the contribution of pioneers in the psychology of gender, such as Jean Baker Miller and Carol Gilligan, to moral development research and to relational theory has been of major significance to a number of fields. The foundation for what we now call gender-specific, gender-sensitive, or gender-responsive treatment for girls and women is here in these theories. Nevertheless, Gilligan's theoretical model has been criticized by some feminists for its "difference feminism," its emphasis on male-female psychological differences as well as the claim that women's decisions are not based on a notion of justice.

SOCIOLOGY OF GENDER

The focus on girls' needs shifted during the latter part of the twentieth century, as the literature and media shifted focus away from the neglect of girls' special needs to the neglect of the needs of boys. It was not girls whose needs were being neglected by the school system, according to the stories in the popular press—it was boys. The title of Christina Sommers' (2000) widely publicized book summed up the shift in sentiment: *The War Against Boys: How Misguided Feminism Is Harming Our Young Men*. A barrage of newspaper articles cited psychologists and other commentators to redefine the crisis in our educational system as a boy, not a girl, crisis ("Eleven-Plus to Be Abolished," BBC News, 2004; Tyre, 2006). The statistics seemed to bear the commentators out. Boys drop out of school, are diagnosed as emotionally disturbed, and commit suicide 4 times more often than girls; they get into fights twice as often, they murder 10 times more frequently and are 15 times more likely to be the victims of violent crime (Kimmel, 2000). Attention deficit hyperactivity disorder, autism, and dyslexia are far more prevalent among boys than among girls.

By 2008, the AAUW came out with a second report drawing on statistical data of educational achievement that refuted claims of a boy crisis and pointed to social class and ethnicity as the major factors in school failure (Strauss, 2008).

Shaywitz (2003) attributes the focus on boys' as opposed to girls' problems in growing up to their more troublesome behavior. Her own research in the schools found that teachers identified boys as the ones with learning problems. Yet when children were tested individually, comparable numbers of boys and girls were having problems. Arguing over which gender has the most problems is counterproductive. Education needs to be individualized to support the learning needs of both girls and boys and of students who do not conform to gender role expectations.

From the earliest age, little boys and girls have a sense of gender role expectations and the behaviors that pertain to their own gender. This sense is constantly reinforced by family members, what Saleebey (2001) refers to as "that steady hum of voices that tells boys and men to do everything we must to ensure that we are not girls" (p. 381). The masculine ethos, accordingly, is very strong and has a significant impact on behaviors. What are the typical norms for male adolescence? Saleebey lists: drinking four cans of beer in 30 minutes, picking fights, playing sports, driving recklessly, and making unsuccessful sexual advances. Where the father-son relationship is unhealthy or nonexistent, a constriction of emotions apart from expression of anger is often the result. In Latino culture, the code of male honor, or *machismo*, prevails; the man is defined as the provider, protector, and head of household (Colon, 2007).

In her later work on gender, *The Birth of Pleasure*, Gilligan (2002) shares insights on what happens to a five-year-old boy—repression—and the adolescent girl—repression as well—that reveal much about detrimental forces in the cultural landscape. Masculinity, she notes, often implies an ability to stand alone and forgo relationships, whereas femininity connotes a willingness to compromise oneself for the sake of relationships. Since the initiation of boys into the codes of masculinity intensifies around the age of five, while girls are given more leeway to express themselves until adolescence, there is a common ground here that is rarely recognized. The difference is that the girl, when she comes face-to-face with societal norms—what Gilligan calls "a process of revision"—the girl is more likely than the boy to name and openly resist the loss to her freedom.

Women share a common bodily experience of femaleness as well as the social oppression of sexism whether they are consciously aware of the fact or not. Girls are often socialized to assume subordinate roles and to value sexual attractiveness over academic or career success. Stereotyping of women's roles furthers oppression by making it hard for individuals born female to develop a sense of self-worth and to find validation of their own needs.

GENDER DIFFERENCES IN OFFENDING

Just as the risk factors for female offending is gendered—related to trauma, relationships, and so on—so too are the offenses themselves. Research shows, for example, that girls and women are less physical in their aggression than boys, and their violence, when it occurs, is often rooted in significant relationships, whereas male violence is often related to dominance issues, gang rivalries, or the commission of other crimes (Okamoto & Chesney-Lind, 2003). The increasing use of detention for girls who in earlier years would have been treated in the community often mandates treatment according to the standard (male-centered) juvenile justice model.

For girls and women, the most common pathways to problematic behavior are based on matters of survival (psychological survival from abuse and physical survival in the face of poverty) in conjunction with substance abuse (Bloom, Owen, & Covington, 2004). Often the precipitating factor in a woman's criminalization is childhood trauma. The underlying depression related to the trauma may lead into later alcohol and other drug use and unhealthy relationships. This process of criminalization is most evident in the lives of (1) abused and runaway girls, (2), battered women forced to live and work on the streets, and (3) women addicted to substances, especially women of color (Gilfus, 2002). Part II of this volume—"Pathways to Crime"—explores the role of early childhood victimization in later substance use, unhealthy relationships, and criminality. This personal history of victimization provides further support for the argument that female offenders have issues unique to their gender that must be addressed.

According to the National Institute of Corrections, to help offenders become productive citizens, "we must revisit some of our efforts and acknowledge that gender makes a difference" (Sydney, 2005, p.1). The institute makes these recommendations for effective gender responsiveness:

Acknowledge and accommodate differences between men and women.

Assess women's risk levels, needs, and strengths and construct supervision case plans accordingly.

Acknowledge the different pathways through which women enter the community corrections system.

Recognize the likelihood that women offenders have a significant history of victimization.

Build on women's strengths and values, including recognizing that relationships are important to women.

> Acknowledge and accommodate the likelihood that women are pri-
> mary caregivers to a child or other dependent. (Sydney, 2005, p. 3)

To summarize the discussion so far, the evidence presented of male-female gender differences in behavior and values, argues for specialized treatment tailored for girls' and women's special needs. Facilities and interventions already are designed with males in mind, and, although some improvements might be in order to help humanize those establishments for all offenders, our concern in this book is with the restructuring required to reflect the treatment needs of the minority of offenders who are female.

KEY CONCEPTS

The next concepts, except for the first one, are foundational to gender-specific policies and the gender-based therapies that are discussed in the following pages of this book.

Female Offender

I must admit to strong reservations about use of this value-laden term. It refers to girls and women who have gotten into trouble for behavior that is against the law. Included here are juveniles whose behavior, such as running away, are status offenses rather than crimes. The incongruity of this term with the strengths perspective is obvious because of the negative connotations and the fact that the label puts the sole responsibility on the girls and women for being in trouble with the law. Canadian feminist writers use the less pejorative term *women in conflict with the law*. That term does not include girls, however, and makes for clumsy wording in the sentence structure. *Convict* has certain advantages in this regard in that it puts the onus on the state for the label and can be appropriately used for persons who are innocent of any wrongdoing, as many so-called offenders are. The term could not be used to refer to juveniles, however, and the connotations are more negative than even the term *offender*. So for want of a better term and because other feminist criminologists and the federal government use the term *female offender*, I reluctantly have decided to use it as well.

Gender Sensitive, Gender Specific, Gender Responsive

These terms, which I use interchangeably in this book, refer to policies and interventions that take into account girls' and women's special needs by virtue of their gender. As the reader will note, this chapter utilizes the term *gender* in its biological as well as psychosocial sense. This is in contrast to the focus of most other feminist scholars who study gender in terms of economic and social disadvantages and differentiate gender, which is social, from sex, which is used in a biological sense (Belknap, 2007; Robbins, Chatterjee, & Canda, 2006). *The Shorter Oxford English Dictionary* (2007) defines *gender* in two ways: as a form of grammar as masculine or feminine for a noun, and for sex. *Gender* relates to the categories of "the two sexes." The term is derived from Latin from *genus* for "race, stock." According to this definition, it does not seem incorrect, therefore, to study biopsychosocial aspects of gender, to refer to both physiological and social attributes of this sex category. A focus on female gender usually refers to behaviors that are culturally based, whether they are derived from biological distinctions or not. Consider rituals surrounding pregnancy and childbirth, for example, which differ across societies. My point is that the category of female gender often brings our attention, at least indirectly, to aspects of female physiology and developmental issues, such as menstruation and childbirth, and vulnerabilities to certain crimes, such as rape.

An article on gender in *Social Work* by Barb Burdge (2007) argues that social workers should reject the traditional dichotomous constructs of gender altogether in favor of a more accurate and affirming conceptualization. Greater flexibility in this regard would be a means of eliminating gender oppression, as Burdge further suggests. From her perspective, the traditional either/or concept that dichotomizes gender into male and female is merely a social construction "supposedly reflecting 'natural differences'" (p. 246). Indeed, there is much overlap between the characteristics traditionally assigned as male and female, while society does tend to exaggerate gender distinctions. And we can certainly agree that patriarchal culture punishes gender nonconformity and "spawns a hierarchy of gender categories in which the non-male category is devalued" (p. 246).

Burdge's recommendation that our conceptualization of gender be expanded to include transgendered persons (people who are anatomically of one sex but who strongly feel that they belong to the other sex) is well taken: Many individuals do exist "outside the gender binary," and we need to provide a viable identity option for such persons. Some Native American tribes had a revered category for "two-spirited" persons who were believed to possess spiritual powers. This is in sharp contrast to the dominant U.S. society's attempts to force individuals to conform to the gender to which they were ascribed at birth. The American Psychiatric Association (2000), for example, includes in its listing of mental disorders "gender identity disorder."

In recognition of the fact that a flexible understanding of gender is essential to be inclusive of all personality types and identities, we still need a female-centered approach to meet the needs of girls and women in the system. These needs are related both to socio-emotional concerns and to health issues.

Programming that is gender sensitive would offer a comprehensive, gender-based design that incorporates both the treatment interventions and the physical environment, including the architecture of the building in which the treatment and/or confinement takes place. Gender-sensitive treatment can of course be oriented toward males to help them work on issues related to their sex, such as masculinity and stresses pertinent to being a boy or man in our competitive society. Much of what passes for gender-neutral programming, such as boot camps and medium-maximum-security-level prisons is really oriented toward training and punishment of male offenders. Whether this kind of tough treatment is apt to bring out the best qualities in offending males or whether it is more likely to reinforce their worst qualities is a matter that deserves consideration.

Most definitions in the correctional literature speak of gender-specific or gender-responsive programming as programming tailored to the special needs of girls in detention. For example, the project of the Annie Casey Foundation on detention reform describes gender-responsive practices in this way:

> Gender-responsive detention reform should include practices, policies, and programs that address: (1) systemic inequities that result in inappropriate confinement of girls (for minor offenses, technical violations, family chaos, and as the result of lack of cross-system collaboration); and (2) girls' needs and pathways into detention that are different from those of boys. Reform of systemic inequities and development of gender-responsive detention and disposition alternatives should minimize girls' returns to detention, prevent detention "dumping," and reduce detention awaiting placement. (Sherman, 2005, p. 40)

Exemplary programs described in Sherman's report provide community services that are strengths based (offered in San Francisco and Boston) and the providing of home-based alternatives to detention such as that offered by Philadelphia's Department of Human Services.

For the purposes of this book, it is helpful to delineate what gender-sensitive treatment is not. (See Table 1.1.)

A basic assumption of this book and of gender-based counseling is that in the pathway to crime for an adolescent, there is no clear-cut dichotomy between victim and offender, that victimization and offending are interactive and interconnected. A disproportionately high percentage of women in prison

Table 1.1. What Gender-Sensitive Treatment Is Not

- Maternalistic or paternalistic treatment, such as that which existed up until the 1970s, in which female offenders in the system were infantilized in institutions and denied equality in employment.
- Advocating a double standard in sentencing practices in the belief that girls need more protection than boys, such as from running away.
- Treatment solely for females. (There are gender-specific programs being developed for males as well.)
- Necessarily feminist. (Many legislators and other public officials and treatment providers advocate gender-based therapies for female offenders based on their knowledge of gender differences rather than out of a feminist philosophy.)
- A focus on just one aspect of a girl's or woman's life (e.g., on cooperative behavior or relationships).
- A therapy that attributes all personal problems to gender-related stresses and gender roles. (This treatment attends to a combination of factors, such as race and class, simultaneously.)
- Hierarchical. (Consistent with women's leadership style, a collaborative relationship is developed between the woman and the treatment provider.)
- Focused exclusively on the "here and now" to the neglect of concerns from past experiences.
- Limited to the psychological dimension in therapy to the neglect of other concerns—for example, educational and relational.

are victims of early childhood sexual and physical abuse. As described earlier, the link to crime might have been via substance abuse originating in adolescence and/or self-destructive relationships with drug-dependent criminal men. Each negative choice or entanglement reinforces the others.

Gender, Race, and Class

Woven into this book is the theme of power relations in the society that must inform all our discussions of criminal justice. Just as the relationship between the personal and political is interactive, so is the link among gender, race, and class. In working with women of color, of any color, it is necessary to be aware of the intersection of gender, race, and class rather than the power of each factor separately. It is on the basis of gender, race, and class in combination that an individual is deemed deserving of protection and respect or as a threat and/or burden to society. Our understanding must be multidimensional, therefore. Thus we can come to see that a woman, say, a victim of domestic abuse, who is both African American and poor inhabits a world in which the forces of gender, race, and class reinforce each other simultaneously; the effect of membership in multiple categories is synergistic rather than additive. Beth Richie's (1996) notion of *gender entrapment* of battered Black women reveals how behaviors that are highly functional in one milieu can be problematic in another. Richie, who based her understanding on in-depth interviews with battered African American women at the Rikers Island Correctional Facility, defines this term in this way:

> I use gender entrapment to describe the socially constructed process whereby African American women who are vulnerable to men's vio-lence in their intimate relationship are penalized for behaviors they engage in even when the behaviors are logical extensions of their racialized gender identities, their culturally expected gender roles, and the violence in their intimate relationships. (p. 4)

Gender, race, and class are constructs highly relevant to criminology in that the ultimate social control of the oppressed is carried out in the criminal justice system. All the state's institutions—the law, the social welfare system, and the media—are controlled by the dominant group. Inequality is built in the system and legitimized through the mass media. The most striking exam-ple at the present time is the typical female offender: a drug-dependent, poor woman of African American or Latino heritage.

Equality with a Vengeance

This term, introduced in criminal justice literature by Chesney-Lind and Pollock (1994) and Bloom and Chesney-Lind (2000), refers to the gender-blind treatment of women by the major institutions of society. Such treat-ment was an outgrowth of the liberal feminist theme of seeking equal treatment for men and women since they were equal under the law (Failinger, 2006). Unintended consequences have resulted. Gender-neutral policies have dumped single mothers off the welfare rolls while gender-neutral mandatory sentencing for drug law violation has brought unprecedented numbers of women and especially poor and minority women into prison. Strict adherence to an equality standard for these women subjects them to discipline according to the male model without allowance for their mother-hood roles or in many cases their history of personal victimization. A flawed notion lurks beneath the current policies: the assumption that women have achieved full equality and that men are suffering the consequences. The brunt of the backlash against policies of affirmative action that have bene-fited women at the higher echelons is borne by the women least able to take

advantage of the new professional opportunities and the least likely to identify themselves as feminist. Negative press claims of violent girls and women
further aggravates the situation (see Chapter 3).

PARADIGM SHIFT

The history of social justice is a history of paradigm shifts related to our con-
ceptions about the nature of crime and the purpose of punishment. From the
1980s through the first part of the twenty-first century, the ascendancy of the
conservative right in conjunction with corporate business interests built on
the doctrine of free market principles contributed to the development of
backlash politics. The erosion of social service benefits in the welfare state
has been matched in the criminal justice system by the passage of draconian
laws against drug use and the mass building of medium- and maximum-security
prisons nationwide. The personal targets of the attack included racial and
ethnic minorities, immigrants, women on welfare, and users of illicit drugs.

Within the criminal justice system, the antifeminist, anti–minority rights
backlash has been disguised through various code words, such as equality,
without any allowance for gender differences, family values, and the war on
drugs. In the writing of the mandatory sentencing laws and laws related to
women's reproductive functions, the patriarchy joined with conservative politicians to reinforce class, gender, and race privilege. The contemporary media
focus on male victimization and female violence did not help the situation. In
response to a negative portrayal in the media of the founders of the women's
movement, the younger generation grew wary of the term *feminism* itself.

Change in ideology often precedes changes in practice, and vice versa. For
example, public intolerance of secondhand smoke helped spawn new laws;
new laws in turn reinforced attitudes about public smoking. Today, regarding
the treatment of offenders, there is evidence of pending change at both levels.
From grassroots activity to the highest levels of government, rehabilitation is
returning to the national consciousness. Although the statistics concerning
incarceration rates would seemingly indicate otherwise—in 2008, the total
jail and prison population soared to over 2,300,000 (West & Sabol, 2009)—
there is some indication that America's long-standing fervor for harsh punishment is on the decline. Evidence for the shift in national consciousness is
revealed in these developments:

- The number of executions in the United States has declined markedly
  each year from 1998 (BJS, 2009a).
- Surveys show that a large majority of respondents favor drug treatment
  over incarceration (Curley, 2009).

- Congress passed the Second Chance Act to help inmates return to their communities ("Shrinking the Prison Population," *New York Times*, 2009).
- The new drug czar favors greater funding for drug treatment including drug courts instead of the war on drugs (Leinwand, 2009).
- Congress is expected to soon reauthorize the Juvenile Justice Delinquency Prevention Act, which emphasizes gender-responsive treatment for girls (American Bar Association, 2009).

At the same time as these promising developments are taking place, however, arrest rates for juvenile females are soaring, and conditions in confinement for girls and women continue to be poor. In light of the difficulties of transforming a male-based system to one responsive to the needs of females, there is a great deal of work to be done.

SUMMARY

The case for offering gender-sensitive treatment to girls and women in trouble with the law was bolstered, in this chapter, through a review of biological, psychological, and social facts about female growth and development. Gender-sensitive treatment, following Gilligan's insights, means attending to women offenders' experiences as relational human beings and recognizing a primary problem that girls and women face is fear of being alone without a significant other on whom to depend.

Gender-sensitive strategies in community correctional organizations include attention to such intimate relationships, family-of-origin issues including personal violence, self-concept, cultural issues, addictive and mental disorders, employment, child care, and parenting. Within residential settings, the introduction of gender-specific programming has far-reaching implications for shaping service delivery. From assessment and classification of women in the system to treatment programming and counseling practices, female-friendly strategies can be highly effective in engaging participants. Now we turn to a consideration of the relevance of such strategies for working with girls who have gotten into trouble with their families and with the law.

Part II

PATHWAYS TO CRIME

Chapter 2

TRADITIONAL AND GENDER-SENSITIVE TREATMENT FOR DELINQUENT GIRLS

Barndomen kommer aldrig igen. *(Childhood never comes again.)*
—Traditional Swedish Saying

Historically, the focus on the juvenile justice system has been on prevention and rehabilitation. In recent years, however, a trend toward criminalizing juvenile offenders is apparent. Media attention was drawn to what some were calling an "epidemic" of youth violence; incidents of mass school shootings by boys who were taking revenge on bullying classmates did not help the situation. Girls were more often the victims than victimizers of such aggression, and they attracted little attention in the press until the early 1990s. Then a strange thing happened: Boys' arrests began to decline dramatically while girls' arrests shot upward in certain categories. The arrest increases were not for shoplifting or curfew violations but rather for traditionally masculine offenses, such as assault.

Girls today have become the fastest-growing segment of the juvenile justice population in the United States. According to the Office of Juvenile Justice and Delinquency Prevention (OJJDP, 2009), females now account for about a third of juvenile arrests for assault; this represents a significant increase in their

25

proportion of violent crime since the 1980s. In 2007, the juvenile male arrest rate was just 8% more than its 1980 level while the female rate was 83% more than its 1980 rate. Similarly, while the male arrest rate for simple assault doubled between 1980 and 2007, the female rate more than tripled. Whereas in 1980, 20% of all juvenile arrests were female, this figure has risen to 29% today. Correspondingly, the detention of girls has increased as well.

These facts have not been lost on the media; seeming anomalies and paradoxes of this sort make for interesting headlines. Themes of the masculinization of the female adolescent can be counted on to invite reader interest. The fact that the increase in girls' arrest rates has been evidenced in a rise in violent offenses has been highlighted, without regard to the context within which the arrests are taking place.

Lost among the coverage are the deeper issues: What is the true nature of female juvenile crime? Have girls become more violent, or has society become more punitive? What is the typical path to detention for a girl? Fortunately, there is an extensive literature, including government sources and scholarship, to provide the answers. This chapter draw on this literature as well as on personal narratives to consider questions about girls under the supervision of the state:

- What do official juvenile statistics tell us about patterns of female delinquency?
- Do the self report data on delinquency bear out the trends in the official statistics?
- What form does girls' aggression take, and how does this form differ from male aggression?
- What is the pathway to crime and to status offenses for the girl who is brought before juvenile court?
- How can such a pathway be stymied—what would female, gender-sensitive programming look like?

INTRODUCTION

This chapter is informed by contemporary criminological theory that, unlike earlier approaches, stresses the complexity of female delinquency and the role that gendered family violence as well as race and class play in determining which girls get into trouble with the law and which ones do not. For enlightenment, we examine the trends in juvenile offenses as reported by the U.S. Department of Justice. Our journey in this chapter, however, goes beyond the statistics to an analysis of forces in society that are detrimental to girls and that bring them to the attention of correctional authorities.

In order to understand the renewed focus on girls' violence, keep in mind the backlash against policies promoting female equality as discussed in Chapter 1, coupled with the punitive thrust in U.S. society as is evidenced at all levels of the criminal justice system. Whether girls today are more violent than before or whether we are seeing a change in law enforcement policies is a key issue in feminist criminology and one that is also our concern. From the burgeoning literature on the gender-specific nature of risk factors for girls, we explore the pathways that bring these adolescents to delinquent behavior, a path that typically includes sexual abuse, traumatization, running away, drug use, battering, teenage pregnancy, and unhealthy peer relationships. Next we examine how the juvenile justice process responds to this behavior. We then turn our attention to residential facilities for female offenders, to the worst and the best of these places. We find that, in a system that was designed to deal with delinquent boys, the specific programming relevant to girls' psychosocial development has often been neglected. We also find that some gender-sensitive programs really are making a difference in troubled girls' lives, such as those offered in Minnesota where restorative justice strategies are tailored to the needs of adolescent females. Finally, I argue for a continuum of care for girls' aftercare to ensure a shift from services for adolescents to adult services in the community, to help these former incarcerated girls function effectively in the world outside. I also argue for alternatives to incarceration wherever possible, focusing on intensive treatment of girls at high risk of offending to prevent the need of later residential placements.

WHAT THE STATISTICS SHOW

Although some crimes girls and boys commit, such as property crime, are remarkably similar in terms of goals—to obtain money or an item of some value—other offenses are more clearly gendered. Consider:

- Zack, an overweight boy who was constantly teased at school, first attempted to shed his status as "wimp" by joining the junior high football team, dieting and building up his body, and dressing in a "cool" fashion. When he failed in all these efforts, he sought to pursue his goal of masculinity through molesting his younger cousin, which he did over a three-year period until he was caught. (Case described by Messerschmidt, 2005.)
- Tammy, a White 19-year-old serving 4 to 15 years for attempted murder, had a long history of sexual and physical abuse by members of her family and her father's friend. When she told her father what happened, he called her a slut. Tammy was sent to foster care while the man who

raped her remained in her home. Tammy ran away and hooked up with a boy who shot at her house and wounded the father's friend who had raped her. Tammy, who was driving the car and was 15 at the time, was sentenced to prison. (Case described by Gaarder and Belknap, 2004.)

These two case histories were selected to demonstrate male-female differences in paths to crime and to show the significance of gender roles in delinquency. Other situations that are similarly gendered and could have been used are physical fighting and gang activity associated with peer pressures to be a "real man" in the male delinquent and girls using their sex through prostitution to obtain money or drugs, assault of a female love rival, and offending in conjunction with the crimes of a boyfriend.

The vast majority of cases handled by juvenile courts, according to the OJJDP (2009), involve offenses committed by males. Included in these cases are both delinquent acts and status offenses. *Delinquent acts* are those that would be crimes if committed by adults—person offenses such as robbery and assault—and property offenses—burglary, arson, and the like. *Status offenses* are offenses that if committed by an adult would not be prosecuted; they include offenses such as running away from home and incorrigibility. The female proportion of the total number of cases handled by the juvenile courts increased from 20% in 1993 to 26% in 2002 to 29% in 2007. Still, this means that 69% of the referrals to the juvenile court are of males. Some would argue that girls get off easier than boys at every stage of the criminal justice process, from arrest to disposition of the case in juvenile court.

Whether female offenders receive preferential treatment in court compared to male offenders is an issue that has been debated for some time. In the past, researchers stressed a chivalry or protectionist factor in the juvenile court's treatment of girls (Zahn, 2007). For White girls, before the impact of the civil rights and women's movements, this double standard for White, middle-class females probably was a factor in the disposition of cases. Although many girls probably had their cases dismissed from juvenile court under such chivalrous treatment, it came at a high price to others and to females in society in general. The assumption was that females were the weaker sex and that they needed to be protected. Under this code of chivalry, the inherent belief in female inferiority and dependence often resulted in treatment in the form of strict social controls (Belknap, 2007). Many girls in trouble with the law were locked up "for their own protection" and to control their sexual behavior. A double standard clearly prevailed. Girls charged with status offenses often were treated more harshly than other youth (males and females) charged with actual crimes (MacDonald & Chesney-Lind, 2004).

Is it a myth that girls are dealt with more leniently by the courts than are boys? What does the research say? Empirical research conducted by Mac-Donald and Chesney-Lind (2004) revealed similarities and differences in the processing of juvenile justice cases of boys and girls in Hawaii. Generally, girls were found to receive equal treatment as boys at the earlier stages of the process (petitioning and adjudication). At the disposition stage, however, girls were found to receive harsh sentences for minor offenses such as running away. Clearly, as the authors conclude, the legacy of the past is with us still when it comes to monitoring and controlling girls' lives.

In any case, the growth rate in cases involving females has outpaced the male growth rate in all offense categories. This is especially true with regard to violent offenses against the person; most of these offenses were simple assaults.

Girls and boys are arrested for different crimes, girls more frequently for prostitution and running away, boys for all the other crimes, ranging from robbery and rape to murder. But even when boys and girls are charged with the same crime, the form that the crime takes may be unique by gender. Take stealing, for example. Boys, as Chesney-Lind and Shelden (2004) suggest, are far more likely to steal electronic items and girls to take grooming items, such as expensive clothes or makeup. Both genders are responding to the consumer culture and to advertising campaigns directed at their gender.

To study the extent of female involvement in specific crimes, see Table 2.1, which is reprinted from the OJJDP (2009). We learn from this table that females accounted for 29% of all juvenile arrests in 2007. Of juvenile arrests for aggravated assault, females accounted for 23%, while they accounted for 34% of other assaults and 16% of drug violations. As is clear from these statistics, incidences of both property and violent crime decreased significantly for all juveniles over the last decade of the crime reports. Note that the categories "Under age 15" and "Percent change" include boys as well as girls.

- In 2007, there were an estimated 300,300 juvenile arrests for larceny-theft. Between 1998 and 2007, the number of such arrests fell by one-third (32%).
- Of the four offenses that make up the Violent Crime Index, only juvenile arrests for murder increased in the last year (up 3%).
- In 2007, females accounted for 17% of juvenile Violent Crime Index arrests, 35% of juvenile Property Crime Index arrests, and 33% of juvenile disorderly conduct arrests.
- Youth younger than age 15 accounted for more than one-fourth (28%) of all juvenile arrests for Violent Crime Index offenses in 2007 and nearly one-third (31%) of all Property Crime Index offenses.

Table 2.1. Estimated Number of Juvenile Arrests, 2007

Most Serious Offense	Number of Juvenile Arrests	Percent of Total Juvenile Arrests		Percent Change		
		Female	Under Age 15	1998–07	2003–07	2006–07
Total	2,180,500	29%	28%	−20%	−3%	−2%
Violent Crime Index	97,100	17	28	−14	5	−3
Murder and nonnegligent manslaughter	1,350	8	10	−23	26	3
Forcible rape	3,580	2	35	−32	−13	−2
Robbery	34,490	10	21	6	35	−1
Aggravated assault	57,650	23	31	−21	−6	−4
Property Crime Index	419,000	35	31	−33	−10	4
Burglary	81,900	12	30	−30	−3	−2
Larceny-theft	300,300	43	31	−32	−9	8
Motor vehicle theft	29,600	16	22	−49	−30	−14
Arson	7,200	12	59	−19	−7	−8
Nonindex						
Other assaults	240,700	34	39	0	−1	−3
Forgery and counterfeiting	3,100	31	12	−60	−37	−11
Fraud	7,800	36	16	−26	−6	−2
Embezzlement	1,700	42	4	5	43	25
Stolen property (buying, receiving, possessing)	22,400	18	24	−33	−9	−4
Vandalism	111,800	13	41	−14	4	−4
Weapons (carrying, possessing, etc.)	43,900	10	32	−8	12	−7
Prostitution and commercialized vice	1,500	78	13	6	1	−4
Sex offenses (except forcible rape and prostitution)	15,500	10	48	−15	−18	−4

Table 2.1. Estimated Number of Juvenile Arrests, 2007 (*Continued*)

Most Serious Offense	Number of Juvenile Arrests	Percent of Total Juvenile Arrests		Percent Change		
		Female	Under Age 15	1998–07	2003–07	2006–07
Nonindex (*continued*)						
Drug abuse violations	195,700	16	15	−6	0	0
Gambling	2,100	2	14	−27	9	−14
Offenses against the family and children	5,800	38	29	−46	−16	11
Driving under the influence	18,200	24	3	−17	−10	−6
Liquor law violations	141,000	37	9	−20	2	1
Drunkenness	16,900	25	11	−28	3	3
Disorderly conduct	201,200	33	38	3	−1	−5
Vagrancy	3,800	29	31	51	−33	−21
All other offenses (except traffic)	378,900	26	24	−22	−3	−3
Suspicion	400	24	26	−72	−25	−8
Curfew and loitering	143,000	31	26	−30	3	−5
Runaways	108,900	56	32	−36	−9	−3

Source: Adapted from Puzzanchera (2009, April), *Juvenile arrests, 2007.* Office of Juvenile Justice and Delinquency Prevention (OJJDP). *Juvenile Justice Bulletin* (Washington, DC: Office of Juvenile Justice and Delinquency Prevention), www.ncjrs.gov/pdffiles1/ojjdp/225344.pdf.

We learn from further information provided in the OJJDP (2009) Juvenile Justice Bulletin that during the decade between 1998 and 2007, when the female juvenile arrest rates decreased, they decreased less than male juvenile arrests in many offense categories (e.g., aggravated assault). Moreover, unlike male arrests, they increased for most drug and alcohol-related offenses (e.g., driving under the influence, drug abuse violations) and increased for simple assault.

How does the increase in arrests for assaults for girls compare to arrests for grown women? In fact, according to the *Uniform Crime Reports* (UCRs; Federal Bureau of Investigation, 2007), the total number of arrests for females increased by 4% while the total for males fell by 17.2%. Arrests for simple assaults between

1997 and 2006 for both juvenile and total female arrests increased (10.6% and 18.7% respectively). And this was a time when both juvenile and total male arrests for simple assault decreased significantly (–8.7% and –23.7%, respectively). This implies that the increase in juvenile female arrests for simple assault over the period was a trend for females in general, not for juvenile females specifically.

Is this a true increase in crimes of violence for girls and women? Feminist criminologists such as Katherine Luke (2008) and state department researchers think not. Based on her examination of the evidence, Luke concludes that the public concern over girls' violence is more reflective of cultural anxiety over changing social norms regarding race and gender than an actual increase in girls' violence. Similarly, researchers from the Department of Justice also doubt the claims about rising female violence. If there had been a true increase in such violent behavior among young females, as they point out, the arrest rate also would show an increase in other categories of violent crime arrests, such as robbery. More likely explanations of the increase in assault arrests are the relabeling of girls' family conflicts as violent offenses and changes in law enforcement practices that have resulted in mandatory arrest laws for incidents regarding domestic violence. Documentation from the U.S. Department of Justice (2008) that drew on self-report and victimization data as well as arrest data reveals that gender differences in juvenile offending, including assault, have not changed significantly in the national victimization surveys since 1980. This finding is in sharp contrast to the Uniform Crime Reports official arrest statistics that show a narrowing of genders in arrests for the crimes of assault. "This discrepancy," according to the report, "suggests that increases in arrests may be attributable more to changes in enforcement policies than to changes in girls' behavior" (p. 15).

In gauging the extent of male and female juvenile violence, we also need to look at homicide rates. These rates, as reported by the Bureau of Justice Statistics (BJS; 2007), show great variation by race and by gender among African Americans. The homicide rate per 100,000 for juveniles (ages 14–17) was 7.9 for White males, 64.1 for Black males, 4 for Black females, and 0.7 for White females. Since the 1990s, the number of homicides has declined in all these categories. Among middle-class African American girls, as the U.S. Department of Justice (2008) bulletin from the Girls Study Group points out, relational conflict did not produce physical fighting, but among economically deprived adolescent girls, it did so.

Data from Self-Report Studies

Research based on self-reported data has an advantage over police-reported data in that it can uncover crimes, most of which have not been reported.

The best source at present is the National Longitudinal Survey of Youth, a project of the Bureau of Labor Statistics to determine the extent of juvenile problem behavior. A national sample of nearly 9,000 youths between the ages of 12 to 17 participated in the survey. In his analysis of this vast survey data, McCurley (2006) provides a male-female breakdown that is instructive. Categories surveyed were: being suspended from school, belonging to a gang, vandalism, theft, assault, selling drugs, and carrying a handgun. In every category except for running away from home, males reported more problem behavior. Significantly, the maximum number of offenses occurred at age 16. Additional data gathered from a self-report longitudinal survey revealed a sharp decrease in delinquent acts for both genders by ages 18 and 19 (OJJDP, 2006). This fact is consistent with findings from recent brain research on adolescents. Researchers have found that the prefrontal cortex, which regulates impulse and emotions, develops later than originally thought—well past age 18 and into the mid-20s (van Wormer, 2007). Developmental psychologist Richard Lerner (2007) reports an association between brain function and structure in the maturing brain and the ability to resist peer influence; this association was more pronounced in girls than in boys. More research is needed to determine the exact nature of this relationship.

Chesney-Lind and Shelden (2004) challenge the notion of a rise in female youth violence. Their argument is premised on the fact that the purported rise is not borne out in self-report data, data that are in many ways more reliable than those provided in official arrest statistics. They single out three additional factors at work: "relabeling," changes in enforcement of the law, and "upcriming."

State legislatures today are relabeling girls' status offense behavior from noncriminal charges such as incorrigibility to assault charges so that they can be better controlled. This relabeling of lesser offenses brings the offending girls under the jurisdiction of the juvenile justice system, thus making them available for adjudication and incarceration.

A second factor affecting the crime statistics is the change in law enforcement procedures for handling calls for domestic violence. New dual-arrest policies favor the arrest of both perpetrator and victim if the victim fought back. Similarly, the new policies are brought into play in family fights; when the parents call the police on their children, the children often are arrested for assault. Often the parents desire this outcome to teach the girl a lesson or for other personal motives.

The third factor, according to Chesney-Lind and Shelden (2004), is the "upcriming" of minor forms of youth violence. Upcriming refers to policies such as zero-tolerance policies that have the effect of increasing the severity of the charges. Many jurisdictions, as Miazad (2002) maintains, are detaining girls not simply to maintain public safety but to protect and arrange services for girls who have not committed serious crimes, including many who have run away from chaotic or abusive homes.

Although these system changes decidedly affect arrest and in-custody rates, the fact that girls are getting into trouble with the law at all suggests a need to learn more about their pathways to delinquency. We need, in short, to learn more about these girls' lives.

PROFILE OF THE FEMALE ADOLESCENT

The first fact to consider in our study of the female juvenile offender is that, first of all, she is a girl. Developmentally, girls are unique; their socialization is unique to their gender as well. Relationships are primary and often conflictual. In order to construct or evaluate gender-sensitive programming for girls, delinquent or otherwise, some knowledge of girls' lives within the family and within society is essential.

Relevant to the pressures on female adolescents, Gilligan (2009) reviews her findings from earlier research in which she found that girls often suffered from a loss of voice: "When I observed dissociation among girls entering adolescence and subsequently in boys around the age of five, what I saw was that they were splitting their minds from their bodies, their thoughts from their emotions, and themselves from their relationships in the process of entering a culture that sanctioned these splits" (p. 10).

An empirically based, landmark study by the American Association of University Women (AAUW; 1992) examined the behavior and treatment of girls in the classroom. The AAUW survey included girls of color and all social classes. These findings, which received widespread press coverage at the time, validated Gilligan's (1982) earlier observations about the unique pressures brought to bear on the adolescent girl. The most striking finding in this research was that White girls tend to lose their sense of self-esteem as they advance from elementary school to high school. African American girls, in contrast, were found to maintain their self-esteem but to often become dissociated from school and schoolwork.

Themes found to be unique to the high school–age girl in the AAUW study and in the girls described in the books *Schoolgirls* by Orenstein (1994) and *The Cult of Thinness* by Hess-Biber (2007) were:

- Obsession with physical appearance and popularity based on external characteristics rather than achievement
- Loss of freedom in later adolescence associated with budding sexuality

- Close attention to relationships
- Intense mother-daughter patterns of communication

Inner-city Black and Latina girls were found to have somewhat unique issues related to life in tough neighborhoods; the development of a tough exterior was seen as vital for their protection from gangs and violence. Early pregnancy was a reality for many. In short, girls' victimization, whether from sexual harassment at school or on the streets to full-blown sexual assault, is a fact of girls' lives that has an important bearing on their personalities and later development (van Wormer & Bartollas, 2010).

In their gender-specific guidelines written for the state of Oregon, Patton and Morgan (2002, p. 31ff) suggest that while these points may not be true of every girl and boy, generally speaking, it can be assumed that:

- Girls develop their identity in relation to other people while boys develop their identity in relation to the world.
- Girls resolve conflict based on relationships while boys resolve conflict based on rules.
- Girls focus on connectedness and interdependence while boys focus on independence and autonomy.
- Girls exhibit relational aggression while boys exhibit overt aggression.

This latter point is emphasized by Okamoto and Chesney-Lind (2003). While boys' aggression tends to be more overt, girls' aggression tends to be verbal and "relational," or focused on damaging another girl's friendships or reputation. Gossiping and spreading rumors are common strategies of female adolescent revenge and sources of great pain to the victim.

Gender, in short, has a dramatic effect on most aspects of girls' lives (Chesney-Lind & Shelden, 2004). The rules that govern females' lives are not the same as those governing males' lives, and the impact of the gender conformity norms occurs at different stages of development for boys and girls. Theories of delinquency that are built on male forms of striving for power and dominance, therefore, are irrelevant to female patterns of conformity and deviance.

PROFILE OF THE ADOLESCENT GIRL AT RISK

One positive outcome of the attention that delinquent girls have received in the news, whether misleading or not, is that it has catapulted Congress to make more funding available for research on the treatment needs of female delinquents and to determine what works and what does not (Sherman,

2005). Accordingly, a growing body of research has been devoted to the study of the characteristics of delinquent girls (Lederman, Dakof, Larreal, & Hua, 2004; Zahn, 2007). Researchers have identified basic demographic and offense patterns as well as background characteristics, such as family dysfunction, trauma, abuse, mental health issues, substance abuse, risky sexual behavior, academic problems, and delinquent peers, as common features among girls in custody (Lederman et al., 2004; OJJDP, 2006).

The profile of at-risk adolescent females that emerges identifies common characteristics including histories of victimization, unstable family life, school failure, repeated status offenses, and mental health and substance abuse problems (Bloom & Covington, 2001). These risk factors are similar to those for boys, but they differ in terms of intensity for girls, except for school failure. Further female gender risk factors as singled out by the National Juvenile Justice Networking Forum (2007), a project of the Girls Study Group, are: early puberty and physical development; sexual assault; depression and anxiety; boyfriend influence; and mother-daughter conflict.

Researchers have long known that family dynamics are a key contributor to delinquency for girls and boys both. The research literature, however, according to Cauffman (2008), reveals that among children of substance-abusing parents, parenting disruptions are linked more strongly with delinquency and drug abuse among girls than among boys. Similarly, conflict over parental supervision appears to influence offending more strongly in girls than in boys. The treatment implications are that attention needs to be paid to emotional issues involving families and to improving family relationships if appropriate.

For girls who live in tough neighborhoods, such as inner urban areas, race, crime, and gender come together to raise the risks of offending. Researchers have found that girls sometimes are violent with each other to look tough in an attempt to get a reputation for their own self-protection (Chesney-Lind, Morash, & Stevens, 2008). Girls may be more influenced by romantic partners than boys, especially in the commission of minor delinquent acts. Schaffner (2006) found that many girls in trouble with the law relied on boyfriends more than twice their age for material rewards, and they became influenced by these men to use drugs and engage in other illegal activity.

PATHWAYS TO DELINQUENCY

Sexual and Physical Abuse

Sexual, physical, and/or emotional victimization are among the most important commonalities found in populations of girls and young women involved in juvenile justice (Zavlik & Maniglia, 2007). Sexual abuse and other victimization, in fact, were identified by the National Council on Crime and Delinquency's (NCCD) study of girls in California as the most critical pathway to female delinquency for young girls (Acoca & Dedel, 1998). The report indicated that 92% of the girls interviewed reported a history of physical, sexual, and/or emotional abuse. Similarly, the U.S. Department of Justice (2009) identified victimization as a key issue for female juvenile offenders. A high percentage of female "delinquents," a reported 70%, have a history of sexual abuse, compared to a reported incidence rate of 30% reported incidents for boys.

To better understand the relationship between sexual abuse and justice system involvement, Goodkind, Ng, and Sarri (2006) analyzed survey interviews with 169 young women involved or at risk of involvement with juvenile justice. They found that girls who experienced sexual abuse, as compared to those who did not, had more negative mental health, educational, addictive, sexual, legal, and employment experiences. Their recommendation was for efforts to prevent abuse from occurring and, beyond that, to improve child welfare and social service systems.

In light of the fact that girls experience more physical and sexual abuse, they tend to exhibit psychopathology including posttraumatic stress disorder, suicidal behavior, disassociative disorder, and borderline personality disorder more frequently than do boys (Miazad, 2002).Consistently, interviews with incarcerated female offenders reveal that these women's childhoods were plagued with neglect and abuse (Gilfus, 1992; van Wormer & Bartollas, 2010). Many responded to this abuse by running away from home. Once on the streets, they survived by becoming involved in drug use, prostitution, and stealing, criminal offenses that typically brought them to the attention of the authorities.

Such an explanation is part of what has been termed a "pathways" approach to understanding girls' entry into the juvenile justice system. Since the role of intoxicating substances plays a key role in the typical road from victimization to incarceration, a closer consideration of substance use is in order. The pathway theory as presented here, as we will see in the section under race, is especially relevant to European American girls with problem behaviors; it is a theoretical model that may need to be modified to understand forces that lead girls of other racial and ethnic backgrounds down the path to delinquency.

In her in-depth interviews with African American girls in the inner city of St. Louis, criminologist Jody Miller (2008) reveals how racial equality rather than race creates a situation for girls that is ripe both for sexual victimization by gang members and others in the community and for delinquency involvement. There was virtually no protection from other girls, the community, or the police for those girls who were physically or sexually attacked. Sadly, the racial and gender equalities were so engrained that the youth regard such violence as deserved by the individual victims.

Sometimes the girl in a juvenile institution cannot be released through no fault of her own but because of her potential victimization. Thus we hear from Tricia (not her real name) as told to social worker Renée Barbu during a counseling session (and shared with van Wormer in a log of October 6, 2007):

> I wish I could go home but I'm not allowed to live in the same house with my brother because he had sex with me. I wish they would just forgive him. I did and so did my family, just like what Jesus Christ would do. We just want to be a family again. They say my anger comes from the sexual abuse and that I need to stay in treatment.

Role of Substance Use

Substance use in females is highly correlated with early childhood sexual victimization, especially among White females. The literature consistently reports a strong link between childhood abuse and the later development of alcoholism and other drug problems (Downs, Capshew, & Rindels, 2004; van Wormer & Davis, 2008). As reported in the NCCD study above, at about the same age as the victimization occurred (usually between 13 and 14 years old), the girls started using addictive substances. This is what happened to Carla, who shared these facts with her counselor:

> When I told my mom that my dad was having sex with me she said I was a liar. She had to believe me after my dad started to have sex with my cousin too. People believed my cousin more than they believed me for some reason. (Interviewed by Barbu, shared with van Wormer in a log on November 3, 2007.)

There are two possible explanations for the link between substance use and childhood sexual abuse. The simplest explanation is that alcohol and other drugs serve to dull the senses from emotional pain; temporarily they lift depression by producing a high. The use of these substances, in turn, causes personality changes and induces other risk-taking activities associated with

sexuality and crime. Eating disorders work the same way and are highly associated with sexual victimization in White women (van Wormer & Davis,
2008).

Jennifer, age 17 (interviewed by Barbu on November 9, 2008), sadly is
typical of girls in her juvenile institution. In her own words:

> My mother chooses men over my sister and me. That's why we
> are all messed up. I started prostituting myself. I didn't care. I
> already felt like crap—I might as well make some money. Now I
> feel a little better about myself, here. I told my mom she has to
> make my sister and me a priority, not the man currently in her
> life....
>
> I don't know why I'm always hungry. I do get regular meals here.
> At home my mom would be at work and there would not be a
> thing to eat in the house. I wouldn't have any money. My stepdad
> would get up at 2:00 pm. He worked the night shift. He would
> order a pizza or something for himself and eat it in front of us
> kids. He would not share. He said we didn't need it because we
> were fat and lazy.

A second explanation of the victimization-substance use link, as offered by
van Wormer and Davis (2008), focuses on the impact of trauma on the mind.
This theory, which links early trauma and a later inability to cope with psychological stress, is entirely consistent with recent neurological evidence of
brain chemistry changes that result from early trauma. Because of these
changes, the former victim's stress response is weakened; this fact sets the
stage for future psychological problems, especially under conditions of
repeated stress (Basham & Miehls, 2004). Adolescents and adults who have
been traumatized as children retain their immature responses (fight-or-flight
reactions) to stress. In controlled laboratory situations, survivors of childhood
trauma have been shown to react very strongly to deliberately stress-inducing
situations compared to a control group who did not suffer trauma in childhood (Heim et al., 2000). Further evidence of a correlation between extreme
stress and a tendency to consume alcohol has been demonstrated in animal
studies (Spear, 2000).

Another form of escape, one that may seem more practical, is simply running away. Running away from a home situation often brings many girls into
the dangerous milieu of street life and ultimately to the attention of the juvenile authorities. To survive on the streets, runaway girls often get involved in

drug-related activities, theft, and/or prostitution, each of which is a punishable crime in itself.

Psychiatric Disorders

Closely related to substance use disorders are psychiatric disorders. An extensive review of all the research on the subject conducted by Teplin et al. (2006) of the Office of Justice Programs found that the research was inadequate and contradictory. They devised a study based on use of a standard assessment of psychiatric disorders and substance use. This form was administered to a large random sample of juveniles in detention. About half of the youth met the criteria for substance dependency; more than one-fourth of females and not quite one-fifth of males were found to have affective disorders, such as depression. This finding of a high rate of depression in girls confirms the finding of an earlier study of adolescent girls in Chicago (National Institute of Justice, 1999).

An extensive survey of Chicago neighborhoods found a close correlation between depression and aggressive behavior in girls. Male-female differences were delineated in data gathered on 72 females and 276 males who had been diagnosed with severe learning disabilities and mental disorders and who were about to be released into the community (Unruh & Bullis, 2005). Female juvenile offenders were found to be less likely than males to be diagnosed with a severe learning disability and less likely to have failed at school or to have been diagnosed with attention hyperactivity deficit disorder. Their work histories showed more stability than did the males'. The girls were more likely than the boys to have parented a child, to have a history of abuse and neglect, and to be at risk of suicide and running away. The findings of Unruh and Bullis could be helpful in planning for gender-specific aftercare for both genders. Child care arrangements and a network of interconnected support systems would help girls establish economic independence.

Returning to the 2006 study of mental disorders conducted by Teplin et al., the sample size was sufficiently large to allow for racial/ethnic comparisons. Among the females tested, although non-Hispanic Whites had somewhat more psychiatric problems than African Americans or Hispanics, almost one-third of the members of each of the racial/ethnic groups had some form of depression and over one-third had an anxiety disorder. Substance use was highest among non-Hispanic Whites. Too little evidence of psychoses was found to allow for racial/ethnic breakdowns. Based on their findings, Teplin et al. stress the importance of screening youth for mental disorders and providing mental health services immediately as needed. Many detention centers do not screen their residents, and they fail to link them to community mental health services prior to their release. Such services should address the interconnectedness of mental health symptoms and delinquent behavior while offering integrated treatment to address psychiatric symptoms such as posttraumatic stress disorder and addictive behaviors simultaneously (van Wormer & Davis, 2008).

CHILDREN OF INCARCERATED WOMEN

Many incarcerated women are single mothers of young and preteen children. When mothers are sentenced to long prison terms for nonviolent offenses, such as complicity in drug dealing, the disruption that their children face is often ignored. A second situation falling heavily on women is the dual arrest policy practiced today in many jurisdictions that results in the arrest of both parties when a report of domestic violence has been filed. Children are often placed in foster care, at least temporarily, following a situation of out-of-control male-on-female violence, which is damaging in itself. The blindness to gender-related realities of the facts surrounding the crime means that children typically have to be brought up by relatives or in foster homes. In contrast to the situation in which a father is incarcerated and the children stay in the care of the mother, when a mother is sent away, the home life as the child knows it is totally transformed (Raeder, 2005).

Eighty percent of mothers who are incarcerated go back to parenting once they are released—and more often than not, their daughters follow a similar path to trouble, according to social work professor Darlene Grant (cited by Pace, 2006). Grant said studies show these daughters are six times more likely to land in the juvenile justice system than children whose parents have not been jailed. Due to racism in the drug sentencing laws and the high incarceration rate for African Americans, Black children are nine times as likely as White children to have a parent in jail (Marks, 2003). Allison, however, who described her situation to her counselor (Barbu, October 8, 2007), is White: "I wish my mom wasn't in prison. She always cooked really good. My father doesn't know how to control me or take care of me, that's why I started being bad and how I got here with all the other juvenile delinquents."

ISSUE OF RACE

African American and Latina girls often grow up in contexts that differ markedly from those of their European American counterparts. Young women of color have a history of womanhood that is unique to them. African Americans, for example, historically have inhabited a world in which their menfolk and other men in the society could not or did not protect them (Fordham, 1993). This fact is reflected in unique survival skills that often come across as aggression. In the classic article entitled "Those Loud Black Girls," anthropologist Signithia Fordham presents her observations from a field study of Black schoolgirls, most of whom came from low-income homes. She found a contrast between high-achieving and low-achieving girls, the former of whom were quiet, studied hard, and in denial of their cultural identity. Underachieving females, in contrast, were strikingly visible, socially popular, known throughout the school, and immersed in "the Black egalitarian system" (p. 11).

Pugh-Lilly, Neville, and Poulin (2001) explored Black adolescent girls' perceptions of delinquent behaviors in interviews with 11 girls enrolled in an alternative school. Some had been expelled from the regular school for fighting. All of the girls indicated that they used aggressive behaviors to protect themselves from perceived threats and physical attacks. The environment that they inhabited was perceived as hostile and nonsupportive. They also perceived a high degree of racism in the society.

A national survey of youth conducted by the Centers for Disease Control and Prevention (2006) found that physical violence in the form of fighting was more common among male than female high school students and more common among Black and Latina females than among Whites. Males and minority groups were more likely than White students to be injured in the fights. Girls of color were by far more likely than other groups to feel unsafe going to school.

Another relevant measure of problem behavior—drug and alcohol use—is shown in self-report surveys that a higher proportion of males than females are involved in such use, especially heavy use, and that Blacks have lower drug, alcohol, and tobacco use rates than Whites or Hispanics (OJJDP, 2006). Consistent with these findings, Black females have a disproportionately low rate of drug referrals compared to White females, at only 10%. This is below their percentage of the juvenile population, which is 16%.

And yet, young Black women are picked up by police at three times the rate of young White women (Marks, 2003). Among females referred to juvenile court in 2002 for person offenses, Blacks accounted for 38% of cases—a clear overrepresentation of this population (OJJDP, 2006). This was about the same racial breakdown as occurred among males. The Latina rate is not provided separately but rather included in the rate for Whites.

These official statistics, combined with qualitative observations of the concerns and behavior of African American girls from poor backgrounds, suggest the possibility of a different pathway to delinquency for many of African American girls due to the reality of their lives. Refuting a biological explanation of gender-role differences, Holsinger and Holsinger (2005) refer to cross-racial research that shows socialization of African American girls stresses self-reliance, resourcefulness, independence, and little sex-role segregation. This upbringing is contrasted to that typical for White females, who are more likely to be socialized to be subordinate. This more stereotypically masculine pattern of upbringing may provide a strength for African American girls, especially in regard to self-esteem, but it is one that is not appreciated by the juvenile justice system. Holsinger and Holsinger suggest that the pathway to delinquency unique to Black females may be shaped by negative experiences in a racist and often inadequate school system.

A background of early childhood sexual abuse was found by Katz (2000) to have different consequences for Black and White women. For Black women, the psychological reaction to childhood abuse was associated with externalization of the anger in outbursts of violence, and for White women with drinking. Holsinger and Holsinger (2005), similarly, found a link between abuse and poor mental health among White delinquent girls and between abuse and violence among Black delinquent girls. Given the racial differences in socialization and self-esteem, these differences, they note, are not surprising.

Moving from referrals to juvenile court to actual decisions to place youth in detention, Black females had a higher proportion of person offenses in the detention caseload (41%) than did either Whites (31%) or youth of other races (27%). For White females, drug offense cases accounted for 11% of detained cases, compared with 5% for Black females and 9% for females of other races.

Racial differences in how girls of color compared to White girls are processed through the juvenile justice system are pronounced. Research shows, for example, that White girls are far more likely to be recommended for probation as opposed to a placement in detention by the courts (Okamoto & Chesney-Lind, 2003).

Additional Factor of Class

Race/ethnicity and class need to be considered together, not race/ethnicity alone. The effects are not merely additive—race plus class—but the consequences of multiple oppressions that work to magnify each other and are associated with additional risks. Family structure, for example, is correlated with a youth's race and ethnicity; White non-Hispanic youth are more likely to live in families with two biological parents than are Black or Hispanic youth (OJJPD, 2006). Gang membership, for example, is highly related to weak family structure and instability for both boys and girls. Almost all gang members are drawn from low-income groups (van Wormer & Bartollas, 2010). Connectedness to school and work are protective factors in preventing the development of problem behaviors. All these factors, negative and positive, are highly correlated with social class.

Poverty is a major risk factor for delinquency and often is accompanied by other risk factors related to family disruption (OJJDP, 2006). Lower-class adolescent females tend to confront higher risk levels than youth from the higher echelons, who live in tougher neighborhoods where there is more crime and victimization, and to have unsatisfactory experiences at school, to need to deal with risks of pregnancy and premature motherhood, and to lack supportive networks at home. "Many live in neighborhoods where guns, gangs, and drugs are common," according to Marks (2003). "And many come from families with at least one relative in jail, making prison terms more of a norm than a social rarity" (p. 2). For all races, middle-class children from stable backgrounds typically do not have problems of the frequency or magnitude as those described here.

In the criminalizing of juvenile offenses, therefore, the issues of gender, race, and crime are paramount. The impact of the criminalizing of girls' offenses has a significant impact on girls, especially on minorities and girls from dysfunctional and impoverished backgrounds. When children from families from the middle and upper classes get into trouble, their parents often can persuade the court to sentence them to probation with a referral to outpatient mental health or substance abuse treatment (Chesney-Lind & Shelden, 2004).

Involvement in Gangs

The most comprehensive survey of gang membership is conducted by the U.S. Department of Justice; data are gathered from police reports in a sample of urban and rural areas. According to the most recent report, gang activity has continued at the same pace over the past decade; before 1996 there was significantly more gang activity (Egley & Ritz, 2006). The "lifeblood" and much of the excitement of these gangs come from drug sales. Latinos and African Americans are the groups most active in gang membership.

Few law enforcement–based surveys pay much attention to female gang activity. According to the National Youth Gang Center (2007), this is because the police are less concerned about female gang activity than they are about male gangs. This survey did determine that 1 in 5 of gangs in the cities contained female members compared to about 1 in 3 of rural area gangs.

Much of the discussion in recent years about "the new violent female" has turned to look at girls' violence within gangs (Archer & Grascia, 2005). A review of the literature on gang delinquency shows a gradual shift in the findings from studies of the early 1980s that saw female gangs as basically auxiliaries of male gangs, although they had their own initiation rituals and enforced fierce codes of loyalty (van Wormer & Bartollas, 2010). Studies of girls' gangs in the 1990s found much more active criminal involvement, especially drug trafficking. Still, as Chesney-Lind and Shelden (2004) suggest, a male bias is evident in much of the literature; female members are discussed in the context of "property" and "sex." Female researchers, in contrast, view female gang members as much more than one-dimensional creatures. And their investigations refute media images surrounding the new violent girl gang members and girls beating each other up. Such media representations do not mean there is an epidemic of violence among young women.

One of the Guys by Jody Miller (2001) provides a close analysis of the gender dynamics of gang membership in mixed-gender gangs. Her own research was based on interviews with a sample of 42 female gang members from inner urban areas of Columbus, Ohio, and St. Louis, Missouri. Overall, the girls were in predominantly male gangs. Latina gang members were more likely than African Americans to describe their gangs as female groups affiliated with male gangs. African American girls were more likely to describe their gangs as mixed gender. Miller found that the young women often joined gangs to be with their older siblings in the context of family problems. In the gangs, the girls had two choices: They could choose to be "one of the guys" and expose themselves to fights and risks of injury or arrests, or they could play more feminine roles—a safer choice in terms of external risks but one that is associated with low status in the gang hierarchy and the risk of sexual exploitation within it. Such young women, in effect, reduce their risk of exposure to street violence by not participating in collective criminal activities, but the trade-off is that they then may be regarded as weak by their fellow gang members and be victimized accordingly. Either way, girls in the gang were more likely than other girls from the same neighborhood to be sexually assaulted, threatened with a weapon, and even stabbed or killed. In Getting Played: African American Girls, Urban Inequality, and Gendered Violence, Miller (2008) reveals through the girls' and boys' own stories the social and structural contexts within which such gendered violence takes place.

Since the risks involved hardly make gang membership seem desirable for a girl, why do young females join gangs at all? Archer and Grascia (2005) list these functions of gang membership to the girl:

- Peer relationships and sense of belonging
- Means of survival in a threatening urban environment
- Desire to be close to a boyfriend who is a gang member

Girls may join because of low self-esteem as a way to get respect and as a refuge from dysfunctional home environments. In other words, girls' participation in gangs is in no way a departure from their normal sex-role behavior. Gangs offer family-type membership as well as some protection in a rough neighborhood.

Eghigian and Kirby (2006), who have studied girls in gangs in Chicago, describe roles that girls may play in gangs:

- Holding and transporting drugs and guns since the police are less likely to search them
- Transporting contraband to and from prisons
- Acting as lures with rival gang members to secure information or set them up for murder or violence
- Supporting criminal acts such as selling drugs and engaging in robbery and burglary.

Leaving a gang is difficult, because gang members will fear the leaking of intelligence, and the girl will no longer have the gang's protection from old enemies. If she is to leave, the former gang member must move far away for her protection. Eghigian and Kirby stress the importance of working with girls in gang-infested neighborhoods while they are very young to provide them with positive opportunities and help them meet their social needs so they will not turn to gangs for support.

GIRLS IN CUSTODY

According to data reported by OJJDP (2006), girls are more likely than boys to be incarcerated for simple assault (an actual attempt or threatened attack without a weapon); violations of probation, parole, or court orders; and status offenses. But boys are far more likely than girls to get into trouble and to be incarcerated.

The Juvenile Justice and Delinquency Prevention Act of 1974 (JJDPA) encouraged states to prohibit the incarceration of status offenders and dependent children in secure facilities (Schwartz, Steketee, & Scheider, 2004).

Although the 1974 Act was not a mandate with fiscal incentives, it did bring about a significant decline in the incarceration of girls for status offenses because it set forth specific requirements for states to meet in order to access federal juvenile justice funds (Miazad, 2002). Then, in 1992 and again in 2002, as part of the Reauthorization of the JJDPA, states applying for federal grants were required to identify gaps in their ability to provide services to girls. Applications had to include a plan for providing needed gender-specific services for the prevention and treatment of juvenile delinquency and assurance that youth in the juvenile justice system are treated equitably on the basis of gender. As of 2009, another renewal of the act is pending.

Females in residential placement are most often sent to detention centers, which are less secure facilities designed for short-term stays, in contrast to more secure facilities for long-term stays. Females are a relatively small percentage of the total number of juveniles in custody. Their percentage has grown, however, from 13% in 1991 to 15% in 2006 (OJJDP, 2006). Girls tend to be younger than their male counterparts; the peak age is 15 to 16 for girls and 16 to 17 for boys. The majority of females in custody are minorities (55%) compared to an even higher number—62% among males. Among the females, 45% are Caucasian, 35% African American, 15% Latina, and 1% Asian.

As far as offenses are concerned, 13% of the girls are in custody for status offenses compared to 6% of the boys. When compared to boys, girls are in custody for more minor offenses. The fact that the community is less fearful of female youthful offenders than they are of young males is an additional factor that results in the confinement of offending girls in less secure facilities than would otherwise be the case.

Still, according to a joint study by the American Bar Association and the National Bar Association (2001), girls are more likely to find themselves detained for minor offenses that could be better dealt with in a less restrictive manner. As legal scholar Ossai Miazad (2002) reminds us, international legal standards through the United Nations and many state statutes mandate the use of "the least restrictive alternative" when addressing juveniles in the justice system. Removal of a child from her community for offenses that would likely not result in incarceration if committed by an adult is a clear violation of this standard.

Conditions in Residential Institutions for Girls

Detention centers, as well as alternatives to detention, have historically been designed for boys; existing policies, practices, and training are masculine in every sense of the word. Fewer than half of the states have enacted regulations addressing specific conditions of confinement for girls, and none of them is comprehensive (Sherman, 2005). The difficulty of transforming this male-based culture to one responsive to the developmental needs of girls is exacerbated by the increasing number of girls in detention, a fact that puts pressure on the whole juvenile justice system for scarce resources.

Abuses that a majority of girl offenders experienced in their homes, in schools, and on the streets are often compounded by injuries they later receive within the juvenile justice system. Among the most commonly reported problems reported by Acoca (2004) in her survey of the research literature are:

- Demeaning and foul language used by staff in interaction with the girls
- Overuse of physical restraints
- Strip searching of girl detainees that includes body cavity searches after visits from outsiders and whenever there is a suspected infraction of the rules

In addition, the girls' access to basic hygiene products was highly restricted; they had to make constant requests for such products to obtain them. These invasions of the girls' personal privacy are humiliating and potentially harmful, given that some of these girls may be pregnant and that many girls may relive the trauma of sexual violation and other forms of abuse when treated in this manner.

Sexual Abuse of Girls in Custody

About one-third of female youth in custody are confined in private facilities (OJJDP, 2006). Such facilities are more apt than state facilities to be involved in incidents of mistreatment even though formal complaints may be fewer (van Wormer & Bartollas, 2010). Major factors in the popularity of the privatization of training schools and other correctional facilities are cost (lower pay and fewer benefits for staff members) and reduced liability for the state in cases of mistreatment. As reported by the OJJDP (2006), drawing on BJS data, about one-third of the victims in substantiated claims of incidents of sexual violence in private and state facilities were female. The male-on-male attacks tend to be by other youth, while sexual assaults of the females tend to be by staff members. Compared to adult facilities, the allegation rate of staff sexual misconduct is far greater in juvenile facilities.

As the OJJDP reminds us, however, we have to take into account the fact that sexual assaults on juveniles are more likely to be reported than those on adults due to mandatory reporting laws that require reporting of child abuse cases. Yet one would think staff members would hesitate to complain against their own place of employment, and the girls themselves generally have no opportunity for redress.

Human Rights Watch (2006) conducted a study of two rural New York facilities for delinquent girls and documented three cases in the past five years of staff having intercourse with their wards. There were also reports of staff touching girls in sexual ways and making lewd remarks. Staff sometimes humiliated girls by publicly commenting on their past sexual history, sexual abuse, or infection with sexually transmitted diseases.

An investigation conducted by the Associated Press of each state agency that oversees juvenile facilities found numerous situations in which girls were groped by male officers and subjected to horrendous physical and sexual abuse (Mohr, 2008). The numbers of accusations of abuse against the officers were staggering. Of over 13,000 complaints made in the over a four-year period, 1,343 were confirmed by authorities. No gender breakdown is given in the report, but clearly from the examples provided, many of the complaints were made by girls.

GENDER-SENSITIVE PROGRAMMING FOR GIRLS

Recognition of male/female developmental differences is important in shaping approaches that will tap into the interests and strengths of each gender. Consistent with findings from the social science literature showing the more serious and violent nature of boys' than of girls' offending (Belknap, 2007), we could predict that programs for boys would be more successful when they offer ways to advance within a structured environment, while programs for girls would do better when they focus on relationships and assertiveness within relationships. Girls who have gotten into trouble benefit, as Gilligan (2009) reminds us, as do all girls, when they are given a voice. Through listening to girls caught up in the juvenile justice system, we can best determine their needs.

Garcia and Lane (2009) decided to do just that—organize at-risk and delinquent girls into focus groups to discuss their personal histories and their treatment needs. When the girls were asked to discuss what most often gets girls arrested, the top three reasons were drug and alcohol use, assault (often on parents), and running away. Their counseling experiences were not always positive as they did not believe the information would be kept confidential. Girls who had had good experiences praised the grief and loss counseling and trauma work as helping the most. One theme that emerged in the focus groups was the desire to have a voice; the girls wished to play an active role in the formal proceedings and in other decisions about their care. They all agreed they wanted custody staff who cared about them and who showed it.

Special attention to girls' unique biology and body image concerns are essential areas of consideration for these are major female concerns. In view of the recognition of girls' special needs, the establishment of group homes would provide the supervision needed in a therapeutic environment. Such homes would provide a female-centered school curriculum, caring mentors to offer encouragement in setting realistic educational goals, and special services for pregnant and parenting young women. Individual and group counseling for survivors of sexual abuse trauma should be provided as well; these matters cannot be addressed properly in mixed settings or in gender-neutral programs. Zahn (2007)) stresses the importance of providing discussions of and information about gender, sexuality, and health and information on how to establish nonabusive relationships with romantic partners, including attention to the selection of male peer friendships.

Gender-responsive policy recommends that effective interventions be utilized to address intersecting issues of substance use, trauma, mental health, and economic oppression (Bloom, Owen & Covington, 2004). To this end, the Iowa Commission on the Status of Women has been a pioneer in promoting conferences and trainings on gender-specific programming for troubled girls. Read Box 2.1 for an interview with Kathy Nesteby, the coordinator for the Gender Specific Task Force in Iowa, who articulates the gender-specific philosophy.

BOX 2.1

Interview with Kathy Nesteby, Coordinator for the Iowa Gender Specific Services Task Force, Des Moines, Iowa

What is your role in the Iowa Gender Specific Services Task Force?

I was hired by the Iowa Commission on the Status of Women (ICSW). The mission of the ICSW is to equalize women's opportunities and to promote full participation by women in the economic, political, and social life of the state. We make recommendations for new policy, develop new programs, and provide public information and education. The ICSW contracts with the Division of Criminal and Juvenile Justice Planning to support the Iowa Gender Specific Services Task Force (IGSSTF). I am the coordinator of the IGSSTF.

What does the IGSSTF do?

The IGSSTF are stakeholders in Iowa's juvenile justice system working together to facilitate system changes to meet females' unique needs. Girls' patterns of offending differ from boys. Historically, Iowa has offered juvenile justice services to girls and boys in the same way, and because boys have always been a larger portion of that system, programming has been based on what works for them. However, sameness does not mean equality. Equality of juvenile justice service delivery does not mean simply allowing adolescent girls access to services that have been provided for adolescent boys.

Girls tend to focus more on relationships, and as a result they are more likely to fear a loss of that connectedness. This is one significant difference that defines their motivation for offending.

The IGSSTF provides an annual conference for girl-serving professionals called Whispers and Screams. We publish and distribute a snapshot study of Iowa's female offenders in the state's juvenile justice system. We provide other professional workshops on the gender-specific approach, and we provide information and advocate for policy change with Iowa legislators.

What are some of the components of gender-specific programming?

1. Keeping girls safe from any verbal, physical, sexual, and emotional abuse. This may also mean the girls need to be removed from friends and family that are too demanding of them, and also it is best if the girls are temporarily removed from adolescent boys because girls are taught to put others, particularly boys, first, and this prevents them from focusing on their own needs.

(continued)

2. Because gender issues for girls of color can be different than gender issues for girls who are White, programs need to be prepared to address racial, ethnic, sexuality, class, and other cultural factors.

3. Improving relationships. This does not mean reinforcing gender role stereotypes that they have already been taught: passivity and self-sacrifice. Instead girls must learn assertiveness, safe expression of anger, and healthy relationships with boundaries. Programs need to help the girls value their relationships with other girls and women as much as they value their relationships with males.

4. Addressing trauma. More than half of girls involved in the juvenile justice system have been physically and/or sexually abused. Any program working with system-involved girls needs to be prepared to address issues of previous trauma.

Interview conducted May 26, 2008, by Renée Barbu.
Printed with permission of Kathy Nesteby.

Controversies in the Field

Just as nonfeminist commentators are divided from feminists in taking the statistical findings of the increase in arrests for female-precipitated violence at face value and attributing this criminality to the impact of the women's movement, so feminist criminologists are also divided. Looming through all this literature is ideology, ideology that concerns the fundamental question of how gender is conceptualized. The controversy also concerns the extent to which one stresses difference or sameness in male and female sex-role behavior. In essence, we are dealing with the age-old nature-nurture controversy. Liberal feminism, sometimes called equality feminism, as described in Chapter 1, rejects a focus on the special needs of the female offender; this position argues for equality based on the fact of the similarity between genders (Goodkind, 2005). Radical feminism, in contrast, often promotes a celebration of girls and women as different from men.

The equality-versus-difference debate has important implications for the understanding of female delinquency, both in its explanation for the causes of delinquency and in its treatment. Whereas criminologists of the equality feminist school would more likely criticize treatments that provide specialized, female-centered approaches for girls, criminologists of the radical school would be inclined to advocate for programming for girls with a stress on relationships, parenting, and healing from early childhood victimization. For example, as Goodkind (2005) notes: "Citing abuse as a girls' issue, when it seems to be relevant for many young people in the juvenile justice system, essentializes gender differences and risks limiting help for boys who have been abused" (p. 64). This approach ignores girls' agency, as Goodkind further suggests. Although the gender-sensitive approach that is the guiding framework for this book is more in line with the difference than the sameness principle, I appreciate Goodkind's arguments that relationships are important to boys as well as girls, that parenting preparation is crucial for their development, and that many of the boys who come to the attention of the authorities have been abused, sometimes sexually, in childhood. Who knows? Once we get effective gender-sensitive programming under way for girls, we might realize that troubled boys would do far better in a nurturing atmosphere rather than in a tough-love or boot camp setting.

A major impediment to effective work with girls in the juvenile justice system singled out by Matthews and Hubbard (2008) is the division between proponents of the "what works" school and the "gender-responsive" scholars. Proponents of the former group argue that the correlates of delinquency are similar for boys and girls; their focus is on treatment that is confrontational and focuses on thinking errors that are believed to perpetuate these girls' oppression. The gender-responsive group, as these authors correctly indicate, emphasizes the importance of developing relationships with girls but provides very little instruction on how to accomplish this.

GENERAL COUNSELING STRATEGIES

Although the empirical research on the effectiveness of programs designed for girls in the juvenile justice system is in its infancy, the existing literature does provide suggestions for practices that work the best. This literature makes clear that approaches should be individualized to address mental and physical health concerns, including substance abuse problems, eating disorders, and trauma. Before such issues can be addressed, however, a trusting relationship between the counselor or case manager and youth must be developed. (Refer to Chapter 6 for a detailed description of the essential ingredients in a working therapeutic relationship.) Consistent with a gender-specific relational theory, a strong helping alliance enhances a client's capacity for positive psychological growth (Matthews & Hubbard, 2008). An excellent way to set the foundations for such a helping relationship is through use of a strengths-based approach: Strengths-based models have been found to be effective for engaging youth in talking about their problems. Jody Miller (2008) heard from the girls in gang-dominated neighborhoods that having a relationship with supportive counselors and female role models was immensely helpful to them in working through their issues and in developing self-esteem.

Group work can be an enjoyable experience and a training ground for the learning of life skills and the discussion of issues that arise in a residential facility. Family counselors commonly work with whole families to work toward solutions collaboratively, such as what sort of treatment is best for a child who is experimenting with drugs. Recognition of the importance of family can flow naturally and spontaneously through involvement in mutual aid or support groups focused on a common, all-absorbing task.

From a strengths perspective, the hallmark of the effective group leader is enthusiasm and unshakable confidence in the young women's latent talents and abilities. The leader or social worker's role, as Gutiérrez and Suarez (1999) state, should be that of consultant and facilitator rather than instructor, so as not to reinforce the sense of powerlessness that victimized and often addicted girls need to overcome. Small groups, according to these authors, have special relevance for empowerment practice with Latinas, because it is in keeping with the Latinos' history of working with one another to provide mutual aid. African American culture is similarly oriented more toward family and community systems than toward individual achievement.

The importance of such group work for the participants is that gaining competency in one area—writing poetry, drawing, parenting—can lead to skills in performing adult roles valued by society. The socially empowering group, even within the confines of the stark juvenile justice setting, can be individually transformative, the more so among women who have been removed from and punished by society, estranged from loved ones, and forced into lockstep with institutional demands. The actively working, fun-loving group can thus represent a strange and powerful anomaly, given where it is and the personal history of its members. Such a group can serve as a bridge to the cultural and social milieu of the larger society (Wilson & Anderson, 1997). And above all, reintegration of the juvenile offender into society is the one thing the current correctional apparatus is often ill prepared to do. The widespread use of a model geared to break convicts of criminal thought patterns can be conceived as a legacy of the previous politically conservative climate and the continuing equating of gender equality with sameness. I concur with Zavlek and Maniglia's (2007) call for a paradigm shift from society's current retributive justice response to the healing model of gender-based restorative justice. Some states, such as Minnesota and Vermont, incorporate a restorative justice approach to help girls make amends for any wrongdoing by enabling them to engage in community service work for reparations in a healing rather than punitive environment.

Researchers have suggested that programs for girls ought to be culturally relevant and sensitive to cultural differences. As Holsinger and Holsinger (2005) concluded from their research on a fairly large interracial sample of incarcerated girls, a life history of abuse is the most relevant variable to address. Reactions to this abuse differ by race, and assessments at the time of correctional placement should identify these differences. Some (more often the White girls) have a propensity to self-injurious behavior ("cutting"), substance use, mental disorders, and even suicide. Others (more often the African American girls) may be more inclined to react through violence. But the acting-out behavior, whatever form it takes, originates from the same source of early childhood maltreatment. The key to breaking the cycle of violence and self-destruction is to create safe places—sanctuaries—where girls no longer perceive the need to be ever ready to fend off the next attacker. That is what female-oriented programming seeks to do.

Innovative Programming

In conjunction with the special treatment needs of girls who have gotten into trouble, Nicole King (2003) in a project funded by the U.S. Department of Justice developed a statewide gender-specific plan for Nevada, one that could apply to any state. As defined in the book, gender-specific programs empower young women; acknowledge and address female offenders' core needs, such as victimization and abuse issues, substance use, mental health disorders, and chronic academic failure; and are family and community oriented.

Consistent with solution-focused therapeutic approaches (see Berg, 1994; De Jong & Berg, 2007), the Nevada plan recommends a focus on what the young woman does well and on creating the opportunity for her to focus her efforts here—on her individual and unique talents. The thinking here is that success in one area can be generalized to other areas and help girls develop effective living strategies and abandon problematic behavior patterns. Aurora Pines is one exemplary program from Nevada that offers opportunities for positive female development and considers the developmental needs of girls at adolescence. The facility is a girl-only environment (apart from staff) and is set in a "wilderness environment" (King, p. 23).

Rudolph Alexander (2000) describes a pilot treatment program at the Santa Monica (CA) Hospital Medical Center developed for girls who have been sexually abused. After engaging in friendly warm-up exercises, the girls played the "Hat Game," in which they all get to answer a question pulled out of a hat, with the questions relating to how they feel their bodies have changed since they were molested and whether they would tell a girl who had been molested that they thought it was her fault. The girls later wrote their own questions: "Have you felt like killing yourself?" "Have you ever felt real crazy?" were examples (p. 208).

In Waterloo, Iowa, group homes that were once coed now specialize in the care of teenage girls, many of whom are already mothers. A system of nurturant foster care has been established in conjunction with Quakerdale, one of the few youth residential facilities in Iowa that accepts pregnant teens. "Patterning with families . . . restoring hope" is the theme of this program that places pregnant teens in trouble with the law in the residential facility. Following their release date, teens have the option of moving into foster care with their babies (Hemenway-Forbes, 2001). Central to all these program innovations is the theme of personal empowerment. In the program, the client is aided to build a positive self-identity and find strength in her own voice and pride in her cultural heritage.

Facility Design

Gender-specific and gender-sensitive are concepts that refer not only to treatment programming but also to the architectural design of juvenile residential facilities themselves. Zavlek and Maniglia (2007) make the case of gender-responsive building construction to enhance girls' sense of safety. These components are integral to such a design:

- Architectural elements, including grilles, registers, fittings, and all fixtures in areas accessible to residents, particularly bedrooms and bathrooms, should be safe and suicide-resistant.
- Procedures such as restraints, strip searches, and intrusive explorations of body parts can induce feelings of victimization to survivors of abuse. Policies and procedures that reflect this knowledge should be adopted.
- Movable furniture can help encourage relationship building by providing a setting conducive to small groups and intimate interactions between staff and girls and by creating a dayroom where people feel comfortable having personal conversations.
- Whenever possible, private interview rooms should be available for intake questioning, which typically includes questions about sexual behavior and abuse.
- Close attention should be paid to the placement of windows and vision panels in the area where body searches are performed.
- To meet privacy needs of girls, appropriate covering for bedroom windows is advised; such covering allows for privacy and yet does not eliminate natural light or prohibit staff monitoring of girls while in their rooms.

- Privacy. Opaque shower curtains in front of multiple single-shower units and saloon doors on bathrooms satisfy privacy needs without compromising institutional security.
- Although closed circuit TV could be used to monitor certain areas, it is important that staff have a direct line of sight to as much of the facility as possible to allow ease of movement and visual supervision.
- Electronic technology may be used in a facility to enhance security and surveillance but must not be substituted for direct staff supervision.
- To preserve family relationships, states should build smaller, locally based facilities that allow juveniles to be kept close to their families and community support systems.
- Above all, juveniles should be provided the opportunity to be in the least restrictive, appropriate environment.

Restorative Gender-Sensitive Programming

Restorative justice practices have become popular in state juvenile justice systems in recent years, with many adopting new practices for handling crime and punishment (Zavlek & Maniglia, 2007). The roots of restorative justice theory can be found in the practices of indigenous peoples throughout the world from ancient times and in more modern times among Canadian Mennonites (Zehr, 2002; van Wormer, 2004). Restorative justice focuses on a philosophical belief that crime should be redefined as harm done to specific victims (including a community) rather than as a violation of arbitrary state laws that identify particular behavior as criminal. Reparation for the harm done is central to the restorative process.

Because of the importance of intimacy and relationships to the growing girl, restorative strategies offer an ideal gendered form of conflict resolution. Typically girls are better able than boys to accept accountability for their harmful actions to others and to confront the difficulties they have experienced in their own interpersonal relationships when they are given the opportunity to connect relationally with service providers (Zavlek & Maniglia, 2007). For girls and young women, adopting a female-responsive philosophy means both allowing them the opportunity to experience meaningful accountability to their victims and restore their own broken relationships (Zavlek & Maniglia). To prepare them for this process, the girls often need to get in touch with their own earlier victimizations and the feelings that were aroused at the time and probably repressed or transformed into anger. This therapy process is all about helping juvenile offenders develop empathy skills for persons they have harmed and to repair relationships in need of restoration.

Since 1993, Minnesota has awarded model program grants to community-based programs that provide gender-specific services. Under the auspices of the Minnesota Department of Corrections, the state has become a leader of gender-specific programming for serious and chronic juvenile offenders. In 2000, the Girls' Restorative Program was launched, which combined restorative justice and gendered principles. Two types of restorative justice circles are used in Minnesota: communication circles and victim offender conferencing circles. Gordon (2004) describes these circles.

> We do restorative justice "Circles." Plainly put, we bring the girls together with the important people in their lives into a safe space, or a "Circle," to speak from their hearts about what has happened in the past, their feelings and thoughts about what is happening now, and their hopes for the future. A trained Circle Keeper or facilitator (in our case, the AMICUS Circle coordinator) works with the girl to prepare for the Circle, invite the members, and create a safe—even sacred—environment for speaking and listening. A "talking piece" (an object of significance to the girl, such as a stone, feather or even a teddy bear) serves as a visual representation of this safe space and is passed from hand to hand. Only the person with the talking piece talks....

> We also attempt to conduct a Victim-Offender Circle with each girl, where a girl sits in a Circle with her victim(s) and support people to speak about the offense and work to repair the harm. (p. 11)

A major challenge of the restorative program is to help the girls, hardened by abuse and negative experiences within the criminal justice system, learn to trust. Through the restorative justice programming, they are asked to sit in a circle—along with their peers, family members, victims, and staff—and to trust the truth that will emerge from the circle. The next case example of a victim-offender process is provided on the program's Web site by Gordon (2004).This passage follows personal testimonies from school officials of how they felt at the student Sarah's offense. (Sarah was serving time in a long-term residential juvenile facility after she had threatened a police officer, who had been summoned to the school, with a knife.)

> Sarah then responded [to the account of her behavior]. She said she was very sorry. She said that she never thought about what a serious offense bringing a knife to school was, and that she would never do it again. She said that she really wants to be home again, but agreed

that she was getting what she needed right now. She also agreed that when she is on her meds, her life goes much better.

The Circle Keeper then asked the group if there were any ideas of what Sarah could do repair the harm. There was a silence, and then one teacher said that the apology was all she needed. The principal agreed and said that he felt that it was over. Another teacher asked if Sarah would keep her informed of her doings. "The best thing you could do," she said, "would be to promise us you will stay on your meds. And, when you are out and about, let us know how you're doing! Send me a card." Sarah promised to do those things. Then the adults wanted to know her plans, so she told them. They applauded her ideas.

She then thanked everyone for coming and we ended the conference, 32 minutes later. (p. 16)

Another of the restorative justice strategies with relevance for juvenile offenders is described in Box 2.2. This is family group counseling and is modeled on effective programming derived from the Maori indigenous populations in New Zealand, an approach that has now been institutionalized by New Zealand child welfare and correctional departments.

BOX 2.2

A Family Plan Forged Out of Commitment and Love

AN FGDM STORY

by Lynn M. Welden

Alyssa (not her real name), 18, made some unfortunate choices over the last few years, some with legal consequences. But her situation improved recently, thanks to a Family Group Decision Making (FGDM) conference facilitated by the Community Service Foundation (CSF) in Pennsylvania, USA, one of the IIRP's (International Institute's Restorative Practices) demonstration

(continued)

programs. By involving Alyssa's family and friends and tapping into their collective feelings of responsibility and concern, FGDM encouraged her to commit to positive changes in her life.

On probation and unable to function in school, Alyssa was in and out of alternative programs, youth detention facilities and group homes. Bucks County Juvenile Probation Supervisor Dean Hiestand brought Alyssa to the attention of CSF's Conferencing Program, thinking that she and her family were ideal candidates for an FGDM conference. Laura Rush, conferencing program coordinator, and Jolene Head, conferencing staff member, agreed. Alyssa was very enthusiastic about the idea of a "family meeting," as were her mother and father. With juvenile court concurring, the FGDM process began.

Twenty people attended Alyssa's FGDM conference, invited by Alyssa and her parents. Said Head, the FGDM's main facilitator, "This family wanted to do this. They owned it and wanted it to happen," adding, "The more committed people at the FGDM, the greater the resources and number of ideas generated."

When the family group met, Rush, Head, and Hiestand were present. "The professionals had been invited to this part of the meeting. They wanted us to be a part of their starting prayer," noted Head.

Everyone stood and held hands for the prayer, led by Alyssa's mother, who then read letters from friends offering her daughter work. Hiestand provided information and answered questions. Alyssa jumped in to share her own feelings, take responsibility for her past behavior, apologize to her parents, and ask forgiveness from others she had hurt. At this point, Rush, Head, and Hiestand left the room so the family could get to the heart of the matter: where Alyssa would live and get an education.

Two and a half hours later, the professionals were asked to rejoin the group. The family had come up with a plan for Alyssa, outlining solutions for her living situation, education and work requirements, and legal obligations, and stressing reconciliation with family, church, and community. The group planned to meet each month to review Alyssa's progress and to circulate a report to keep everyone informed. This FGDM was an acknowledged success, with everyone proud of having had a voice in the process.

"I was excited about the FGDM concept," said Alyssa's aunt. "People talk about doing it, but nobody ever pulls 'the village' together formally. To actually have family and friends volunteer to take responsibility, to participate, is great. The FGDM was about bringing our village together in a formal process. It strengthened our relationship with Alyssa and with each other and acted as a reminder of how we have to stick together as a family. There are more kids, younger than Alyssa, coming through our family pipeline, so whatever we can do to save them from making bad choices is important."

The FGDM participants are determined that Alyssa will follow the plans they devised, because they were directly involved in developing them. "We all know she cannot deal with every point right away," said Alyssa's aunt. "But we are happy and hopeful that this conference has encouraged her to take these steps."

Alyssa now realizes that everybody who was at the FGDM that night loves her. They had met to help her examine her missteps and to contribute constructive ideas for her future.

Hiestand presented the family's plan for Alyssa to the juvenile court judge, who accepted it. Alyssa is now attending a local high school and is taking cosmetology courses. "No one has a crystal ball," said Hiestand. "But if the family sticks to the plan, I think Alyssa will be fine."

Source: *Restorative Practices E Forum*, October 10, 2007. Reprinted with permission of the International Institute for Restorative Practices. Retrieved July 2008, from www.iirp.org/pdf/csffgdm.pdf.

AFTERCARE SERVICES

Community-based services are crucial to help the adolescent from an unstable family background find a pathway out of destructive behavior into a mature and independent lifestyle. David Springer et al. (2007), writing for the task force to transform juvenile justice in Texas, advocates a shift from a parole model to a reentry model of aftercare. Money saved on continued incarceration can be spent on aftercare services provided in the youth's home community. Community-based providers should be allowed to contract with mentors, coaches, teachers, and churches to provide parole services. Aftercare strategies that offer appropriate counseling, vocational, and mental health services should help ensure that the youth matures out of delinquency.

One highly creative solution to helping young teen parents who are too immature to assume parenting duties is the Quakerdale foster care program described earlier. In this unique program, the teen learns how to parent within a safe and nurturant environment while she pursues her education to prepare to take responsibility for her and her child's life.

SUMMARY

What emerges from this review of research on young female offenders is a portrait of young women in trouble with the law who find themselves trapped by their families and the social environment. This chapter addressed the gendered aspects of girls' offense patterns, their unique pathways into delinquency and incarceration, and their behavior and needs while in the juvenile justice system. In our study of government statistics including self-report surveys of criminal and other problem behavior, we found no evidence of an increase in violent behavior among girls, as is commonly claimed in popular media. Arrest rates are up in certain categories, however, due to a toughening up in juvenile law.

Because a disproportionate number of girls referred to juvenile court are minorities, special attention needs to be paid to background factors in the pathways that lead to the detention center and training school. In locking up youth who do not need to be locked up, whose backgrounds of poverty and victimization are implicated in their survival strategies, the system is failing our girls. Such girls in juvenile justice settings need to feel physically and psychologically safe. We need to end inappropriate detention of these girls while providing safe, homelike environments and intensive treatment for their mental disorders and substance use. And we need to choose core strategies that are gender and culturally relevant. Otherwise the pathway to delinquency may be the pathway to self-destruction and crime.

Chapter 3

THE NATURE OF
WOMEN'S CRIME

*But from the ashes of destruction, mayhem, and oppression may emerge
the human spirit, the capacity for the heroic. So we can never dismiss the
possibility of redemption, resurrection, and regeneration.*
— Dennis Saleebey (2006), p. 9

Crime is a socially constructed category and often says more about the
society's values and traditions, even hang-ups, than about the individuals
whose behavior is defined as criminal. In other words, society gets the criminals it creates and even, in a sense, deserves. In this chapter we see from the
statistics how gender, race, and class intersect in the correctional sphere. We
see how much women's crime is directly related to their disadvantaged economic and social condition, and to their pasts. And to drugs. Not to mention
to their relationships with men.

As a background for working with female offenders and helping them turn
away from a life of crime or from returning to a high-risk environment, a
basic knowledge of how they got into trouble in the first place is essential.
And as a background for correctional policy makers and administrators, an
ability is needed to refute the myths sometimes promoted in the mass media
about "a new breed of female criminal." Are women today becoming more
violent? Is there a new breed of female criminal, as is sometimes claimed?
What do the official statistics tell us about male/female differences in crime?
These are among the questions addressed in this chapter. Consistent with a

holistic approach to crime, biological, psychological, and sociological explanations for female crime are considered.

That even a seemingly neutral offense such as theft or assault may have a different meaning to a man than to a woman is a theme of this chapter. More pronounced differences in gender would be expected to occur, of course, in the crimes of prostitution, murder, and sexual abuse and molestation.

ANTIFEMINIST ACCOUNTS OF FEMALE CRIME

The "bad girl" of cultural stereotypes is masculine, tough spoken, of low socioeconomic status, aggressive, male looking. Her characteristics have endured for generations (Comack & Brickey, 2007). Although murder, as Chesney-Lind and Pasko (2003) note, is predominantly a male activity, when a woman is the perpetrator, her crime is apt to be rooted in cruel circumstances. Let us consider some more headlines that are characteristic of contemporary attitudes:

> "The Boy Crisis" (Cover, *Newsweek*, 2006)
> "Men Are More Likely than Women to Be Victims in Dating Violence" (*University of New Hampshire Media*, 2006)
> "Middle School Girls Catching up to Boys in Delinquency" (*Research, Health, Family, Law, Gender*, 2005)
> "Women Just as Violent as Men: Survey" (The Age.Com, 2006)
> "Violence among Girls on the Rise" (Rowe, *Seattle Post-Intelligencer Reporter*, 2004)

Such media pronouncements as these are overblown (the headline about a "boy crisis") and extremely misleading (the implications of the other four headlines). Headlines about crime are important generally in that they not only grab readers' attention but also influence their understanding of the topic (Jackson & Banks, 2007). And the press invariably chooses to feature crime stories that are unusual in some way so as to grab readers' attention. The most interesting feature of these articles in the popular media, according to Pollock and Davis (2005), is that they are cyclical and seem to be discovered at least once every decade. Although there are far fewer stories of this type in the past few years than a decade ago, the memory of the earlier rash of news headlines about female violence persists. Accordingly, an insight offered by Pollock and Davis is that this cyclical "discovery" of the violent female criminal has affected public policy. Because the general public and their representatives in law enforcement now view women as likely perpetrators of violence and men as hidden victims of such violence, girls and women are arrested much more often along in domestic situations, even when they are the ones who call the police in the first place. Policy and decision makers apparently have come to believe the myth that women are more dangerous than was previously believed. Hence the increase in arrests of women for aggravated assaults and simple assaults, according to Pollock and Davis.

A little history is useful at this point. Feminism was a popular force in the 1970s; this was a time of sweeping social change. The expectation, therefore, was that, as career opportunities abounded, women would become more like men. Freda Adler (1976) quickly vaulted to fame in 1976 with the timely publication of *Sisters in Crime: The Rise of the New Female Criminal*. A sudden fascination with the liberated woman as criminal was spawned. A highly readable book, *Sisters in Crime* opened with examples of infamous violent female criminals, such as assassins and revolutionaries. On the surface her argument was plausible: No one was interested in petty criminality, of course. Examples of infamous dangerous and violent female criminals in the early pages of the book introduced the reader to what was later known as the "liberation hypothesis" of female crime. In Adler's words, "females are cutting themselves in for a bigger slice of the pie" (p. 29). When their goals of sexual equality are denied them, however, these frustrated women get involved in aggressive and violent acts. "The movement for full equality has a darker side," claimed Adler (p. 13).

Adler's hypothesis was put to rest in the late 1970s when the reported rise in characteristically male types of crime failed to materialize. The reported increase in women's crime actually was a fraud, a fact that was related to a crackdown on women committing welfare fraud, poor women who were far from liberated in any sense of the word. Adler herself conceded this fact and indeed stated that female inmates more often than not are downright hostile to the goals of the women's movement.

Largely ignored by the popular media, feminist scholars of the time, such as Crites (1976) and Feinman (1980), expressed outrage at Adler's hypothesis. The law meanwhile was coming down harder on women than before. Any chivalry that had once been accorded to White women of a certain class was now mostly a relic of the past (Bloom, Owen, & Covington, 2003; Bloom & Chesney-Lind, 2007). It became hard for women to request special treatment and fight for equality at the same time. We can call this the equality paradox, a phenomenon that still plagues the women's movement. In any case, prosecutions of women for larceny and fraud soared.

The "liberation hypothesis" was revived in the late 1990s, about three decades later (Belknap, 2007). Films about mean girls and YouTube clips of girls beating up other girls helped perpetuate an image of female violence.

Appetites for misbehaving girls are seemingly insatiable, with a weekly barrage of reports in the press (Ringrose, 2006). Recently, the female norm of developing close relationships has been viewed in terms of cliquishness; unprecedented media attention is devoted to relational aggression among girls. Ringrose refers to this sensationalizing of gender difference and preoccupation with the cruelty of "mean girls" as a "way of re-pathologizing the feminine" (p. 419). In fact, such relational aggression among members of the female sex is nothing new.

PROFILES OF FEMALE OFFENDING

From the literature on female criminal behavior, we can construct a profile of the average female offender. She is likely to be plagued with poverty and to lack an education and job skills. She is generally young, unmarried, involved in unhealthy sexual relationships, and the lone caregiver of small children (Chesney-Lind & Pasko, 2004; Franklin & Lutze, 2007). She has had a tough upbringing characterized by physical and sexual abuse; such victimization has continued in adulthood in the form of rape and battering and is associated with emotional problems and severe stress reactions (Belknap, 2007; Failinger, 2006; Franklin & Lutze, 2007). Transcending all these attributes of the woman involved in the criminal justice system is the impact of relationship—relationship and trauma. From a gendered perspective, formative relationships, later attractions, and the drive to stay in a given, even threatening relationship comprise an important part of a woman's being. This reality significantly influences whether women are victimized and ultimately criminalized. We can sum up this truth in this way: Trauma breeds trauma and hardship more of the same.

For a quantitative source of data on criminal activity focused on gender, we turn to those provided by the *Uniform Crime Reports* of the Federal Bureau of Investigation (FBI) (2009). This report is based on all crimes known to the police. Most precincts across the United States maintain arrest statistics and report annually to the FBI. Table 3.1 (which is Table 42 in the Uniform Crime Report) gives the arrest rates by gender for 2008. The arrest rates are a far more accurate gauge of crimes committed than conviction rates because many of the offenses are later reduced through plea bargaining. A study of this statistical table reveals for us facts of much interest to criminology researchers and to feminists and non-feminists alike. As we can see in this table, the total number of arrests for both males and females was highest for the less serious offenses. For women, the arrest rates in 2008 were highest for property crimes, which includes fraud and larceny, drug abuse violations, driving under the influence, and less serious assaults. Prostitution is a mainly female form of offending that, as we know, is related to drug use.

Table 3.1. Arrests, by Sex, 2008

- Nationwide, 75.5% of the 10,709,361 persons arrested in 2008 were male.
- Males comprised 81.7% of those arrested for violent crimes and 65.2% of those arrested for property crimes.
- Of all persons arrested for murder in 2008, 89.2% were male.
- Males accounted for 81.6% of all persons arrested for drug abuse violations.
- Females accounted for 51.7% of all persons arrested for embezzlement in 2008.

Source: FBI, Uniform Crime Reports (Washington, DC: U.S. Department of Justice, 2009), Table 42.

IS FEMALE CRIME INCREASING?

One strategy to determine if women are engaging in more criminal behavior today than formerly is to compare the female percentage of crime from earlier times with today. We learn from Table 3.1 by subtracting from the male rate that the female percentage of all arrests in 2008 was 24.5%. We can compare this figure to the rate of total arrests across all offenses for 1965 when the female percentage of total arrests at that time was significantly less—only 10% (van Wormer and Bartollas, 2010). And by 1980, the female rate had risen to 15.8% (Bureau of Justice Statistics [BJS], 1980, Table 34).

What was happening? The media blame the rise on women's increasing liberation from traditional roles, while feminist criminologists pointed to the crackdown on welfare fraud and an increased willingness of stores to prosecute shoplifters (Chesney-Lind & Pasko, 2004; Feinman, 1980). This was indeed borne out in the statistics for arrests for fraud and minor theft, not crimes of violence. From 1987 to 1998, however, the arrest rate for crimes of violence for young adult women had increased by 80%, and the juvenile arrest rate had risen substantially as well (BJS, 2000). Most of the increase, as the BJS report indicates, was in arrests for aggravated assault "perhaps reflecting increased prosecution of women for domestic violence" (pp. 5–6). In 1997, women's share of crimes of violence was 16% (FBI, 1998). As we learn from Table 3.1 (subtracting from the male rate), by 2008 the female proportion of arrests for violent crimes had risen to 18.3%.

Looking at conviction as opposed to arrest trends shows that the offense composition among women in state prison was changing rapidly during the last two decades of the 20th century (BJS, 2000). The number of both men and women who had been convicted of violent and property crime decreased while the proportion of drug and public-order offenders has been growing. These convictions were related to the emphasis during this period on the war on drugs. Between 1990 and 1998, the women's imprisonment rate increased 88%; the increase for male offenders was also pronounced but not as dramatic.

The most notable trend in the years since 1997 has been the continuing rise in the female share of persons arrested for the violent crimes of simple assault (without injury or use of a weapon) and aggravated assault. The *Uniform Crime Reports* (FBI, 2009), which calculated 10-year arrest trends from 1999 through 2008, found that the total arrest rate for adults declined around 3% for males during this period and rose by 11.6% for females. Women showed an increase in arrests for robbery, possession of stolen property, and simple assault. The fact that the homicide rate was down by around 6% and the aggravated assault rate by 2.5% seems to indicate that women are not more violent than formerly. The robbery rate increase is hard to explain, but we have to keep in mind that these crimes are often committed by women with their male partners as well as the fact that only 11.6 of arrests for robberies are of females, so a slight increase in the raw numbers looks like a major increase in the percentage.

Arrest and conviction rates are a function of both the occurrence of criminal behavior and of law enforcement measures of the society. With regard to women's offending behavior, the level of tolerance of that behavior may vary from time to time. Changes in attitudes toward offending women would be reflected in the arrest and conviction rates. How can we prove whether women are changing, for example, by engaging in more instances of less serious assault than they did in the past? One thing we can do is consult a source of crime reports that is in many ways even more accurate than the FBI arrest data. I am referring to data collected from the National Crime Victimization Survey (NCVS) that is conducted annually on a random sample of the U.S. population. Because this survey collects information directly from persons on their own victimizations, the crime of homicide is not a consideration. The NCVS results are useful, however, as an indication of the frequency and severity of other forms of violence. We can also discover from the interview data the percentage of crimes in which the perpetrators were male or female. As reported by the BJS (2008), the interviewees identified perpetrators of violent crime as female 19.7% of the time; these were cases of single-offender crimes. For the crime of robbery, for example, the perpetrator was identified as female in 19.7% of the cases. For aggravated assault, the figure was 17.6, and for simple assault, 22.1.

Steffensmeier, Zhong, Ackerman, Schwartz, and Agha (2006) examined NCVS data over time to determine if the increasing female arrest rates reflected actual changes in women's behavior or if they reflected changes in policy. What they found was that since 1979, male and female assault rates rose through the early 1990s and declined significantly in recent years. These researchers conclude, therefore, that recent policy shifts have affected the apparent increase in women's violence, since no such increase is revealed in the survey data. In fact, victims' reports indicate sizable declines in female-perpetrated assaults since at least the mid-1990s in contrast to the *Uniform Crime Reports* arrest data.

RACE AND CLASS

While nearly two-thirds of women under probation supervision are White, nearly two-thirds of those confined in local jails and prisons are minorities (BJS, 2000). Hispanics account for about 1 in 7 women confined in state prisons and nearly 1 in 3 female prisoners in federal custody. Relevant to occupational status, about 60% of women in contrast to 40% of men were unemployed at the time of arrest; 30% of the women were receiving welfare assistance. This "racialized feminization of poverty" (Sudbury, 2004, p. 230) limits women's survival options and sometimes leads to involvement in illegal moneymaking activities. Poor and minority women are the major casualties of America's war on drugs; many of those incarcerated in the federal sector are immigrant women who were transporters of drugs, or "mules" (van Wormer & Bartollas, 2010).

The overall incarceration rate for Black women was 3.75 times the rate for White women. Latina women were 1.6 times more likely than White women to be incarcerated. Across age groups, African American women were incarcerated between 2.8 and 4.3 times the rate of White women (West & Sabol, 2009). Since the majority of female prison inmates are women of color, the stridency of the attacks on the "new violent criminal females" can be perceived as a thinly veiled instance of institutionalized racism. The situation here is the same as that which occurred during the crackdown on women on welfare, which also had racist overtones.

THEORIES OF FEMALE CRIME

Who are these women in trouble with the law? What are their individual personal histories? What forces led them down the paths of seeming self-destruction? To answer questions such as these, I have filtered out from the literature on crime and crime causation (even male-centered theories) whatever facts or theories are relevant to an understanding of female criminality, no holds barred.

Biological Theories

"Most criminologists," as Vito, Maahs, and Holmes (2007) indicate, "regard biological studies of crime with a mixture of indifference and ridicule" (p. 82). This rejection of biological factors includes genetic factors in crime-related behavior and probably of drug use, gender, and age as well. Perhaps these researchers associate biological theories of crime with the early criminologists, such as Cesare Lombroso, who equated women's physical characteristics of heavy eyebrows, enormous jaws, and "neck-muscles exaggerated as in oxen" with criminal behavior (Lombroso & Ferrero, 1895, p. 89). These views reflected the societal belief that a fallen woman was a lower species than a male criminal and therefore less capable of reform. Later studies on sex chromosomal abnormalities in delinquent girls are of little value as well (see, e.g., Gibbens, 1971). A major problem with the early biological theories of criminal behavior is that they were all created by men and were highly misogynous.

And yet biology is a crucial component in much that is human (van Wormer, 2007). Functional magnetic resonance imaging of men and women under stress reveals gender differences in response to stress. Whereas the area of the male brain that is associated with fear is activated during stress, in women the limbic system, which is associated with emotional responses is affected ("Men Are from Mars," 2008). Although this research can explain the male tendency to react violently to situations, it does not explain female crime. A later report on antisocial behavior in girls found that girls who were antisocial were judged by their teachers to be apt to develop depression in adolescence ("Anti-Social Behavior in Girls," 2009). Such signs of early childhood depression and antisocial behavior in girls may prove to be an important precursor to later offending behavior (Cauffman, 2008).

Brain research is the province of psychologists, psychiatrists, and neurobiologists who today are on the threshold of discoveries related to such biologically based disorders as antisocial personality, addiction, and compulsive risk taking. Antisocial personality, which used to be called psychopathy, is a mental disorder listed in the *Diagnostic and Statistical Manual of Mental Disorders* (4th ed.) Text Revision (*DSM-IV-TR*) (American Psychiatric Association, 2000). Persons who qualify for this diagnosis are impulsive, blaming of others, and seemingly unable to feel empathy or guilt. Eight times as many men as women receive this label. Research shows that the rate that this character disorder is manifest in correctional populations is about 10 to 15% among females and 25 to 30% among males (Strand & Belfrage, 2005). Traditionally, caretakers have been blamed for causing this disorder through abuse. Research also is looking toward biological explanations—for example, in twin studies conducted at the University of Southern California and brain studies at the University of Iowa (Barovick, 1999). This disorder may be of some relevance to those who work with female offenders and with some of their partners and family members as well.

A rare, empirically based study of 26 psychopathic offenders (13 male, 13 female) incarcerated for alcohol-related crimes measured the existence of psychopathy based on scores on the Psychopathy Checklist—Revised (Walsh, 1999). This device, developed by R. D. Hare, determines the presence of psychopathy in terms of attitudes that are exploitative and blaming of others and the lack of empathy, affect, and remorse. Interviews with female psychopathic offenders revealed the tendency to react violently to seemingly trivial personal insults. One 43-year-old female, for example, reacted to her neighbor's racial slur in this way: She pulled out her knife and slashed the offending women's face several times, which required the woman to have over 100 stitches. A 26-year-old offender who was serving time for assaulting a police officer described feeling "psyched" when engaging in violence. Several of the women, moreover, reported feelings of power and excitement in "beating the defenseless," such as dogs and children. The recommended treatment for such individuals is a cognitive approach to enable them to plan, rehearse, and practice alternative ways of reacting to slights other than through the use of violence. A significant finding is that many women labeled antisocial because of their alcohol-induced criminal behavior were misdiagnosed; they did not possess the underlying character pathology that their alcoholic behavior seemed to indicate.

Strand and Belfrage (2005) examined gender differences in antisocial characteristics in samples of hundreds of male and female offenders in Sweden. Through testing, the authors found that the men scored high on the items impulsivity, adolescent antisocial behavior, and lack of empathy. The women were found to display antisocial characteristics through relational aggression, lying, deceitfulness, and lack of impulse control.

The influence of testosterone levels as a link to criminal behavior in both males and females resurfaces from time to time. The link between testosterone and aggression in animals is well established (Anderson, 2007). Much-cited research by Hargrove and Hargrove (1997) and Dabbs (1998) measured the testosterone levels via saliva samples taken of 87 female inmates of all ages. In the prison context, women who had the highest levels of testosterone tended to have been convicted of violent crimes and to evidence dominant, aggressive behavior in prison. The findings by Hargrove and Dabbs are similar to those in studies of male prisoners. Testosterone levels were highest among male inmates convicted of violent crimes such as rape, homicide, and assault. These men also violated more prison rules. Keep in mind that men have on average 10 times as much testosterone as women do. Cortisol, an important hormone, is sometimes called the stress hormone because it is secreted in response to stress. Women who are low in this hormone have been found to be prone to commit antisocial behavior, including acts of violence (Anderson, 2007).

A mental disorder that does occur frequently in female offenders and especially adolescent girls is depression (Bloom, Owen, & Covington, 2003). Obeidallah and Earls (1999), in a project from the Institute of Justice, confirmed the link between depression and delinquency. During childhood, males' and females' rates of depression are similar and relatively low; early adolescence is a time when the rates clearly diverge with girls showing a pronounced increase. Difficulty in concentrating, loss of interest in previously enjoyed activities, feelings of hopelessness and low self-worth—all may contribute to self-destructive acts and alliances. To document a relationship between depression and antisocial behavior in an ethnically diverse population, interviewers gathered self-report data on 754 girls in urban Chicago. Comparing the antisocial behavior of girls who were depressed with those who were not, Obeidallah and Earls found that 40% of nondepressed girls engaged in property crimes compared to 68% of girls with depression. Fifty-seven percent of depressed girls engaged in seriously aggressive behavior compared to only 13% of those who were not depressed. Overall, these findings suggest that depression in girls may put them at high risk for antisocial behavior. Smith, Leve, and Chamberlain (2006) further validated the role of a background of trauma and health-risking and delinquent behavior in their assessments of 88 girls referred to Oregon juvenile services.

Addictions researchers, similarly, are devoting attention to brain chemistry. The research is two directional: focused on the impact of drugs on the brain and the risk factor of addiction susceptibility. Thanks to sophisticated new imaging techniques such as positron emission tomography scans, scientists can view the brain today in ways never before imagined. In fact, today's scientists know more about how drugs act on the brain than we do about anything else in the brain, according to Nora Volkow, director of the National Institute on Drug Abuse (National Institute of Health, 2009). What we know the most about is the extent to which substance abuse can cause severe, and often irreversible, damage to brain cells and to the nervous system in general.

Over the past decade, similarly, scores of American scientists have been diligently mapping the brain waves of alcoholics and their offspring. Promising research conducted by scientists from the National Institute on Drug Abuse (NIDA, 2007) compared DNA samples from a large group of heavy-drug-using subjects with a control group. The researchers were able to identify 89 genes that are associated with addiction. Many of the genes have an impact on brain regions implicated in memory processes. Other research consistently shows that low levels of the neurotransmitter serotonin are linked to both addiction and aggression (van Wormer & Davis, 2008). When individuals self-medicate with cocaine, for example, the brain adapts to the artificially induced highs, and an unbearable craving for the drug results. Thus brain biochemistry is a factor in addiction, in regard to both its etiology and its continuation.

In women's lives, the connection between addiction and crime is both direct and indirect—direct in being associated with uninhibited lawbreaking behavior, not to mention perhaps careless use of the illegal drug itself, and indirectly through involvement in destructive relationships, relationships with people who are involved in the criminal underworld.

Other personality factors related to criminal behavior in myriad and curious ways are traits such as hyperactivity and a tendency toward risk-taking behavior. Unless their energy is channeled elsewhere, hyperactive, high-risk-taking girls and women can be predicted to "take a walk on the wild side" every now and then and perhaps pay the consequences. Since males are far more prone to manifest each of these traits than females, traits that are almost synonymous with getting into trouble, one would expect males to have a comparably higher crime rate, and they do.

Brain damage is another area of recent research advances. A traumatic brain injury can cause cognitive problems and lead to anger management problems (Centers for Disease Control, 2007). Injuries to the prefrontal cortex can cause drastic personality changes and reduce one's ability to perceive, remember, or understand risky situations that could lead to an incident of physical or sexual violence.

Psychological Theories

Psychological aspects of offending include modes of thinking, a background of personal trauma, and emotions such as anger and depression. Feelings are, of course, closely linked to biology. We consider theories relating crime to criminal thought patterns (male-oriented theories) and explanations for female offending that stress a history of trauma and victimization.

The work of Yochelson and Samenow (1976) and of Samenow (1984) would be of little relevance to the topic of female offenders were it not for the fact that these theories and therapy techniques shape the treatment that many inmates, male and female, receive in prison. Yochelson and Samenow derived their ideas through studies of the criminally insane at St. Elizabeth's Hospital in Washington, DC. After probing the psyches of hundreds of inmates, they decided that the criminals were not sick; they were just masters at manipulation. Change comes only through a drastic alteration in thinking patterns; however, only a few criminals, from this perspective, are amenable to change.

Samenow's theories have been adopted by prison psychologists and counselors who learn of them through workshops and in-house training programs. Although the concepts were derived from work with male psychopaths, many of these concepts are applied for work with female offenders. A focus on individual wrongdoing and criminal thought patterns is based on the assumption that women in trouble with the law are markedly different from other women. Canadian social scientist Maidment (2006) is highly critical of this treatment approach for its negativism, which permeates prison life and pathologizes women.

The second major psychological approach to female criminality is exactly the opposite of Samenow's male-centered approach for breaking down criminal thought patterns. Meda Chesney-Lind and Pasko (2004) and Joanne Belknap (2007) are key proponents of a far more empathic approach related to women's subordinate role in society and personal history of severe childhood abuse.

The prevalence of physical and sexual abuse in the childhoods and adult backgrounds of female offenders has been consistently supported in the research literature (Bloom, Owen, & Covington, 2004). Among men and women on probation, the BJS (2000) found that 6 in 10 women in state institutions experienced physical or sexual prior abuse. A similar rate of such abuse is reported among men and women in treatment for substance abuse (van Wormer & Davis, 2008). The Canadian rates for incarcerated women are 68% suffered physical abuse and 53% sexual abuse at some point in their lives (Comack & Brickey, 2007). Among Aboriginal women, the rates are much higher.

To understand male/female differences in motivation for crime, we need to consider not only female pathways to crime but also research on masculinity and male identity in addition to female pathways to crime. Mullins, Wright, and Jacobs (2004), in their study of young urban male offenders, found that most of men's interpersonal disputes with other men were grounded in the need to build and maintain gendered reputations. They further found that the men held gendered perceptions of appropriate and inappropriate behavior that served as a trigger for retaliations. Retaliation following a threat was practiced as a key street survival strategy.

Social Theories

The best known of the crime causation theories are rooted in sociology. Such theories range from explanations such as economics and class at the macro end of the spectrum of causation to socialization and labeling at the spectrum's center. These theories were all geared toward males. Whether they have any relevance for female delinquents and criminals is debatable.

Opportunity theory states that blocked opportunity in a society that stresses material success leads to antisocial forms of behavior. Certainly the economic marginalization of women and the feeling by those without skills or education that they will never "make it" are factors that might play into crimes such as theft, fraud, or drug dealing. Women offenders, when released from prison, are often not equipped, due to their lack of skills, to fit within the dominant economic and social structures that law-abiding citizens can (Failinger, 2006). Freda Adler, professor of criminal justice at Rutgers University, who decades ago developed a liberation hypothesis for female crime, continues to use this sociological explanation. As before, she continues to be widely cited in news commentaries on female crime. A *New York Times* article on women's imprisonment by Butterfield (2003) states:

> "With women taking on the social roles of men, they have the same opportunities to commit crime," especially crimes like embezzlement.

> And as time passes, Ms. Adler said, women are committing more serious crimes and have longer criminal records, like male criminals. This means they are more likely to be sent to prison and given longer sentences if they are arrested.

> "The police, prosecutors and judges can't just look aside anymore and say they are women," said Ms. Adler, whose book "Sisters in Crime," published in 1975, was widely attacked by other scholars as antifeminist. (p. 2)

Sociological theories of gang delinquency argue that peer group affiliation and living in crime-ridden neighborhoods promote crime. Jody Miller's (2001, 2008) work showed how strategies of survival in a crime-ridden neighborhood could lead to trouble. Beth Richie's (1996) research on gender entrapment of battered Black women showed how race and class intersect in the lives of incarcerated women. The pathway to crime for the battered women was that they felt compelled into illegal behaviors through their menfolk. Inmates who were not battered, however, were apt to blame the system for their arrests. Their road to crime was usually through drug-related activities, burglaries, and theft.

In an exhaustive empirical research comparing the attitudes of male and female prisoners toward the law and justice, Edna Erez (1988) found that the women had far more positive attitudes toward law and justice, although not necessarily toward the legal authorities, than did men. This, as she concluded, is in accordance with gender role socialization and societal expectations that women obey and respect authority. Sometimes this obedience is to male authority, however, often the obedience is to their lovers and spouses who themselves may be operating outside the law. However, their very close relationships often spell trouble for them. Often they get involved in crime and in trouble with the law due to their close connections with men; this is especially true at the lower echelons of society. La Tanya Skiffer (2009), a sociologist who grew up in South Los Angeles, developed an interest in crime causation. For her book, *How Black Women Offenders Explain Their Crime and Describe Their Hopes*, she interviewed 30 African American prisoners at the California Institution for Women. The majority were serving time for murder. She found that the women cited external factors such as abuse or being introduced to drugs by their partners and peers. Many of the inmates, however, took responsibility for the criminal activity themselves.

Consider these cases described in a law journal by Failinger (2006):

- "Chris, a 22-year-old woman, was arrested for permitting her husband to sexually abuse her five- and nine-year-old nieces. Chris's father was an alcoholic and was abusive to his wife and children.... When she was 21, she married a 35-year-old trucker. In accounting for her failure to stop her husband's abuse of the children, Chris suggested that she acted to please her husband, so he would love her."
- "After Betsey dropped out of school, her live-in boyfriend's mother, Marlene, encouraged her to work in prostitution in the streets near a naval base.... She went through many men in her descent into drugs" (p. 487).

Neighborhood is a key factor here. Belknap (2007) cites research that reveals the significance of geography in determining the influence of crime and drug use. Women brought up in crime-ridden neighborhoods and surrounded by role models who devalued education and working within the system to earn a living are more likely than others to be initiated into illicit drug use and violent crime (both as victims and as perpetrators).

Labeling theory has the advantage of linking the sociological to the psychological. When kids or adults are labeled as bad, according to this theory, the label becomes a self-fulfilling prophecy. The concept is consistent with the strengths approach of social work, which shows how trust and positive rather than negative interpretations of people's acts can bring out the best in them (see Saleebey, 2009). Kai Erikson (1966) gave life to this notion in his historical analysis of records left by the early Puritans of Massachusetts Bay Colony. His investigation led him to the stories of women, rebellious in some way, who received the label of deviant and whose behavior accordingly grew more extreme. His words can still inspire us today:

> People in this society do not expect much in the way of reform from those who are labeled "deviant." And this, historically, brings us back to the Puritans, for it is then their image of deviation, their belief in the irreversibility of human nature, which may be reflected in that expectation. (p. 205)

INTEGRATED THEORY OF WOMEN AND CRIME

Carol Gilligan (1982) conceptualizes gender differences multidimensionally: "Clearly these differences arise in a social context where factors of social status and power combine with reproductive biology to shape the experience of males and females and the relations between the sexes" (p. 2). To take one example from the life course of a female offender: Sally, a hyperactive girl with a short attention span cannot sit still at school and drives her teacher and parents crazy. Internalizing the negativism around her, she joins a group of outcasts, experiments with drugs, and drops out of school. She may or may not gravitate toward crime and be arrested. However, she is at high risk for trouble-prone and self-destructive behavior. Biological attributes combine with the psychological process of internalizing negative adult reactions, which combine, in turn, with social influences in her environment, including peer group culture and ultimately lead to the acquisition of a deviant, "bad girl" label. Each of us is a unique individual; our personalities and behavior can be understood only in terms of the interaction of a combination of factors. As summarized by Bloom et al. (2004), women's most common pathways to crime are based on survival of abuse, poverty, and substance abuse. And let me underscore the word *survival*.

Feminist criminology is an exciting new area of research. Kathleen Daly (1994) introduced a typology of female offenders that differentiated the roads to crime for street women, abused women who had turned to drugs, women who got into trouble with drugs through a significant other, and battered women who were essentially forced into crime. Richie's (1994) typology, based on her interviews with women confined at Rikers Island, New York, explored differences in pathways to crime for battered and nonbattered African American women and abused White women. A key difference between the battered women of the two races was that the African Americans were more protective of their batterers than were the White women who had grown up in a more patriarchal home environment and more accepting of their subordinate gender status. The African Americans also were more likely than Whites to seek help when battered.

More recent research on pathways to crime is provided by Simpson, Yahner, and Dugan (2008). They differentiated early-onset from later-onset offenders in a large mixed racial group. More than half of the women in the sample came to crime later in life and had had a fairly stable lifestyle until they got involved with criminally-prone men.

Unlike these contributions by feminist criminologists, which are inclusive, some of the classic theories from sociology discussed earlier are narrow in that they explain one kind of crime but not another. Opportunity theory, for example, is far more relevant to economic crimes such as embezzlement than to crimes of personal violence or drug possession. The fact that the crime of embezzlement has risen steadily for women since the 1970s undoubtedly relates to career changes for women as well as to their increasing involvement in gambling. The remainder of this chapter briefly describes various types of crime with special relevance for women.

CRIMES OF VIOLENCE

Robbery

Robbery, unlike burglary, is a crime of theft that involves violence or a threat of violence against a person. According to the *Uniform Crime Report* (FBI, 2009), offenders who commit robbery are about 88% male. Although the motivation of robbery—to obtain goods or cash—is the same for both genders, the male/female differences in the modus operandi of robbery has been found to be pronounced. In her in-depth interviews with 37 African American offenders operating on the streets of St. Louis, J. Miller (2008) found that compared to women, men were more apt to view robbery as one means of expressing their masculinity. Men relied on violence, often using a gun and injuring their victims, who were usually men. Women often robbed other women whom they viewed as weak and easy targets. If their targets were men, however, they manipulated the men into thinking they were willing to engage in sex, got them off in a hotel or some other indoor setting, then robbed them when they were the most vulnerable. Sometimes the women worked with men as a team. Miller sees the urban backgrounds of poverty and lack of legitimate opportunities as powerful incentives for robbery for both genders. Belknap (2007) cites obtaining money to buy drugs as a motivation for many habitual criminals.

Murder

The relative scarcity of female-perpetuated murder is what makes female murderers, women such as Bonnie Parker (of Bonnie and Clyde fame), Jean Harris (a high school headmistress who killed her ex-lover), Susan Smith (who killed her children), Karla Faye Tucker (a born-again Christian who was executed in Texas for her drug-fueled axe-murder), and Casey Anthony (charged with the murder of her two-year-old daughter) so intriguing.

In 2006, although both male and female homicide rates had declined significantly, the rate of males committing homicide was at least nine times the rate for females (FBI, 2009). Research has revealed that, compared to men, women arrested for homicide are less likely to have previous criminal histories, are more likely to have committed the offense alone, and are more likely to have killed as the result of domestic conflict (van Wormer & Bartollas, 2010).

Domestic Homicide
The victim-offender relationship differs substantially between female and male murders (Califano, Smith, Snyder, & Rand, 2009). Whereas men are more apt to kill a stranger or be killed by a stranger, homicides by and of women generally involve intimates or other family members.

According to the BJS (2007) data, the number of intimate homicides for all races and genders declined between 1975 and 2005. The number of Black males killed by intimates dropped by 83%, White males by 61%, Black females by 52%, and White females by 6%. The most recent report indicates the African American intimate partner homicides have continued to decline (Catalano et al., 2009). It should be pointed out that in previous years the numbers of Black partners and spouses killed by women was extraordinarily high; now these numbers are considerably down although they still are well above the White murder rate. According to my calculations from the 2007

BJS data, the Black male spouse victimization rate is four times the comparable White rate, and the boyfriend murder rate is seven times the comparable White rate. Until 2007, White women were still victimized at almost the same level as earlier. Across the board, guns were the most common weapon used.

In 2008, 700 males and 1,640 females were killed by their intimate partners, according to the BJS (Califano et al., 2009) report. This means that men are significantly more likely to kill their spouses and partners than are women to kill theirs. Interestingly, in the early 1970s, before domestic partner shelters and other victim protection services were introduced, about as many women killed their intimate partners as their partners killed them, and the number was well over 1,200 homicides committed by each gender. The most frequently offered explanation for the striking decline in female homicides of their male partners is that since most of these murders committed by women were done out of self defense or anger over being beaten, now battered women have an alternative means of escape from a dangerous or otherwise intolerable situation. Wells and DeLeon-Granados (2004), for example, explain the striking decline in homicides of men by their wives/partners in terms of "exposure reduction theory" (p. 233). *Exposure reduction theory* is the notion that the availability of mechanisms that allow a woman to sever her ties with an abusive partner will spare her from seeking a violent solution.

Unfortunately, since men's motives for killing their wives/partners are different—not for defense but for retaliation after a breakup—when the woman does escape, her life still may be at risk. Sometimes the end result is murder-suicide; virtually all of murder-suicides that arise out of intimate partner situations are perpetrated by men. Research shows that the individual who is dangerously violent and also prone to depression is at risk of killing his partner and himself when the threat of a breakup occurs (van Wormer & Bartollas, 2010). There are almost two murder-suicides a day in the United States, three-fourths of which involve domestic partner situations (Violence Policy Center, 2006).

In cases of female-on-male intimate partner homicide, the power imbalance between men and women comes into play. Women who kill, as Karlene Faith (1993) explains, generally do so when the man is in some way incapacitated— asleep or drunk, for example—and thus the defense of being in immediate danger does not apply. These women serve long prison terms, accordingly. Recent research showing that women engage in violence against their spouses to the same degree as men do are erroneous and fail to take into account women's structured vulnerabilities. Weapon availability, of course, figures in, boosting American murder rates far above those of their European and many Asian counterparts (Violence Policy Center, 2006).

What are the personalities like of women who kill? Since these women likely end up serving long prison terms, they are available to be studied by sociologists and observed over the years by correctional workers. In a classic study, Ann Jones (1980), the author of *Women Who Kill*, observed that although the act of killing, especially by a woman, may be extraordinary, most women who commit this act are ordinary in every way. In fact, women convicted of murder, as it is universally acknowledged, are often the most compliant women in prison, the most middle class, and the most likely to lack criminal records (Faith, 1993). My prison participation-observation study in Alabama confirms this observation (if we overlook the behavior of two self-proclaimed "hit ladies"). (See Chapter 5.)

In one of the most intriguing studies up to that time, Hamilton and Sutterfield (1998) compared a sample of 20 battered women who murdered their partners with a sample of 29 battered women at a women's shelter who did not do so. The key difference between the groups was not personality but their earlier treatment by police and whether they were referred to a shelter. These findings are consistent with recent statistics from the U.S. Department of Justice and Statistics Canada that show a decline in female partner murder rates but not in women killed by their partners.

Albert Roberts (2007) examined data drawn from a sample of 105 women in prison convicted of killing their husbands/partners and 105 battered women in a sample from the community in New Jersey. The imprisoned women had a history of being battered. These women were far more likely to have received death threats from their partners than the battered women who did not kill their partners; these threats were specific as to time, place, and method. In addition to a history of partner violence, the majority of the women prisoners had a history of sexual abuse, a substance use problem, had attempted suicide, and had access to the batterer's guns.

Child Murder (Filicide) and "Fetal Abuse"

If women who murder their spouses are considered an anomaly, women who kill their children are regarded as downright monsters. Mothers and stepmothers kill about half of all children murdered. Whereas mothers tend to kill infants, fathers more often kill children age 8 or older. Mothers, of course, spend a great deal more time with children, especially small children, than fathers do. Studies of women in psychiatric populations who killed their children document high incidences of psychosis, social isolation, depression, lower socioeconomic status, suicidality, substance use, and difficulties in their own childhood (Friedman, Horwitz, & Resnick, 2005).

McKee (2006), a forensic psychologist and author of *Why Mothers Kill*, evaluated over 30 girls and women who had killed their infants and children. From his research, he singled out five categories of parents who take the lives of their children. They included those who were: abusive/neglectful, psychotic/suicidal, psychopathic, detached, or retaliatory. The first three categories are self-explanatory. Detached mothers are defined as those who fail to bond with their newborn infants, and retaliatory mothers are those who kill to get revenge on someone. Actually, as McKee informs us, parents who kill their children for revenge are almost always fathers.

An estimated 50% to 80% of new mothers suffer from mild depression after giving birth; major postpartum depression, however, is a rare yet serious psychological issue affecting fewer than 1% of new mothers within the first year after giving birth (McKee, 2006). What distinguishes this condition from the milder variety is the mother's obsessive concern about hurting the baby. Because the woman is at risk of harming herself or her baby, postpartum psychosis is a medical emergency. It has been recognized by the law as an element in infanticide for 50 years in England. Women suffering from this condition are given intensive hospitalized treatment for the psychosis until they recover.

The mother who kills her newborn does not see the infant as human but more as a foreign body needing to be destroyed. McKee (2006) refers to "ignored pregnancy cases" (p. 27) committed principally by young women who denied or concealed their pregnancies. Mothers who kill older children may be acting out of anger and hatred or out of a suicidal impulse. Some women, such as Susan Smith, who drowned her children in a car, kill their children, then plan to kill themselves. Smith had many of the risk factors for suicidal murder: There was a high rate of suicide in her family, including her father, who died when she was a child. Susan was sexually abused by her stepfather and diagnosed as having bipolar personality disorder. Her marriage was shaky and her children were very young.

In the old days, killing babies for rational reasons used to be much more common. Abortion was illegal, and children born out of wedlock and their mothers were stigmatized. Today, in India, female newborns are at least three times more likely to be the victims of neonatal murder than are boys (McKee, 2006).

Property Crimes

The most significant gender difference in arrest profiles is the relatively greater involvement of females in minor property crimes, such as shoplifting and fraud, and the relatively greater involvement of males in major property crimes and crimes against persons (Steffensmeier & Schwartz, 2004). The economic marginalization of women may help account for their relatively high involvement in larceny, theft, check and welfare fraud, and forgery. Although men still dominate in property crimes, the women's steadily high rate of criminality here undoubtedly is linked to the "feminization of poverty" (Belknap, 2007).

Shopping and shoplifting tend to go together for some women. The gender factor here is evidenced in the types of merchandise that are taken. Men steal items that express their manliness, to impress their peers. Girls and women, however, are drawn to take luxury items they feel they need but cannot justify spending household income on, items such as cosmetics and jewelry.

Embezzlement is a crime that, on the surface, is not related to poverty but rather to opportunity for women. The overwhelming majority of bank tellers today, for example, are women. In that sense, there is more opportunity for them to take money than they had before.

Women's embezzlement rate rose by 23% between 2004 and 2008 (FBI, 2009) compared to a somewhat smaller increase in the rate for men. As we can see from Table 3.1 presented earlier in this chapter, women make up just over half of all arrests for embezzlement. This does not mean, however, that women are responsible for half of the money and resources that are confiscated in this manner because such women rarely have access to the vast sums of money that some men do (Belknap, 2007). Studies of embezzlement reveal that most women charged with this crime often worked as tellers or in clerical positions; many of their male counterparts were in managerial positions (Daly, 1994; Steffensmeier & Schwartz, 2004).

Theories of crime causation for white-collar crime are often very different from the explanations offered for crimes of poverty. For example, fraud is associated with welfare programs, such as Temporary Aid for Needy Families and other entitlements, and there is fraud at the higher echelons in accounting and investment schemes. Although the high-status female offender clearly does not share the personal lifestyle of the typical female offender, the two groups of women do share something in common that is often overlooked: loyalty to a man who is breaking the law. Jacobs (2006), in her analysis of six recent cases of women who have been convicted in connection with major corporate crimes, such as the Enron scandal, describes a common pathway to women's crime that crosses class lines. This pathway involves loyalty to a man engaged in wrongdoing, often in regard to a request for assistance in some form of cover-up. This characteristic, Jacobs argues, is one that is shared with women who are the wives and girlfriends of street criminals. Of the six case studies of female white-collar criminals that Jacobs studied, only one individual emerged as truly independent, and that was Martha Stewart, the well-known homemaking entrepreneur. Unlike the other five prosecuted women, Stewart was at the helm of the company, not at a lower level of a hierarchy. To summarize what we learn from Jacobs's analysis, even white-collar crime is shaped by gender.

Current research suggests that whether it is theft on a grand scale or a small one, it is property crime, not crimes of violence, that will continue to be women's domain for the foreseeable future. Much of this crime is related to poverty; much of it is also related to drug use. Prostitution, our next topic, is also related to drug use.

Prostitution

Described by some as the "oldest profession" for women, prostitution seemingly provides a lucrative environment for the exchange of sex for money between mutually consenting adults (Valandra, 2007). Prostitution is illegal in all states except for Nevada; about twice as many women as men are arrested for this crime. Managing prostitutes in the criminal justice system neglects the fact that for many women, their prostitution is the result of numerous and complex psychological stressors (Arnold, McNeece, & Stewart, 1999; Websdale & Chesney-Lind, 2004). The social aspect is explored in graphic terms by Vednita Nelson (1993):

> Racism makes Black women and girls especially vulnerable to sexual exploitation and keeps them trapped in the sex industry. It does this by limiting educational and career opportunities for African-Americans in this country. It does this through a welfare system that has divided the poor Black family....

> Today, middle-class White men from the suburbs drive through the ghettos of America to pick out whatever Black women or girls they want to have sex with, as if our cities were their own private plantations. (pp. 81, 82)

When we think of prostitution, most of us think of street prostitution. Street prostitution, however, is estimated to account for only about 20% of prostitution in major cities but for the majority of prostitution arrests (Arnold et al., 1999). The organization COYOTE (Cast Off Your Old Tired Ethics) is a high-class prostitutes' rights group that advocates the legalization of prostitution (what they describe as "sex work") (Rauch, 2006). Currently they are protesting recent restrictions imposed by the government's new anti–human trafficking laws. Legalization such as exists in the Netherlands and in several other European countries provides for regulation of prostitution, health checkups, and protection for women in this trade who can call the police, for example, if they are victimized. In order to combat the problem with trafficked women that was rampant in Sweden, the government passed legislation that criminalized the buying of sex but not prostitution itself (De Santis, 2007). The thinking behind this law, which was strongly supported by Sweden's organization of women's shelters, is that women prostitutes are not criminals but victims. This is a shift in viewing prostitution from the male to a female perspective. Sweden chose this route over its tradition of legalization, which had only expanded the sex industry. The results in Sweden have been favorable, especially in cutting down on sex trafficking and organized crime.

In neighboring Norway, conditions for women who are imprisoned are so agreeable that the police have had to stop taking Russian prostitutes into custody. Jail conditions did not deter the women from crime. Prostitution, then, is essentially legal in Norway. Government officials have grown increasingly worried about the scores of foreign prostitutes on local streets in recent years ("Buying Sex Can Yield Jail Term," 2007). They believe most are victims of human traffickers who have forced the women into prostitution and seize the vast majority of their earnings. The new proposed law forbidding the purchase of sex is aimed at prostitutes' customers and alleged White slavery operations.

The life of a street prostitute, according to Stout and McPhail (1998), is one of pain and terror. Battering and rape from pimps and johns "goes with the territory." Pimps often take prostitutes' earnings or stop them from seeking other employment; johns use economic and physical power to make them comply with their demands. They know that prostitutes have no legal protection. Like other women, prostitutes are more at risk of contracting the AIDS virus than of spreading it; they often contract AIDS from use of dirty needles to inject heroin or cocaine into their bodies. Crack cocaine is most commonly used by African American and heroin by European American street prostitutes. Exchange of sex for drugs is common.

Many prostitutes are arrested and enter jails and prisons on drug charges. Others, however, are prosecuted by AIDS-specific laws targeting prostitutes who receive positive test results for HIV antibodies and are subsequently arrested for prostitution. Critics of these laws argue that this is a punitive strategy aimed at vulnerable women and that there is no epidemiological evidence that prostitutes contribute significantly to the sexual transmission of the AIDS virus (Luxenburg & Guild, 2007).

The psychological side of prostitution is addressed by studies of posttraumatic stress disorder (PTSD) and other mental health problems in this group. PTSD is extremely common in prostitutes, a fact that is not surprising given the level of violence members of this group have experienced (Valandra, 2007; Websdale & Chesney-Lind, 2004). Interviews with 130 San Francisco prostitutes revealed that over half reported sexual abuse in childhood and about half reported having been physically assaulted (Farley & Barkan, 1998). Many more had experienced rape, threats with a weapon, and physical assaults as adult prostitutes. Most met the *DSM* criteria for a diagnosis of PTSD.

Arnold et al. (1999) observed a support group in a Florida case management program for former prostitutes with substance abuse involvement; these researchers also interviewed staff and outreach workers. Most of the women reported they were substance abusers first and prostitutes second but that they sought treatment in groups of women who had engaged in street prostitution so that they could discuss their problems honestly. Some had severe mental health problems for which they were referred for treatment. Although histories of physical and sexual abuse were common, the participants did not at first view themselves as victims. In treatment, however, they were encouraged to explore their vulnerabilities and how they had used drugs to cope with their problems. Staff members reported that the challenge was to encourage women to pursue a vocation that was realistic for them but one that also paid sufficiently, as prostitutes are used to handling large amounts of money. A follow-up study of recidivism conducted by the authors revealed that only 1 individual in a sample of 12 returned to the streets. A key aspect of success in the program was the police/social work collaboration that occurred. This program, in its propensity to help people find a better way rather than focusing on punishment, is consistent with many of the principles of restorative justice.

Sex work is an extremely dangerous occupation worldwide. Among the dangers to which sex workers are exposed are drug dependence, venereal disease, violence, discrimination, debt, criminalization, and exploitation (Rekart, 2005). Across the world, children and young women are kidnapped into sex slavery. An article in the British medical journal *The Lancet* advocates a harm-reduction or public policy approach to help women who have chosen this line of work and that prostitution be decriminalized in such cases. The goal of harm reduction is to save lives by making health and social services readily available. Successful and promising harm-reduction strategies are health education, empowerment, prevention, care, occupational health and safety, and human rights–based approaches.

Valandra (2007) studied former African American prostitutes who were engaged in a voluntary healing program in their own neighborhood. In personal narratives, the women described how kin support, "hitting bottom," and religious faith were factors in getting them off the streets. Barriers were being stigmatized and lack of economic resources and job skills. The descriptions of their life on the streets are gripping. Consider this one:

> The majority of my johns were White men. One time, a White john, trying to pick me up, told me, "Once a ho always a ho." I decided to pick up a White trick for myself. I made him do for me what I had to do. He worked for me cleaning house, preparing meals, and turning tricks. He fell in love with me, but I only knew money, sex, and drugs. I asked God's forgiveness for this, and now I see myself as an ex-prostitute, recovering addict [who is] working every day to make a change. (p. 203)

The healing program was provided at an Afrocentric agency, and it helped maintain the women's decisions to leave the profession.

Other Sexual Offenses

Research Findings

National criminal justice statistics reveal that of all adults and juveniles who come to the attention of the authorities for sex crimes, females account for less than 10% of these cases (FBI, 2009). Specifically, arrests of women represent only 1% of all adult arrests for forcible rape and 6% of all adult arrests for other sex offenses. The figures from the United Kingdom and Canada are comparable (Ford, 2006). The number of adolescent girls coming to the attention of the juvenile courts for sex offenses has increased significantly, however, in recent years (Snyder & Sickmund, 2006).

Because of the sudden increase in adjudicated female sexual offenders and the reluctance of many states to release sex offenders into the community, treatment programs are being set up specializing in gender-specific sex offender treatment (Maison & Larson, 1995; Vandiver, 2006). Sexual offenses for which women are incarcerated include sexual abuse, rape, and child molestation. Those women arrested for rape are usually accomplices to the crime (BJS, 2000).

The limited research available on this population compared to male sex offenders shows that females lack compulsive sexual fantasies about children; are often completely dependent on men who initiated abuse; seem strangely unconcerned about loss of parental rights; and had suffered childhood damage of an extreme nature themselves (Maison & Larson, 1995; Vandiver, 2006). Because of their backgrounds of victimization across the life span, women sexual offenders do not respond well to traditional methods for working with sex offenders that are highly confrontational (Vandiver). Such traditional treatment designed for male sexual offenders reinforces feelings of low self-esteem in this highly victimized population.

Minnesota provides specialized treatment for female sex offenders behind prison walls at Shakopee Correctional Facility, which opened in 1984. One year later, an outpatient treatment center, Genesis II, opened to meet the needs of female offenders placed on probation (Taylor, 2001). Most of the women had victimized their own children. In the counseling program at Shakopee, prostitutes are included along with others whose offenses were of a sexual nature (Maison & Larson, 1995). One fascinating finding of therapists at the Minnesota program was that whatever age the sex offenders were, the age that they saw themselves as "being on the inside" was closely related to the age of their victims, often small children. "Diane," for example, who "aged" herself at 13, molested her 12-year-old son. Therapists' strategies were to look beyond the damaged little girl inside, provide emotional mothering for her for a while, and model a healthy, mature relationship—in this case, between the therapists, who were old friends.

Teacher-Student Sexual Offenses

In the well-cast and superbly acted British film *Notes on a Scandal*, starring Cate Blanchett and Judi Dench as an art and history teacher respectively, a major theme is the affair between the Cate Blanchett character, Sheba, and a 15-year-old student. The boy, who has a mad crush on the young teacher, tricks her with a false sob story to get her sympathy. Sheba, struggling under the weight of a long marriage to an older man and two children, knows her relationship with the boy is wrong but seems unable to resist. The sexual scenes are explicit. When the truth comes out, thanks to the Judi Dench character, the boy's parents are outraged, and the plot proceeds to its inevitable tragic end.

Judging by media accounts, female teacher liaisons with their male students in real life are an increasingly common occurrence. "U.S. Teacher Sexipidemic Spreading Across the Planet" (2005) is a gripping headline provided by an Australian news source. This article lists over 50 cases from the past 10 years of prosecutions in the United States of female teachers reported and prosecuted for have sexual relations with a student. All of the students were male except for one. Most of the cases described involved only one student who was over age 16 at the time; most of the women were in their late 20s.

Americans might well remember the hubbub surrounding the case of Mary Kay LeTourneau. "Mad about the Boy," proclaimed the headline in *Time* magazine (Edwards, 1998) that gave details on this provocative case. The former Seattle teacher, Mary Kay LeTourneau, 36, was imprisoned on two counts of second-degree child rape for having a sexual relationship (and a baby) with a boy, then 13, who had been her student in the second and sixth grades. The boy repeatedly denied being a victim; his mother expressed no anger as well (Tate, 2004). Unlike the typical offender who is a predator, LeTourneau did not see herself as exploiting a victim but of being in love and wanting a baby for a bonding experience. Also unlike the typical male offender who preys on small children, LeTourneau was involved with an older youngster who seemed mature for his age. She did well on medication for a manic-depressive disorder, but, once released, she went off the medication and broke the orders not to see the boy. She was found by police making love to him in a car and was reimprisoned. She gave birth a second time. Because of the public fascination with the case, a TV movie *The Mary Kay LeTourneau Story: All American Girl*, was shown on the USA Channel. It received a mostly positive review for the sensitive handling of the subject matter (Bianco, 2000). LeTourneau was in solitary confinement for her offense when the movie was aired. Today, LeTourneau is free and her former student is grown. They are married and live together with their two children.

Ever since the LeTourneau case hit the news, the number of cases of female sex offenders has increased significantly, perhaps due to greater awareness that such women-boy liaisons are a crime (Levine, 2006). In Britain, as well, following a new awareness of female sexual abuse of children, there are increasing prosecutions of what the British call "female paedophiles" (Burrell & Wallis, 1999). One case of a 30-year-old teacher who had an affair with a 15-year-old boy whom she enticed with drugs parallels the LeTourneau case. As a result of such cases, a new prison unit has been set up in Britain for the first time to treat female sexual offenders; a cognitive-behavioral treatment approach is to be used, probably modeled on the male offender program. Ford (2006), in her book on British women convicted of abusing children, believes the numbers are vastly underreported and notes that in the United Kingdom, the number of female sex offenders serving time in prison has increased from 14 in 1996 to 37 in 2005.

Gormley (2007) reports on a seven-month investigation conducted by the Associated Press into records on teacher discipline in all 50 states. Of the 446 cases discovered from over the five previous years, most involved sexual misconduct with students, and 9 out of 10 of the accused educators were male. The teachers were often caught when their seductive e-mails and digital photos were discovered. Most of the students were in high school, and in many cases relationships extended over years.

Drug-Related Crime

The most obvious trend over the years is related to arrests for drugs and drug-related offenses (Butterfield, 2003), and often arrests and prosecutions for other crimes, such as violence, robberies, and prostitution are drug related. According to the U.S. Department of Justice (BJS, 2006) approximately half of female and male federal prison inmates were using drugs in the month before the offense. In state prisons, the numbers were 60% and 42.8% respectively. More women used methamphetamines (meth) than men during this time period—15% (federal) and 17% (state) compared to 10% in both federal and state facilities for men. Interestingly, as an earlier BJS report (2000) states, nearly 1 in 3 women serving time in state prisons said they had committed the offense in order to obtain money to support their need for drugs.

The war on drugs, as stated previously, has emerged as a war on minority and poor women, a war that is packing nonviolent women into prison in record-breaking rates. Central to understanding the creation of the sentencing guidelines for crack cocaine—the cheaper, smoked alternative to powder cocaine—is the role of the media. The social reality of crack was shaped and presented to the general public, at the time relatively unconcerned about the drug problem, along with President Reagan's declaration of the war on drugs in 1986 (Sudbury, 2004).

In constructing and presenting the problem of crack, the media focused on three general themes:

1. The claim that crack was more addictive than powder cocaine, leading to such problems as "crack babies"
2. The strong link to the violent crime world of inner city gangs
3. The low cost and ready supply of the drug.

In conjunction with the much-publicized sudden death of basketball star Len Bias, who died of a cocaine-induced heart attack (in fact, the culprit was powder cocaine), there was a public and political outcry for action. Without the usual committee hearings, therefore, a bill swept through Congress. This bill culminated in the 1986 and 1988 Anti-Drug Abuse Acts establishing harsh mandatory minimum sentencing guidelines within the federal system and targeting crack cocaine. Possession of 500 grams of powder cocaine, but only 5 grams of crack, triggers a mandatory minimum sentence of 5 years for possession: This is the 100 to 1 ratio that people are talking about, a ratio that has been considered racist and classist by most observers. The penalty for drug dealing (trafficking) is higher. States followed suit and increased their penalties as well. For this reason, the number of Black women incarcerated for drug offenses increased 828% between 1986 and 1991 (Bush-Baskette, 1998). This increase was more than three times that of White women. Unlike men, women typically are convicted of drug possession rather that drug dealing.

The facts were contained in testimony before Congress by American Civil Liberties Union representatives Fredrickson and McCurdy (2008). Part of the testimony focused on the toll that the mandatory minimum and harsh drug sentencing laws is taking on women of color.

Such sentencing laws fail to consider the many reasons—including domestic violence, economic dependence, or dependent immigrant status—that may compel a woman to remain silent. In fact, as we learn from a study of gender differences in drug market activities based on extensive arrest data, women's earnings in this illegal enterprise are low, they tend to procure drugs in their own neighborhoods, and drugs are generally acquired by means of trading sex for drugs (Rodriguez & Griffin, 2005). The drug market, according to these researchers, is thus highly gendered, with men playing the leading roles and with women who are connected to these men vulnerable to arrest and prosecution. Despite a Supreme Court ruling in 2007 to give judges more discretion, the mandatory minimum laws still are on the books in most states.

Promising developments at all levels of government—the Supreme Court's ruling to give judges more discretion over sentencing, Congress's numerous bills to end the disparities, and the Obama administration's announcement of plans to endorse treatment over incarceration for drug addicted offenders— are taking shape. In April 2009, the Justice Department endorsed for the first time a plan that would eliminate vast sentencing disparities between possession of powdered cocaine and rock cocaine (Johnson, 2009). A shift of funding into treatment, counseling, and job training is anticipated. This announcement has followed several other developments geared to remove the drug sentencing inequity that human rights groups, academic scholars, politicians, and even the U.S. Sentencing Commission have been fighting for years. The drug czar and former Seattle police chief Gil Kerlikowske has endorsed this shift in focus.

Until the impact of the anticipated sentence reform is felt, women with drug problems will still be present in large numbers in correctional institutions. Women such as Kemba Smith, a Black college student, whose case is described by Sudbury (2004), will still be behind bars. Smith received a 24-year sentence just for knowledge of her boyfriend's drug dealing. She was pregnant and feared for her life. This case, according to Sudbury, represents the gender entrapment experienced by many African American women entering the criminal justice system.

Women charged with dealing drugs sometimes wind up with longer sentences than the drug-dealing men they are involved with because they lack the information about the drug-trafficking operations the prosecutors want or they are unwilling to go undercover or snitch on family members. Women engage in what would otherwise be noncriminal activity that is identified as "aiding and abetting," such as accompanying a male intimate to a drug sale, answering the phone when a drug deal is taking place, or spending money obtained through drug sales (Failinger, 2006).

The interplay of race, class, and gender is at its most pronounced in the prosecution of drug-addicted mothers. Under the rationale of protecting the fetus, poor, Black, drug-addicted mothers are being hauled into court. This is part of an alarming trend toward greater state intervention into the lives of pregnant women. And poor women of color are the primary targets of government control; they are the least likely to obtain adequate prenatal care yet the most vulnerable to government monitoring, and they are the least able to conform to middle-class standards of motherhood. The prosecution of drug-addicted mothers thus becomes more than an issue of antifemale backlash. Poor Black women have been selected for punishment as a result of an inseparable combination of their gender, race, and economic status.

The media excitement over "crack babies" that appeared in the early 1990s and that was later found to be scientifically questionable was embodied into law due to a landmark case, *Whitner v. South Carolina*, which became law in 1997 (Sagatun-Edwards, 2007). This case upheld the prosecution of an African American woman, Regina McKnight, who was homeless and who ingested crack cocaine during the third trimester of her pregnancy. She was convicted of homicide and sentenced to 12 years in prison when her baby was stillborn. After the baby was found to have cocaine in his bloodstream, McKnight was prosecuted under child abuse and endangerment statutes. The National Association of Social Workers had joined 18 other health-related organizations in an *amicus curiae* (friend-of-the-court) brief asking the full court of appeals to hear the case (O'Neill, 2000). In 2003, on appeal, the South Carolina Supreme Court upheld the conviction based on laws recognizing a viable fetus as a person for the purpose of homicide laws and wrongful death statutes (Sagatun-Edwards, 2007). The U.S. Supreme Court denied to hear the appeal of this verdict.

The implications of the South Carolina decision are far-reaching. Maternal substance abuse during pregnancy has, in effect, been outlawed, and some patients have found themselves shackled to their hospital beds immediately after giving birth. Under this law, pregnant women with substance abuse problems will be highly reluctant to seek treatment. In light of the South Carolina decision, some states are introducing bills to make fetal abuse a felony. (There is no mention of charging men who batter their pregnant wives with fetal abuse, however.) Mandatory reporting of cases of suspected child abuse and neglect involving maternal drug use are now increasingly common. Since drug testing occurs only in publicly funded healthcare facilities, such laws, needless to say, fall chiefly on poor and minority women.

By 2004, hundreds of women had been arrested nationwide for their addictive behavior while pregnant (Paltrow, 2004). Many more have lost custody of their children because some states consider "child neglect" to include prenatal exposure to controlled substances. A new federal law passed and signed by President Bush in 2004—the Unborn Victims of Violence Act—makes it a crime to cause harm to a "child in utero." Many states have followed suit and passed such laws of their own.

Mandatory reporting of cases of suspected child abuse and neglect involving drug use are now increasingly common in many states. Drug testing of women occurs regularly in publicly funded healthcare facilities; there has been no comparable effort, however, to test for the role of sperm in causing birth defects (van Wormer & Davis, 2008). One could argue that the criminalization of maternal conduct during pregnancy violates a woman's rights to equal protection under the law inasmuch as evidence of a newborn's positive toxicology screen is used only in cases against women.

One positive outcome from the outcry over these prosecutions, according to Sagatun-Edwards (2007), is that many states have placed a priority on making drug treatment available to pregnant women. And increasingly prenatal substance use is treated as a public health matter rather than as a criminal justice matter.

Many other countries do not criminalize drug users in this way. The prevailing belief in Europe is that drug addiction is an illness, not a crime. European countries, according to a report by the Drug Prevention Networks of the Americas (DPNA, 2002) are searching for alternatives to prison. Treatment options are widely available. Even Sweden, which has some of the most stringent policies against drugs, offers a suspended sentence for minor drug offenses in return for treatment. Treatment options are no longer limited to detoxification or methadone treatment. Several nations, including Switzerland, offer heroin maintenance programs. The goal is to regulate drug use through regular contact with the users.

Since the 1950s, Norwegian law has allowed treatment as an alternative to prison for those convicted of drug offenses. In 1991, Norway introduced compulsory treatment for offenders. In 1996, the Norwegian government went a step further to include compulsory treatment for pregnant drug or alcohol users (DPNA, 2002). Under the new provisions, the unborn child's safety and health are placed above the abuser's freedom to choose whether to seek treatment.

Public benefits that often are denied to individuals on the basis of a drug conviction or drug use include welfare, educational loans, and public housing. Although federal law authorizes these policies, several states have begun to reject such punitive measures (Drug Policy Alliance, 2007).

SENTENCING OF WOMEN FOR CRIME

A note on page 1 of the BJS (2000) special report on female offenders states that women were serving shorter sentences than men for comparable crimes. The explanation provided later in the BJS document is that men had a higher prior conviction rate than women.

The belief that women receive lighter sentences than men for similar crimes and criminal histories persists; from this perspective, women offenders are seen as getting away with more lenient treatment than men in the belief that they are the weaker (and less dangerous) sex. Objective research seems to bear this belief out. Economists Sarnikar, Sorensen, and Oaxaca (2007), for example, formed this conclusion based on their analysis of data obtained from the United States Sentencing Commission's records. Their research, which was based on over 45,000 sentencing cases between 1996 and 2002, used sophisticated formulas to weigh variables such as prior criminal record. The results showed that women had an advantage of 9.5 months less in the length of their sentences; therefore they received more lenient sentences than did men with a similar crime and history. One serious flaw in their study, however, was that these researchers used only cases of White women. This was, as stated in the article, to rule out the factor of racism. This finding is interesting in that it seems to indicate a small degree of chivalry accorded to White women. But we cannot generalize the findings when the majority of sentenced offenders are members of minority groups.

When it comes to the death penalty, it is true that women are less likely to be sentenced to death row or executed than are men. Yet, there is convincing evidence that women who are perceived as masculine and gender inappropriate in their demeanor in court are treated more harshly than are women who seem more feminine in their appearance and behavior (Belknap, 2007). Prosecutors of women in capital cases (cases for which a death sentence is possible), for example, have been known to emphasize masculine characteristics and lesbianism to turn the jurors against defendants (Baker, 2007). Farr (2004), in her study of women on death row, found that the media had portrayed these offenders as "manly" and "man-hating" women who were the personification of evil. Many had engaged in felony robbery (a male-associated crime) in connection with the murder. As a result of homophobia in society and in the criminal justice system, about half of the women on death row are lesbians. In his analysis of women who have been executed in recent years, Schulberg (2007) likewise discovered several gender-based factors that singled these individuals out from offenders who have committed crimes of a similar nature. It is not the crime, as Schulberg argues, that is the determining factor, but the individual's demeanor—the degree to which she conforms to society's expectations for appropriate sex role behavior. Wanda Jean Allen, for example, was convicted of killing her lesbian lover; her lesbianism and masculinity were exploited by the prosecutor during the trial. She was executed in 2001. This prejudice by jurors probably applies to noncapital cases as well and may explain why certain types of women are more apt to receive prison terms than others.

The gender of the judge also is a factor in sentencing patterns. Female judges, far from overidentifying with female defendants, may hold them to a higher standard than male judges do. One study found the higher the proportion of female judges in a district, the less the disparity in male and female defendants' sentencing (Schanzenbach, 2005).

Although more research is needed on sentencing practices, we probably can conclude that White women who are feminine in demeanor have the best chance of receiving somewhat more lenient treatment than African American females and males of all races. As a rule, research shows that women of color, poor women, younger women, immigrants, and known lesbians are accorded less leniency than other women (Bloom & Chesney-Lind, 2007). And we also know from reports throughout the literature that conspiracy laws unfairly impact persons who are minimally involved in criminal behavior but who are the partners and wives of men who are actively engaged in lives of crime. Under conspiracy laws, the context of the relationship is not taken into account; nor is the impact on the children of sending both parents to prison (Gaskins, 2004). The gender-neutral sentencing laws fail to recognize the distinction between major players in drug organizations and minor ancillary players (Bloom & Chesney-Lind, 2007).

SUMMARY

In this chapter we have examined the nature and context of women's crime and the treatment of women in the criminal justice system. The pathway to crime for a female offender was seen to have biological, psychological, and social components. Childhood victimization and trauma have been identified consistently as primary pathways that lead girls and women into the criminal justice system. A pattern of poverty, involvement in unhealthy relationships, and initiation into drug use and other illicit activities is part of the typical scenario. Because racism and poverty often go hand in hand, females from poor, inner city backgrounds are often forced to deal early with problems of violence, prostitution, drugs, childhood pregnancy, and rough treatment by the authorities. The intersection of gender, race, and class is thus a highly evident component in female crime, both in regard to the form that the crime takes and the punishment that is meted out.

Many of the facts of their lives that form the web of circumstances of their lawbreaking are specific to women: childbirth and child care, care of the elderly, abuse by men, and dependence on men or the social system for economic aid. To lump female lawbreakers together with male lawbreakers without regard for these details of their lives is to blur the experiences of two disparate groups. Empathetic counseling for troubled women and their placement in nonpunitive, nurturing group homes could perhaps save them from their worst, most self-destructive instincts.

Part III

WORKING IN CORRECTIONAL INSTITUTIONS

Chapter 4

WOMEN IN PRISON

Make of my past, a road to the light.
Out of darkness, the ignorance, the light.
　　　　　　　—**Langston Hughes,** "The Negro Mother," 1931

M y dissertation study at the women's prison at Wetumpka, Alabama, was
entitled *Sex Role Behavior in a Women's Prison* (1979). The focus was
on characteristics of masculinity and femininity and how relationships among
the women were stratified. The rationale for the women's prison setting was
this: To learn about gendered role behavior, I needed to study women in a
unisex environment. There was no better place to conduct such research than
a women's prison. Then I could compare the women's behavior with what we
know about how men treat men in similar all-male settings. Today I can draw
on what I learned in that comparative study to bolster the case for a specialized treatment for women, in respect to both treatment interventions and sentencing options.

This chapter brings us into the world of the total institution, a world
strangely shut off from the outside, in which the rules that govern civil society
and personal respect for freedom and privacy no longer apply. Prison is memorably described by one of the tough women convicts in the classic movie
Caged (1950) "like a big cage in the zoo, only you clean it up yourself." The
cage analogy is apt, but the women locked on the inside are not animals—
each woman has a story that is filled with personal tragedy.

Work within a woman's prison can be both exciting—because of the drama
of the setting—and gratifying—because the needs of the women are so great.

This work, whether as correctional officer or counselor or administrator, is shaped not only by the society of women in the prison but also by federal and state criminal justice policies. And those policies are shaped by the political and economic climate of the times.

The focus of this chapter is on the contemporary prison environment in which correctional officers and counseling staff work. To present an accurate picture, government statistics and facts drawn from investigative reports by nongovernmental organizations used to present a contemporary profile of the prison population as well as the facts pertaining to their confinement.

To determine attitudes of prison administrators toward their charges, I summarize results of a national survey that I conducted in 2001. These results are followed up with a recent interview of an innovative prison warden who has fought to give her charges the help they so desperately need. Given the special concern of health issues to women in confinement, sections on health and mental health care are included. After discussing these healthcare issues, we turn our attention to a matter that has been long concealed from the general public until a spate of lawsuits and human rights investigations made the facts known: the sexual abuse of incarcerated women by male officers. Next we turn to an overview of women's inmate society, a social construction that is uniquely female. Narrative writings from women behind bars and from correctional workers highlight this portion of the discussion. The chapter concludes with a description of exemplary programs from abroad that were designed to meet women's special needs.

FROM A REHABILITATION TO A PUNISHMENT FOCUS

Correctional history shows that in the early days, in England and the United States, prisons for women were an afterthought. At first women were incarcerated with men; sexual abuse of the women was rampant. The story of women's imprisonment in American (and European) history is the story of people who were hanged, beaten, and starved. It is the story of women (and men) convicts who were treated worse than animals. At times chivalry was accorded to White women only. Gradually, there was a shift from the male prison model of treatment for all inmates to a consideration of needs based on gender. Women were appointed as wardens of women's prisons.

During the 1960s, rehabilitation was the primary goal of corrections. Programs in counseling, education, and training were set up for the purpose of "correcting" inmates' behavior to help them lead law-abiding lives upon their return to society. Inmates were even called "residents" at one point in the federal system. From this time until the 1970s, female inmates generally got special treatment in accordance with their gendered needs; however, they tended to be treated more like children who had gone astray than as adults.

A key factor that put an end to the impetus for progressive reform was sociological research of the nothing-works school. Liberals became cynical about forced treatment and argued for an end to indeterminate sentencing so that inmates would know exactly when they would be released. Conservatives used the new sociological research findings that seemed to point to the ineffectiveness of treatment to disparage the belief that criminals could be rehabilitated. The various progressive juvenile and adult rehabilitation programs were deemed to be a waste of the taxpayers' money. The end result was that over the next two decades, punishment was back in full force, and with a vengeance. The Federal Bureau of Prisons abolished parole, as did many of the states. As the progressive ideals were abandoned, reformatories and custodial prisons were merged into the medium-security design for women's incarceration that we have today.

The modern era, which we can describe as the legalistic age, is characterized by an emphasis on gender equality—in building designs, hiring practices, and vocational opportunities. The feminist movement was largely responsible for many of these developments that culminated in several landmark cases to provide women with parity in treatment with men. New legislation was passed to provide women (staff as well as inmates) with the same opportunities available to men (Rasche, 2003). The flip side of this privilege of equality is that women inmates also received the same harsh treatment that society had been meting out to male convicts. And security became the emphasis in both women's and men's facilities, even though the public fear of escaped female convicts has never been that high. Historically speaking, punishment for women had come full circle and mirrored the punishment for men. Guarded, as earlier, by male officers, sexual exploitation of women inevitably returned and has become a major source of lawsuits today.

In some of the more progressive prisons in the United States, men and women were housed together in co-correctional facilities in order to solve the female inequality problem. This solution was found to be flawed in various ways, although having a female presence was beneficial for men who were deprived of healthy, heterosexual contact (Belknap, 2007; Faith, 1993). With women forever in a tiny minority, the problems—conflicts, jealousies, sexual tensions, frequent pregnancies, double exploitation of women as sexual objects and nurturers—seemed to outweigh the benefits. Male dominance of prison leadership and emotional and sexual exploitation of female inmates by male inmates are additional drawbacks to co-corrections (Feinman, 1994). In Swedish prisons, however, where prisons resemble college dormitories and

sexual contact is not forbidden, male/female mixing is not viewed as problematic or even an issue.

In recognition of the problems associated with the U.S. absolute equality
ideology, the Canadian system introduced a new approach—*substantive
equality*—which focused on situational diversity, including the unique needs
of Aboriginal women (Goff, 1999). The need for programming to help women
recover from their past experiences of abuse and to promote healing, self-
esteem, and self-sufficiency was formally recognized, although this philosophy has not always been honored in practice. Dell, Fillmore, and Kilty (2009)
examine whether the promises of gender specialized treatment have been
kept and argue to the contrary, that the old male, security-focused model still
operates. Aboriginal and other women, for example, are treated as misbehaving and manipulative inmates for self-harming behavior when this behavior is
related to their early life victimization. When these women are placed in solitary confinement, such punitive practices have the potential to trigger past
experiences of abuse and trauma.

The Women's Prison Population

The documentary film *Perversion of Justice* (Mummert, 2007) records Hasan's
tragic story of arrest and imprisonment that begins with a battered woman
who escaped from her husband and moved her family in with her cousin in
Nebraska. She occasionally wired money for her cousin and performed other
errands for him. When he was arrested for masterminding a crack cocaine
operation, Hasan was arrested as well. Her refusal to testify against him got
her a mandatory sentence of 100 years. Her story and the grief that her daughters felt are now recorded on film for the public to see.

This case illustrates how a relatively innocent person can get caught up in
the sweep of zero-tolerance laws. Most women prisoners—about 75 percent—
are serving time for nonviolent offenses, often due to the mandatory drug-
sentencing laws. The majority are from backgrounds characterized by poverty
and personal pain. That female prisoners are drawn from the ranks of the economically marginalized is revealed in the fact that only about 4 in 10 women
in state prisons were employed full time prior to their arrests; this compares to
60% of male inmates. Furthermore, 30% of female inmates were receiving
welfare assistance (U.S. Bureau of Justice Statistics [BJS], 2000). The racial
aspect of crime and punishment is revealed in the fact that African Americans
and Latinas are more likely than Caucasian Americans to be imprisoned.

For years, women have been only a tiny fraction, usually only around 4%,
of the total prison population. Part of the reason, of course, is women's

relatively low crime rate compared to men's. Historically, women were much less likely to be imprisoned unless the female offender did not fit the stereo-typical female role. Such differential treatment of women, sometimes referred to as chivalry, seems to have become a thing of the past, as Chesney-Lind and Pasko (2003) observe.

Although women's rate for serious crimes continues to be low, the rapid growth in the incarceration of women continues. The profiles of women in prison, in contradiction to the myth of the new, violent female offender, confirm the detrimental impact of mandatory sentencing guidelines.

At every level of the social system, the effects of racism and classism leave their imprint indelibly on the later stages. Today, as Chesney-Lind and Pasko (2003) suggest, street crime has become a code word for race. The singling out of the one drug used most frequently in the inner city for harsh penalties creates a situation with desperate consequences for Black and Latino women. Women of color singularly bear the brunt of the new mandatory drug-sentencing laws.

When their spouses and partners are arrested for drug dealing, women are often brought down with them. Equality under the law may thus fail to take into account the inequality in most of these male/female relationships. In any case, today's harsh sentencing practices weigh heavily among the young women of color, most of them mothers, who are serving time in the nation's prisons.

Whereas women were only 4% of the U.S. incarcerated population in 1980, by 2000 women comprised 6.4% of the prisoner total (in local jails and prisons), and by 2008 women comprised 6.9% of the prison total (West & Sabol, 2009). The growth rate for the last two years has leveled off. In Australia, the female percentage of the prison population has expanded, similarly, from 3.9% in 1984 to 6.8% in 2003 (Australia Bureau of Statistics, 2004). In the United Kingdom, the incarceration rate for women has increased 50% from 1998 to 2009 (Morris, 2009). The increase is pronounced among older women who are serving short sentences of several months for nonviolent offenses such as shoplifting. Canada similarly has seen an increase; over the past five years there has been a 30% increase in the number of women in custody awaiting trial, and the percentage of the federal prison population that is female has gone from 5% to 6% since 2001 (Babooram, 2008). In Japan and New Zealand, an upsurge of women prisoners is in evidence as well ("Women in Prison," 2008). In Europe, the percentage of female prisoners is on the rise, generally, growing from 2% to 3% of the total in the 1990s, to around 5% to 6% by 2003 (Walmsley, 2007). These trends are universal.

In the United States, prisoner and jail inmate profiles can be best revealed through recent studies from the BJS (2000) West and Sabol (2009), and the American Civil Liberties Union (ACLU) (2005). From these respected sources, we learn that:

- White women were one-third as likely as Black women to be incarcerated and slightly more than half as likely as Hispanic women to be incarcerated in 2008 (West & Sabol, 2009).
- The proportion of Black female inmates has steadily declined since 2000, while the numbers of White and Hispanic female inmates has risen by about 30% over the past 8 years (West & Sabol, 2009).
- Approximately 65% of women in state prisons have young children; about two-thirds of the women lived with their children before entering prison (BJS, 2000).
- Nearly 60% of the women reported they had been physically or sexually abused (BJS, 2000).
- About 6 in 10 women in state prison were using drugs in the month before their offense (BJS, 2000).
- In most cases, when a woman is imprisoned, her child is displaced; when the father is incarcerated, the child is more likely to live with the mother and not be displaced (ACLU, 2005).

These statistics, which are beyond dispute, provide documentation of the racism, sexism, and classism that exists in contemporary society. Part of the reason for the racial lopsidedness, as we have seen in Chapter 4, is the harsh sentencing practices that punish users and dealers of crack cocaine, a drug associated in the public mind with inner city crime. Past mandated minimum sentencing for involvement with this drug has filled up jail and prison cells with African American and Latina women. Sexism, as we have also seen, is played out in the harsh sentencing of women and their removal to prisons far from home. Classism is evidenced in the poor educational backgrounds and high poverty rates of these women.

The rapid growth in the number of U.S. women who are sentenced means that departments of corrections are not able to focus on treatment and rehabilitation but rather on the warehousing of people; worry over finding the next cell is the predominant concern. Jail and prison construction has become the major expense to counties all across the nation. Ironically, the prison building boom is occurring at the same time that the crime rate has steadily decreased, especially rates of the violent crimes so often sensationalized in the news. The more prisons that are built, inevitably, the more people will be sentenced to fill them. "Build them and they will convict" is the common refrain. States that once managed with one or no prisons for women now are building several. And the repercussions of women's growing rate of incarceration will be felt well beyond prison walls. Experts point, in particular, to the children of inmates who are far more likely than other children to end up in the juvenile justice system or prison (Petersilia, 2003).

PSYCHOLOGICAL PROFILE

The linkages between female offenders and victims of gendered crimes such as rape and partner abuse are profound. In addition to the female offender's likely personal history of victimization, there is common ground between the victims and offenders with regard to:

- Mutually dehumanizing encounters with agencies of social control
- The impact of racism and classism in victimization and the prosecution of crimes
- A common recognition by international organizations and others that one's human rights have been violated
- The theme of sexual objectification and sexual abuse of vulnerable women in and outside of custody
- A joint history of reform efforts generated by the women's movement to protect women in their dealings with the court
- Mutual needs for empowering and crisis intervention counseling, advocacy, and consciousness-raising efforts

Approximately 80% of women in U.S. prisons and almost 66% of women in Canadian prisons have a serious problem with alcohol and other drugs, and substance abuse is associated directly or indirectly with the crimes for which they were convicted (van Wormer & Bartollas, 2010). Perhaps because of the association of the use of the illicit drug methamphetamine with Whites, the most recent incarceration statistics reveal that the incarceration rate for Black women has declined since 2000 from 6 times that of White women to 3.7 times that of White women (West & Sabol, 2009). There are increasing numbers of White women sentenced to prison and a reduced number of Black women so sentenced.

Related problems are eating disorders and other mental health problems, such as depression, high anxiety, and compulsions for self-mutilation. The refusal to conceptualize substance abuse as a healthcare issue rather than a law enforcement problem is at the heart of the phenomenal growth rate of the U.S. prison population.

Because of this psychological prison profile, female prisoners are often viewed solely as losers and in negative terms. Former inmate and social work researcher Kathy Boudin (2007) urges us not to focus on the statistics and stories of victimization, but rather to be aware of the fact that "women in prison are filled with ideas, energy, dreams, and possibilities. Women in prison can be critical agents of their own change.... They can redirect their lives" (p. 16). Boudin provides vivid descriptions of how the women at Bedford Hills Correctional Facility effected institutional change through advocacy and organizing. Through their persistence, the inmates arranged to have HIV/AIDS volunteers provide educational sessions on this disease. Inmates also worked together to improve the care of child visitors and the infants who lived in the prison nursery. With the support of the administration and people in the community, a group of women arranged for a full college curriculum to be offered to the inmates. "These stories," concludes Boudin, "can alter the narratives of screaming newspaper headlines about women arrested, sent to prison, or trying to come home.... [H]elp create conditions that develop their potential, and recognize women whose potential has been realized" (pp. 21–22).

PRISON CONDITIONS

"What do you want for your girls now, a swimming pool, a beauty parlor?" This question was asked of the progressive warden in the movie *Caged* (1950) by a member of the board of directors. This attitude of resentment toward prison inmates who might have an easier life than some law-abiding women on the outside is still common. This attitude ignores the fact that the physical isolation from society in conjunction with the loss of freedom is a serious punishment in itself. Punitive legislation in recent years took away privileges after public outcries. Nationwide, weight-lifting programs for male inmates were canceled; color televisions were replaced with black-and-white screens; and eligibility for certain entitlements, such as Social Security benefits, was disallowed. When Congress removed prisoners' eligibility for Pell Grants for college education, most inmates could no longer afford to take the courses that had so fulfilled their lives. And yet research shows that female inmates who have access to college classes are four times more likely to stay out of prison after their release than are inmates without this opportunity (Talvi, 2007).

Because of the relatively small size of the women's population compared to the men's—a fact true the world over—woman's prisons tend to be geographically isolated, and women of all kinds, sentenced for all varieties of crime, from drug offenses to "hit lady" murder, are locked up together. Program offerings and vocational opportunities, such as well-paid work release programs, tend to be severely restricted as well. Regarding programming for substance abuse problems, treatment is provided only at the end of time served, a year or so before eligibility for parole so inmates serving long sentences get left out.

In 1979, to ensure a cheap labor pool, Congress began a process of deregulation that allowed private corporations to exploit the captive labor market for profit. Prison labor as it exists today, as Levin (1999) argues, bears a frightening resemblance to slavery. With wages as low as 11 cents an hour in some places and no benefits or vacations, the prisoners must choose between labor and longer sentences, since "good time" policies subtract days from one's total sentence for good behavior and days worked. In fact, involuntary servitude as punishment for crime is legal under the U.S. Constitution (Thirteenth Amendment) but not under the Universal Declaration of Human Rights (1948), which outlaws slavery of all forms.

Some inmates are relatively well paid by the companies that employ them—well paid, that is, by prison standards. Corporations ranging from J.C. Penney and Victoria's Secret, to IBM and TWA utilize prison labor to cut costs and increase profit margins (Levin, 1999). In several other countries with better welfare systems, such as Sweden and Norway, prison workers are well paid, unionized, and get paid vacations. In Canada, prison workers are paid a living wage even for attending school. These kinds of incentives for work and education are immensely helpful to correctional authorities in the smooth running of a women's institution.

Consistent with the trend toward sexual equality, the courts have determined that the disparate resources and treatment traditionally provided to female inmates infringed on their Fourteenth Amendment right to equal protection under the law. Women prisoners therefore can file lawsuits, and do, to claim their right to parity of treatment with male prisoners (Rasche, 2003).

One problem with the lawsuits by women demanding vocational equality with men in prison is that the men in U.S. prisons do not have it so good themselves. In areas where men were put on chain gangs, this was tried for a while for women too. And the boot camp option also was made available to women. Chesney-Lind cynically refers to this development as turning female inmates into "a correctional version of GI Joe" (Chesney-Lind & Pollock, 1994, p. 167).

Are women in prison treated as if they are men? I posed this question to a former correctional officer who had worked in both men's and women's institutions. This is what she said (in personal correspondence of February 15, 2000) in part:

> I disagree that the women are treated more like the males. In fact, they are treated more harshly and discriminated against by their "guards." Many female administrators resent these women being in prison. And you know how women think, they're far more nasty than any man could be. I think that female personnel are much nastier to females than to males. At the Ohio Reformatory for Women they have rules (swearing will get you a hole shot) whereas in a male prison, FU is common jargon.

I can confirm the comment about female bashing as typical from my dealings with prison officials. That women offenders are far more conniving and treacherous than men is the commonly voiced belief. Rasche (2007) devoted a whole chapter to this phenomenon with the compelling title "The Dislike of Female Offenders among Correctional Officers." The almost unanimous desire on the part of correctional officers, male and female, to avoid working with female offenders or in women's prisons is probably due to their lack of specialized training, as Rasche suggests. Indeed, as she states, the very supervisory techniques that are taught emphasize intimidating tactics that may backfire when applied to female prisoners.

Prison overcrowding is another major problem in women's institutions due to the surge in female incarceration rates. The impact of prison crowding on male and female imprisonment rates was studied through longitudinal data analysis of sentencing and early releases in the state of Minnesota. Stolzenberg and D'Alessio (1997) found that, compared to their female counterparts, male offenders are more likely to receive expedited departures when crowding in male prisons reaches intolerable levels. This fact is true even though the woman's prison in Minnesota is actually more overcrowded than the male prison, a finding that casts doubt on the frequent claim that female defendants receive more lenient treatment than male defendants.

Media reports from the United Kingdom reveal a similar problem with overcrowding in women's prisons following a rapid increase in the confinement of seriously disturbed women (BBC News, 2007). A rash of suicides among imprisoned women in 2002 scandalized the nation and led to a public inquiry by the United Kingdom Parliament (2004) in the House of Lords. Among their findings:

- There were three times as many women prisoners in 2003 as in 1993, yet the crime rate is not rising.

- Nearly half of the women are mothers of young children.
- Almost half of the women were imprisoned for drug offenses.
- About 18% of the women in U.K. prisons are foreign, often serving drug sentences for having been used as drug carriers, or "mules."

As a result of the media focus on prison conditions and the earlier incarceration of children, the United Kingdom has set up modern juvenile homes with professionally trained staff and is providing specialized treatment for the girls. Methadone maintenance programs for female addicts are under way, and extensive mental health and substance abuse treatment will be provided.

HEALTHCARE NEEDS

Leslie Acoca (1998), director of the Women and Girls Institute of the National Council on Crime and Delinquency, observed these scenes: a terminally ill White woman in a wheelchair baking in the midday sun because no one is there to move her and a young Hispanic inmate pleading for help for medical services for her HIV-positive toddler. Talvi (2007), who also has toured prisons across the United States and other countries, reports firsthand horror stories of medical incompetence and neglect until it was too late and untreated diseases that proved to be fatal. For some women in prison, therefore, their 10- and 20-year sentences become death sentences as chronic illnesses become terminal.

When women's prison advocates seek gender-responsive healthcare for women, they are often told that women cannot be treated differently from men. Yet, as Raeder (2005) indicates, there are valid biological reasons why women do not use urinals or why one-piece jumpsuits are a major inconvenience. Differences in policies also need to take into account women offenders' histories of physical and sexual abuse and the proliferation of mental disorders among them. Of course, there are specific concerns related to women's reproductive functions: menstruation, pregnancy, and postpartum healthcare. In an official investigation of one of the most progressive prisons for women in the United States—Bedford Hills Correctional Facility in New York state—complaints were made concerning the allotment of toilet paper, which had to be the same at male and female institutions. This requirement ignores the fact that women, especially because of their monthly periods, require more toilet paper than men. There was a reported shortage of sanitary napkins as well (Correctional Association of New York, 2006).

The failure of the state to provide adequate medical care to meet the special needs of female prisoners is highlighted in the report of the General

Accounting Office (GAO; 1999), *Women in Prison: Issues and Challenges Confronting U.S. Correctional Systems.* Focusing on the nation's three largest correctional systems—the Federal Bureau of Prisons, the California Department of Corrections and the Texas Department of Criminal Justice, a system collectively holding over one-third of the nation's female inmates—the report found serious deficiencies in the areas of treatment for substance abuse and mental health problems and HIV infection. Compared to men, women in prison have higher rates of illness in all three areas. For mental illness, for example, 13% of female inmates in federal prisons and 24% in state prisons (compared to 7% and 16% of men) report having a mental disorder or having spent time in a mental hospital. The GAO report revealed that the prisons surveyed provided ready access to female-specific health-care services and that initial physical and pelvic examinations, mammograms, and routine pregnancy screening were done. Many of the prisons were under close external scrutiny due to lawsuits over neglectful health-care in the past.

Substance abuse treatment is the area of most striking deficiency; despite the fact that an estimated 60% of female state prisoners (and 43% of federal prisoners) were dependent on or abusing drugs at the time of arrest, only around 9 or 10% are in treatment at one time (Rand , 2006). More White than Black female offenders have alcohol and other drug problems; today, as mentioned, methamphetamine addiction is bringing large numbers of White women into prison.

We must keep in mind that attendance at self-help group meetings such as Alcoholics Anonymous is counted as treatment in most prison surveys. These groups are important but cost the system nothing and are not capable of providing the in-depth therapy that most offenders need. The formerly male-oriented curriculum is being revised in some states, such as Texas, to include relationships and trauma work of specific relevance to women.

In California, a recent scandal has emerged concerning dental treatment in the women's prison system (Garcia, 2008). To gain access to desirable programs, including special housing where they can live with their children, women must be cleared of any preexisting health problems. Yet dental care apart from teeth extraction is not readily available. As a result, hundreds of inmates are choosing to have their teeth pulled so they can enter the programs. Keep in mind that many of the inmates, from poor backgrounds and a history of methamphetamine use, have severely damaged teeth. About 9,000 teeth are pulled each year in California's three female institutions, according to prison system records.

Upon release, these partially toothless women are having great difficulty finding employment.

HIV/AIDS AND HEPATITIS C

Two of the most life-threatening diseases for prisoners are HIV/AIDS and hepatitis C. Compared to 1.6% of male inmates, 2.4% of all female inmates in state and federal prisons are HIV positive (Maruschak, 2008). This rate has declined steadily since its peak in 1999. The decline reflects a decline in the general population. In some states, such as New York, Texas, and Maryland, the rates are much higher. A high correlation exists between HIV cases and tuberculosis and being HIV positive and having hepatitis C.

According to the Correctional Association of New York (2006), which toured and researched conditions at Bedford Hills Correctional Facility, 56 inmates were HIV positive (around 14%) at the time of the visit, 50 of whom were getting treatment. Special counseling and advocacy for these women was provided through the highly respected ACE (AIDS Counseling and Education) program.

In New York state, where pregnant women inmates live with their infants for a specified period after giving birth, care of newborns of HIV-infected mothers is a complex and daunting task, particularly if complicated by drug dependence in the infant. HIV, like other female inmates health problems, is often a part of the cultural baggage women bring to prison with them. Because of the women's dire poverty and the failure of the United States to offer universal healthcare, jails and prisons paradoxically are in the position of providing access to healthcare services unavailable in the women's home community.

About 7% of the 607 women screened for HIV at the Washington, DC, jail in 2006 were found to be infected with HIV/AIDS (Levine, 2007), compared to 2.7% of men. HIV-specific programming and medical treatment are provided at the facility, which gives inmates an incentive to get tested.

Hepatitis C, which is spread through infected blood and can lead to chronic liver disease, affects 20% to 50% of women's jail and prison populations (Talvi, 2007). Hepatitis C is especially prevalent among women incarcerated for crimes related to sex work and drug addiction (Correctional Association of New York, 2009). Unlike HIV medications, which are often subsidized, hepatitis C medications are highly expensive. Some prison systems fail to test for this disease. In New York facilities, for example, around 62% of women who test positive for HIV receive medical treatment while only 4% of inmates with hepatitis C receive comparable medical treatment. At the Bedford Hills facility, 23% of the inmates have hepatitis C.

Health and Human Rights

Legal cases based on medical abuse and neglect abound. Whereas prison administrators insist they are doing their job, healthcare-related allegations from female inmates and their legal advocates indicate otherwise. The denial of adequate medicine for chronic diseases, lack of timely treatment for spreading cancers, and dangerous delays in care for pulmonary and cardiac problems are among the allegations made (Talvi, 2007). At the California Women's Facility at Chowchilla with a population of over 4,000 inmates, for example, come reports of mentally ill prisoners locked in solitary confinement 23 hours a day, a rash of suicides, a total lack of privacy even when women are on the toilet, and brutal "cell extractions" of noncompliant inmates.

Just as we in the United States look at other countries to gauge their level of enlightenment, so they look to the United States to see how humane and rehabilitative prisons are in this, the richest country in the world. According to international nongovernmental organizations such as Human Rights Watch and Amnesty International, descriptions of the treatment of women in U.S. prisons are far from laudatory. The fact that male correctional officers are placed in such close physical contact with female inmates is considered an anomaly from the foreign perspective.

That other states are also guilty of medical neglect is highlighted in the Amnesty International (1999) report on human rights violations of women in custody. Florida, Virginia, and Washington, DC, were singled out for their routine medical neglect of female inmates. Amnesty International calls attention to these healthcare failings.

- Partly because of the explosion in the female prison population, there are too few staff to meet physical and mental health needs.
- There are long delays in obtaining medical attention. Disrupted and poor-quality treatment causes physical deterioration of prisoners with chronic and degenerative diseases like cancer. Prisoners are overmedicated with psychotropic drugs.
- Women who attempt to access mental health services are routinely given medication without the opportunity to undergo psychotherapeutic treatment.
- Women in security housing units (SHUs) spend between 22 and 24 hours a day in small concrete cells. A large proportion of women in SHUs have been diagnosed with mental health problems. One California

psychiatrist told Amnesty International that the harsh conditions there can induce psychosis or exacerbate existing mental illness.

- Shackling of all prisoners, including pregnant prisoners, is policy in federal prisons and the U.S. Marshals Service and exists in almost all state prisons. Shackling during labor may cause complications during delivery, such as hemorrhage or decrease in fetal heart rate.
- Inmates with HIV/AIDS do not receive life-saving drugs.

Amnesty International makes these recommendations:

- Local, state, and federal authorities should provide resources to ensure the identification of the physical and mental health care needs of all inmates upon admission and while in custody and the provision of necessary services and treatment.
- Healthcare should be provided without charge.
- Healthcare should accord with professionally recognized community standards for services to women.
- Authorities should establish standards of adequacy and appropriateness for prison and jail health services and conduct periodic, independent external reviews of the services.
- People suffering severe mental illness should not be in jails and prisons but in mental health institutions.
- The federal government should fund a study to look into mental health services for women in jails and prisons. One element of the study should be the use of psychotropic medication.

Talvi (2007) reports on the dire situation facing frail elderly inmates. Some have terminal illnesses yet are still treated as high-security risks — "they are handcuffed and even shackled by their ankles to their deathbeds" (p. 114). The only pain medication given to women suffering from chronic and terminal illnesses was aspirin or Tylenol.

In their in-depth study of medical care through the eyes of inmates at a detention center in Arizona, Moe and Ferraro (2003) found that some women were pleased to get any healthcare at all because none had been available to them on the outside. In interviews, many others told chilling stories of near-fatal neglect in prison. Fear of contracting diseases in the enclosed space of the prison was a constant among the women.

MENTAL HEALTH CARE

With the dismantling of public mental hospitals beginning in the 1960s and the incarceration boom of the past decade, prisons have become home for alarming numbers of the mentally ill. Jails today have become the poor person's mental hospital, the dumping grounds for people whose bizarre, unmedicated behavior lands them behind bars.

In its investigation of the treatment of prisoners with mental illness, Human Rights Watch (2003) devoted special attention to the plight of female inmates. The government statistics on the extent of mental illness in this population are probably an underestimate, according to Human Rights Watch. In New York, for example, 26% of the women are on the active mental health caseload compared to 11% of men, and in Pennsylvania, Georgia, and Vermont, over a third of female prisoners are on that caseload.

Mental health treatment is clearly substandard and especially so for female inmates, who often are simply tranquilized into silence. In their evaluation of inmate treatment in Arizona, Moe and Ferraro (2003) said that the only time inmates received treatment for their mental problems was when they threatened suicide. Then they were locked up on "suicide watch." In testimonials from a tall Rastafarian woman incarcerated at the York Correctional Institution in Connecticut, we get this firsthand description:

> Hollering went on all day long and arguments broke into fights that sent the COs [correctional officers] running. Because I was a battered woman with emotional scars, these conditions were like triggers back to my worst days...I was tranquilized three times a day with Elavil.... that made me withdrawn, suicidal, and obese. I had entered [the prison] at...110 pounds, down from my normal 140.... Nine months after my incarceration, I weighed 240. (Jessamy, 2003, pp. 192–193)

In her investigative book *Crazy in America*, Mary Beth Pfeiffer (2007) records the tragic case of Shayne Eggen, which received much publicity in Iowa. Eggen, diagnosed with paranoid schizophrenia, was prone to self-mutilation and had a pattern of violent outbursts. In an earlier confinement in jail, she gouged out one of her eyes. Since she was also subject to such outbursts in prison, she spent her time in solitary confinement, where she gouged out the other eye. Pfeiffer used Eggen's story to illustrate the impact on mentally ill individuals and the prison system of the closing of hospital beds across the nation. The closings occurred in conjunction with the passing of the federal Supplemental Security Income law that was designed to support ex–mental patients living in communities. Cutbacks in Medicaid for institutional care for psychiatric patients followed. The discovery of new antipsychotic medications prompted these changes. While hospital closings pushed mentally ill women onto the streets, their behavior (such as illicit drug use) sometimes drove them into prison and kept them there. Psychiatric treatment, apart from the provision of medications, is rare within the prison setting. Protecting the public from crime and maintaining discipline within prison walls are the major goals of prison, not healing the sick.

This low standard of treatment violates the Fourteenth Amendment requiring equal treatment under the law. Even worse is the brutalization and victimization of mentally ill inmates whose vulnerability and noncompliance place them at great risk at the hands of officers and often inmates. The use of chemical sprays, shackles, handcuffs, and stun guns are routine with this population. Depression, anxiety, claustrophobia, and paranoia—all are exacerbated in the total institutional setting.

SEXUAL ABUSE OF FEMALE INMATES

As a result of the affirmative action laws and lawsuits by women seeking to work in all correctional institutions as officers, just as women went to work in men's prisons, men were hired to work in women's prisons. This set the stage for a rash of sexual scandals by male officers who took advantage of women's vulnerability. This happened in the early days of prison history, was a well-known pattern under slavery, is a fact of life in military conquest, and is a problem that inevitably arises in situations where men have absolute power over girls and women. I am talking about sexual abuse, rape (from the Latin word *to seize*), and sexual exploitation of the dominated by those who control their lives and resources. Writing in a law school journal, Brenda Smith (2006) offers psychological insights into the power dynamics of controlling women who were enslaved in the 19th century and the norms of imprisonment today, which she views as "a modern corollary of slavery" (p. 571):

> At base, both slave owners and correction officers used sexual domination and coercion of women to reinforce notions of domination and authority over the powerless. Like women slaves, women prisoners are seen as untrustworthy, promiscuous, and seductive. They are the archetypal "Dark Lady" who is responsible not only for her own victim-hood, but also for the corruption of men. Like women slaves, women in custody have sometimes "chosen" to align with their captors—for reasons of convenience, sexual expression, desire, material need, or survival. Because she is the "other" woman, poor and often Black, she is relegated to the margins, outside of the coalition by traditional feminists, Black men, and those advocating for poor people. (pp. 605–606)

Deprived of the comforts and often necessities of life and at the mercy of correctional officers, women in prison today are prime targets for sexual abuse and exploitation. The scandals, human rights reports, and lawsuits that have been generated by cross-gender guarding of inmates have come almost exclusively from complaints by legal aid lawyers and other advocates on behalf of female prisoners.

The facts are daunting, and the individual stories more so. The stories come to light in lawsuits, histories described in Human Rights Watch (1996) and Amnesty International (1999) reports, aired on national TV, and in personal correspondence from prisoners. If it had not been for the idealism and determination of legal aid lawyers and feminist organizations such as the National Women's Law Center, the stories might never have emerged. The stories of rape, revenge deprivations, forced nudity in lock-up, pregnancies in a closed system where the males were the only guards, forced abortions, and solitary confinement of complainants and witnesses barely received notice until seven or eight years ago. Across the country, there were incidents of prison or jail staff sexually molesting inmates with impunity (Siegal, 2004).

According to Stop Prisoner Rape (2003), the sexual abuse of female inmates at the Ohio Reformatory for Women was widespread and persistent. Reports of such abuse were brought by a therapist and confirmed by a nurse administrator and former inmates at the facility. The extensive investigation conducted by Stop Prisoner Rape, which was bolstered by widespread media coverage in Ohio, further revealed that female inmates who complained were locked in solitary confinement.

Rathbone's (2005) interviews with women confined in the Massachusetts women's prison at Framingham provide details of sexual relationships between inmates and guards, often the trading of sex for small privileges. A further account of prison scandals from the popular literature is provided by Amy Fisher (2004), who at age 16 shot her lover's wife at his request. In prison, as a celebrity murderer, Fisher was sexually abused by correctional officers. Today, now a free woman, she is active in prison reform.

Official reports both echo those from the scholarly and popular literature and provide additional information. Survey results from the sexual violence report conducted by the U.S. Department of Justice and analyzed by BJS statisticians Beck and Hughes (2005) provide some rather startling information about sexual misconduct in the nation's jails and prisons. Female staff members were frequently reported for sexual misconduct in men's prisons. The statistics are these: With regard to inmate-on-inmate nonconsensual sex acts in prison and jail, males comprised 90% of the victims and perpetrators. In local jails, 70% of victims were female and 65% of perpetrators were male. In state prisons, however, 67% of those involved in sexual misconduct were female, as perpetrators, and 69% of the victims were male. No specific illustrations are given, but one can speculate from other studies that some female officers who work in men's prisons may be psychologically susceptible to being manipulated by the men in their charge.

To understand this phenomenon, we turn to a special report from the U.S. Department of Justice (2005). This inquiry, the first of its kind, was undertaken as a requirement of the Prison Rape Elimination Act passed by Congress and signed into law in 2003. Among the cases it described were that of a female psychologist who was overheard discussing her sexual relationship with an inmate and of a letter that was intercepted describing a female teacher's sexual relationship with a male inmate. What stands out in these cases is that the male inmates were not the ones filing the complaints, whereas we know from other reports many of the women who get sexually involved with their male correctional officers do feel victimized and do complain. And the U.S. Department of Justice report on prison rape confirms that male inmates do not file complaints against female officers who have engaged in sexual misconduct with them. The report also states that criminal prosecution of such cases is rare.

A Human Rights Perspective on Prison Sexual Abuse

To learn details of prison sexual abuse that took place previously, read the 347-page report of 1999. In its updated *Stop Violence Against Women*, Amnesty International (2007) recommends that authorities take these measures:

- Incarcerated women should be guarded only by female officers. Male staff who provide professional services in female facilities should always be accompanied by female officers.
- Sexual abuse of all persons in custody should be expressly prohibited and should be widely defined to include sexual assault and threatened sexual assault, sexual contact, and sexually explicit language and gestures.
- All staff and inmates should be informed that sexual abuse is prohibited and that
  - Inmates have a right to complain if they are abused.
  - Staff members have a duty to report if they know that an inmate has been abused.
- Inmates should have the ability to complain directly to an external office, such as an ombudsman or attorney general, for example, through an 800 number. Internally, authorities must make several methods of reporting sexual abuse available.

- Victims of sexual abuse must be provided with appropriate care and redress. Immediate action must be taken against staff who sexually abuse inmates, including criminal investigation if the alleged misconduct would rise to the level of a crime.
- All complaints must be investigated independently, promptly, and thoroughly in line with best practice for the investigation of sexual assault.
  - All allegations of custodial sexual misconduct that may meet the level of a crime should be referred for external investigation, and impartial prosecutorial staff—not correctional staff—should decide whether prosecution is warranted.
  - Inmates and staff must be informed that they have a right to protection from retaliation.
  - Protection from retaliation should not include solitary confinement or lockdown and should not result in the revocation of any privileges previously afforded an inmate.

Further recommendations from Amnesty International include:

- Staff should receive detailed and regularly recurring training about laws and policies prohibiting custodial sexual misconduct.
- Restraints should be used only to prevent escape.
- Policies should prohibit the use of restraints on pregnant women when they are being transported and when they are in hospital in labor and just after they have given birth.

Unlike Human Rights Watch, which does not object to men guarding female prisoners, Amnesty International is calling for female inmates to be supervised by female staff only. Both of these nongovernmental organizations urge that any correctional employee who engages in sexual intercourse or sexual touching of a prisoner be prosecuted to the fullest extent of the law. As Human Rights Watch (2003) indicates, the Prison Litigation Reform Act signed into law in 1996 to curb prison lawsuits has seriously compromised the ability of individuals and non-governmental organizations to challenge abusive prison conditions through litigation. Extensive mass media reports of frivolous lawsuits by prisoners to the neglect of serious suits challenging life threatening health conditions, for example, has fueled public support for legislation to seriously curb the prisoner lawsuits. The most stringent anti-litigation laws were passed in Michigan. In a positive development that has important implications for all prisoners, the state of Michigan agreed to pay $100 to settle a class action suit on behalf of women who were raped while in custody of the government (Nolan, 2009). This victory for the former inmates and their lawyers put an end to the legal battle that has raged for over a decade. According to Nolan, who serves on the National Prison Rape Elimination Commission, this settlement is solid evidence that prison rape will no longer be tolerated.

Recent Developments

Today, across the United States, states are cracking down on sexual abuse of prisoners, as we see in this recent headline from Iowa, for example: "Sex with Inmates Gets Former Jailer 8 Years in Prison" (Strong, 2008). Probably due to the publicity of inmate abuse, many prisons and jails are showing greater sensitivity to the protection of women in these facilities (see results of my survey of prison administrators in the next section). Efforts such as making sure the staff is well trained, educating the prisoners about their rights, eliminating impunity for guards, and following up on reports of sexual abuse, as is mandated in Minnesota, go a long way toward prevention. Toward this end and in reaction to the national outcry over sexual assaults of male and female inmates, Congress unanimously passed the Prison Rape Elimination Act (PREA) in 2003 (Beck, Harrison, & Adams, 2007). PREA aims to establish zero-tolerance standards of sexual assaults; to increase data and information on the occurrence of prison sexual assault as collected by the BJS; and to develop and implement national standards for the detection, prevention, reduction, and punishment of prison sexual assault.

Results from the 2007 BJS data collection showed that males constituted 82% of the victims and 85% of the perpetrators. Whites were 72% of the victims; Blacks were 16%, and Hispanics, 9%. Victims of staff sexual misconduct were 56% female; the perpetrators were 60% male. This effort obtained data from prison administrator reports. A follow-up BJS report on sexual victimization is the first national inmate survey to derive data entirely from the inmates themselves (Rand, 2008). Although most of the prisons in which data were gathered were male facilities, 16 facilities were female. Results were discouraging. For example, at Valley State Prison in California, 5% reported staff-on-inmate sexual contact, and at Rockville, Illinois, 2% reported such contact. On a separate measure of what the BJS report presented by Beck and Harrison (2008) termed "nonconsensual" sexual contact with a staff member, the Julia Tutwiler facility in Alabama was singled out as having an extremely high rate (around 10%) of inmates claiming such victimization. Human Rights Watch (2007), responding to this report, urges the BJS to eliminate reference to inmate willingness with regard to staff sexual misconduct in future reports.

All sexual interaction between staff and inmates, as Human Rights Watch correctly indicates, is inherently coercive because of the inherent disparity in power between staff and inmates. Thus it can never be considered "voluntary" on the part of the inmates.

On the legislative side, there have been promising developments and more probably will be forthcoming. According to a follow-up report by Amnesty International (2007), significant legislative reform has taken place since its original report was published on abuse of women in custody. In 1990, few states had laws criminalizing custodial sexual misconduct. Today, all but Vermont have passed such laws. Many state laws do not cover all forms of sexual contact, however.

Survey of Prison Administrators

Although there is a wealth of information on women's prisons, there is no up-to-date needs assessment survey of women's prison administrators to determine how the special needs of female inmates are being met. To learn the current state of affairs pertaining to incarcerated women, I conducted a survey of administrators of all women's correctional facilities in the United States. (For a full description of the methodology and results, see van Wormer & Kaplan, 2006.) A mailing list was developed of 77 closed women's facilities in the United States. Most states required approval by an official review board. After many rejections (such as by the entire federal system and all prisons in California) and much bureaucratic hassle, the return rate of around one-third can be considered acceptable.

Results from the 28 administrators who responded revealed that prison officials were often critical of the media reports over staff-inmate abuse yet that they were taking measures to protect their institutions from such scandals. As a whole, results showed that administrators are having difficulty coping with troubled and troublesome inmates, many of whom should not be in prison in the first place. The "defensive nature of their crimes," the unreasonably long sentences, and the factor of mental illness were all given as concerns. Prison overcrowding was mentioned again and again as a major problem. Generally the results are consistent with recent reports in the literature that enforcing a male model on women prisoners is inappropriate and political and that the primary concern of women inmates is the welfare of their children. One surprise finding was the effort to restrict male officers' access to their women charges, probably as a result of past experience and recent scandals. The fact that 9 of the 28 respondents said the recent media reports of male officer sexual abuse of inmates was "reflective of reality" is highly significant. Nine of these administrators even agreed that the publicity was probably helpful in the long run. A second surprise to me was the large percentage of respondents who felt women are sentenced to prison today because of increased criminal activity, a statement that contradicts national crime statistics reporting. Further unexpected and significant findings were that almost half of the administrators surveyed felt that restorative justice was a trend for the future and that the majority believed greater funding would be provided for substance abuse counseling. These may portend positive developments. For a recent interview with a progressive prison warden from the state of Iowa, see Box 4.1.

BOX 4.1

Interview with Diann Wilder-Tomlinson, Former Warden of Iowa Correctional Institution for Women

How did you get into this field?

I started with my law degree from the University of Iowa. I then returned to Marshall County where I was from and started a private practice. In 1986 I ran for county attorney and won. I served two terms as the Marshall County Attorney. After losing the third election, I then applied for a position as administrative law judge at Anamosa State Penitentiary. This is how I got into corrections initially. I have been in corrections now for just under 14 years. I held positions as assistant director of policy and legal as well as director of the Civil Rights Commission. After those positions I became the warden of the Iowa Correctional Institution for Women [ICIW] at Mitchellville, Iowa. I was there for 10 years. Just recently I moved into the position of deputy director of the Western Region.

Do you feel that you are respected by others being in this position of authority?

I feel that I am respected in my position. I believe that I had to work harder because I am a woman and because I am African

(continued)

American, but I am very goal oriented and driven and see it as a challenge. When there are barriers, I do not give up. I believe any woman or minority who has a good education and is motivated can do anything that she wants to do.

What kind of mental health and substance abuse problems do the offenders have?

There are probably around 65% to 70% of women who are on psychotropic medications. Many of the women have the issues of past trauma, substance abuse, and mental health needs. They all tend to be interrelated and are a cycle that goes hand and hand.

About how many of the offenders have addiction problems?

About 90%.

Is alcohol or drugs the main problem? Which types of drugs are the most prominent?

Drugs would be the greatest problem, then the alcohol. Methamphetamines are the most prominent then alcohol, marijuana, and cocaine after that. Alcohol/drug problem is the most common top need of ICIW inmates [data as of February 2008], with 59.2% of women at that facility with this need.

About 90% of Iowa prison inmates have a past or current problem with alcohol, drugs, or both. Among female inmates with current or past drug problems, meth was the most common drug abused (52.4%) followed by marijuana (40.9%) and cocaine/crack (35.7%). This analysis is based on 2005 data from the LSI-R [Level of Service Inventory—Revised assessment].

What is the racial breakdown?

ICIW has 20.9% African American; 0.7% Asian; 2.3% Native American; 2.7% Latina/Hispanic; and 73.3% White.

Can you estimate how many inmates have a history of abuse?

Most of the inmates have some form of abuse when they come into prison. There is not an exact statistic on this. The difference with men and women and abuse is that for most men, when they come of age, the abuse stops, whereas with women, the abuse can and does continue. It is vital for these issues to be addressed if there is a change that can be made with these women.

How many women (percentage) do you feel are prepared for parole or complete freedom?

All by the time of release are ready, but they will still face major issues on transitioning back into the community. The majority of the offenders at ICIW are nonviolent. The rate of incarceration of female offenders is twice the rate of male offenders. However, at the same time female offenders tend to work their way into prison after being given multiple chances in the community.

What changes in the system would you recommend that would improve life for the women?

I would have to say gender-responsive programming for both male and female offenders. There is not a one-size-fits-all program for men and women. Reentry programs are also very important. Having more vocational programs in the prison is very important. Currently in Mitchellville there are a few vocational programs, such as Prison Industries, which teach sewing, imaging, assembling furniture, cubicle panels, bottling chemicals, as well as making garbage bags. They also work with Habitat for Humanity. Continuing to add to these programs and teaching more vocational skills so that the women can get out and work a job that would allow for self-sufficiency is very important so that they do not return to the criminal justice system. It is

(continued)

also important to educate employers in the community so that these women are given an opportunity to use the skills that they have learned.

Is there anything else that you would like people to know about the prison system?

That the prison system is nothing like what you see in movies or on TV or read about. They tend to depict the worst and sensationalize. Our staff are humane and want the best for the offenders and want to help them change and succeed and not return to prison.

Source: Interview of Diann Wilder-Tomlinson, currently deputy director of the Western region for the Iowa Department of Corrections. Interview conducted on April 18, 2009, by Mona Krugger, MSW, for this book. Printed by permission of Diann Wilder-Tomlinson and Mona Krugger.

SOCIAL WORLD OF THE WOMEN'S PRISON

Knowledge of the social psychology of the prison captive female environment is crucial for those who work there. The goings-on behind the walls of the female prison—the deep bonds, the love-hate relationships, the sexual intrigues—say more about the inmates as women than about their legal/correctional status. To view masculinity and femininity in pure form, in fact, one can study life in prisons—men surrounded by men and women with women and then compare and contrast the social worlds that have evolved. Compared to male inmates, who may even use the prison experience as an image enhancer and who, in prison, inhabit a macho world where the strong survive and the weak are victims, the concerns of female offenders tend to be centered more on their children, their relationships, and their economic well-being.

Women in prison try to maintain ties with family members on the outside as much as possible. Within prison walls, they often reconstruct family relationships through membership in a sort of pretend family. There is nothing pretend, however, about the emotional feelings that are evoked in such relationships. As Owen (1998) suggests, the emotional intensity characterized by female prison friendships, the willingness to take new and young inmates under their wing, and to pretty well take snitching for granted are totally unlike anything seen in men's prisons, where violence is always just beneath the surface. Men's prisons are characterized by gang loyalty, often along racial lines, allegiance to an inmate code, a clearly defined leadership and dominance structure, and regular instances of homosexual rape.

Prison Families

In my sociological study of the women's prison at Wetumpka, Alabama, a study conducted through freely intermingling with the inmate population (see van Wormer, 1979), I experienced family interaction at close range. In my unpublished journal, I described the network and at times chaos involved in prison kinship ties:

> Whereas Giallombardo (1966) discovered a network of meaningfully related family ties, it was my finding that the Alabama family structure was somewhat weak. Some claimed mothers who did not accept them as daughters and vice versa. There were very few fathers to solidify the family unit; husband figures came and went constantly. The butch types were young and seemingly more interested in "playing the field" than in fathering a family. One case was the exception, however. The couple formally "married" and later adopted a child-like retarded girl as their daughter. The "child" was affectionate but rebellious and always getting into trouble. Most family relationships were actually of the mother-daughter variety. Mothers alternatively were seen hugging and scolding their errant offspring. One woman had chosen for her child a hopeless drug addict, a person who had to be constantly stopped from swallowing any product in sight. The one called "Mamma," on the surface, got little in return.

A correlation between extreme isolation away from society in single-sex environments, a tradition of familialism or strong extended family ties, and the development of prison family forms is evident. As we learn from Bonnie Foreshaw (2003) in her personal narrative from Wally Lamb's inmate writing circle:

> When I arrived in Niantic back in 1986, confused and scared, I was cradled in the arms of the elders who comforted me and helped me survive. Today I serve as a mentor and substitute mom to other frightened women, and as "Grandma" to several youthful offenders, those tough, scared babies whose innocence I can see beneath their masks of defiance. (p. 208)

As long as women are shut away from the world outside and from the close caring (and scolding) relationships to which they are accustomed, the argument can be made that the old, familiar pattern will be perpetuated, only with a different cast. In my research on intimacy in Alabama, I learned first-hand that the functions of the prison families are many: They

- Offer mutual support and protection in a strange and often bewildering environment
- Serve to provide a mutual aid network in an atmosphere of deprivation
- Are sometimes encouraged by female staff and administration for their social control aspect—keeping family members out of trouble
- Above all, create situations for fun, gift sharing, and inevitably, laughter.

Thirty years after I conducted my research, and knowing how much the lives of these women must have changed due to overcrowding at the prison and new laws that had been passed, I wrote to the new warden of Julia Tutwiler Prison informing him of my earlier study and asking for his description of recent events. His reply was enlightening:

We have not used the word "matron" in years. Our officers are called Correctional Officers; we have male and female officers. Yes, women still form families and we still have an "old folks" dorm, we call it the A & I Dorm (aged and infirmed). We still have the same building, however, we do have a new sewing factory and kitchen/dining hall. No, we don't have any criminally insane people running around scaring people. We do have a Mental Health Dormitory. Our count averages about 715 daily.

We have Substance Abuse Programs, programs for abused females, we have AA/NA. We have a Trade School, we have parenting programs and we have a program for the inmates whose children can't come to visit on a regular basis. (Steve Dees, private correspondence, 1998, p. 1)

Since this letter was written, lawsuits against Julia Tutwiler have been filed on the basis of the risk of serious harm caused by the overcrowded and under-staffed open dorms (Human Rights Watch, 2003). According to Human Rights Watch, "the unsafe conditions are so severe and widespread today that they are essentially a time bomb ready to explode facility-wide" (p. 139). More recently, the prison population has ballooned to over 1,000 inmates who endure, in summer, the stifling heat of central Alabama. This fact and the quality of healthcare were found by a U.S. District Court judge to border on the criminally negligent (Elsner, 2006). Cases of guard-inmate sexual abuse were pending.

Prison Sexuality

Estimates of how many women in prison are homosexually involved vary so much that about all that can be said is we do not know. A small minority of inmates are extremely masculine in their behavior; they are prison "turn-outs," women who assumed macho roles whether because of the instant popularity they acquired by being a "he" in the all-female environment or for reasons of material gain. Generally speaking, femmes, who tend to be White and to greatly outnumber the masculine inmates, or butches, often get into fights due to jealousy. Most inmates who are not involved in this volatile situation are highly critical of it.

In her review of scholarly literature on women's prisons, Severance (2004) found that most researchers estimated sexual involvement of inmates with other inmates to be about 1 in 3. In her personal interviews with 40 incarcerated women in Ohio, Severance learned that of those inmates who were sexually engaged, some saw their involvements as limited to prison whereas others planned to continue a lesbian life on the outside. Women who have been beaten by men and/or abandoned by them often do not wish to return to relationships with men (Belknap, 2007; Talvi, 2007). The love that develops between women in prison is often a highly positive development; many women come to see themselves as far more lovable than they ever realized they were.

Among the reasons that inmate interviewees gave to Severance for their prison sexual involvement were a past of abusive relationships with men, loneliness, curiosity, and sexual deprivation. Hensley, Tewksbury, and Koscheski (2002), in their survey of 245 inmates in a southern correctional facility, found that almost half of the women acknowledged engagement in homosexual activities, including kissing and oral sex. White women were less sexually active than were women of other racial and ethnic groups.

Among women forced to live with each other in close and intimate quarters, emotional closeness can be expressed through simultaneous touching and hugging with prison family members without taking on sexual connotations. Significantly, the family ties are made publicly known, presumably so others do not get the wrong idea. If members of the same sex hold hands or caress each other, rumors fly; self-doubts rage. But redefine those acts in terms of mother-daughter, sister-sister, brother-brother exchange, and all is well. In female same-sex institutions, in short, where sexual tensions often get played out as homophobia, a clarification of one's relationship in terms of sisterly and motherly love (and conflict) can serve to legitimize the bonding between unrelated women.

How about inmate-to-inmate sexual coercion among women? Hensley, Castle, and Tewksbury (2003) explored that issue via questionnaires completed by 245 inmates in a southern correctional facility. Over 4% of the 245 inmates reported that they had been sexually coerced by other female inmates, and 2% admitted they had sexually coerced another inmate. The incidents included genital touching or attempts at sexual contact. Although African Americans were more heavily represented as perpetrators than as victims, Whites were sometimes perpetrators as well. Interestingly, for some, perceived change in sexual orientation occurred. Over half of the victims and perpetrators stated that they had identified as heterosexual prior to incarceration. However, the sample size of perpetrators was extremely small—only 5 inmates out of the 245 who filled out questionnaires—so further research is needed on this subject.

The horror that is known as homosexual rape, but which perhaps should be called same-sex heterosexual rape, is absent from the female prison scene except in Grade B movies. Conversely, to be a young man, especially a young White man, in prison is to be exposed to sexual threats, taunting, and assault in an all-male society in which predators subdue their prey. In men's prisons, male rape serves a variety of purposes unrelated to sex, such as domination and control (Rasche, 2003). The horror of homosexual rape is conveyed in an article by Pagnozzi (1999), which described the gang rape of a White middle-class adolescent who spent a night in a Cleveland holding pen because his parents wanted to teach him a lesson. In jail, he found himself at the bottom end of the pecking order where inmates who do not participate in rape likely will be targeted themselves. The article continues:

> He [the inmate] is learning brutality. "He's practicing intimidation and aggression he may act out on women when he gets out," says Dr. Terry Kupers, an expert witness in jail cases and author of the book "Prison Madness."
>
> Men who rape men are mostly heterosexual inside and outside of prison. "If you're the top, you're not gay because the man you're having sex with is a woman in your symbolic world," he explains. Sex with a woman when he gets released? It's just business as usual.
>
> "They're not realizing they are very abusive to women, because in prison what they are doing would have been considered soft," Kupers says. (p. A3)

This disturbing article ends with a description of the violent date rape by an ex-inmate of a woman who had no idea that her date had just been released from prison and that he had learned to associate sex with violence in prison. His words to the victim (as cleaned up for the newspaper report) are haunting: "I have respect for you so I'm going to [have sex with] you vaginally."

Although I am presenting this story to show that the social world male prisoners inhabits is far different from the social realm of female prisoners and that to build women's prisons according to the male model is a travesty, this horror story also points out that violence begets violence. When society brutalizes its citizens, innocent people will pay.

INMATE MOTHERS AND THEIR CHILDREN

Because U.S. society is individualist rather than family based, there has been a serious neglect throughout the system of the consequences when mothers in trouble with the law are ripped away from their children and other relatives by the state. "A woman's first concern is always for the welfare of her children." This comment was made by Sister Marion Defeis (1996, p. 6), New York City jail chaplain and inmate advocate. She was appalled at the grave injustice against women, some of whom have been arrested at Kennedy Airport for transporting drugs. The majority of women are mothers. Whereas the men with whom the chaplain has worked are concerned primarily about their legal cases, Defeis tells us, women's concern is their children. My women's prison survey, similarly, indicated that mothers serving time are concerned primarily about the children they left behind.

When a woman is arrested, her children are sent to relatives or to overburdened foster care system. Consumed by anger and rage, these children are clear candidates for developing emotional and legal problems down the road. Sister Marion realizes that the only way to fight for the mothers and children is to fight against the national drug policy, to fight for treatment rather than for punishment of drug addiction. Her fight has been joined by Catholic chaplains throughout the United States.

Only a minority of the children of women sent to prison remain with their fathers. Grandparents, particularly grandmothers, are the most common caregivers for children during a mother's incarceration (Belknap, 2007). Mothers' feelings of anxiety are sometimes exacerbated when women inmates are forced to place their children in the care of relatives they know are living in dire poverty or who have been abusive in the past. They know also that upon their release, they will have difficulty finding a job due to their felony record. In addition, there increasingly are state and federal restrictions on persons convicted of felony drug charges from receiving various forms of financial aid.

Advocacy to change national drug policy, working at the macro level, is one form of advocacy, the form geared toward stopping the problem at its source. If you keep drug-abusing mothers in the community and monitor their lives, parenting, and substance abuse treatment, a whole generation might be spared from following in their mothers' footsteps into crime. These alternatives are far less expensive to society in both the short and long run than locking up mothers.

Advocacy at the micro level is important as well to help prison inmates preserve family ties as much as possible. For example, in Waterloo, Iowa, a unique youth offenders program is run by a former police officer to break the generational cycle of crime. Family counseling is provided to help the children and spouses of prisoners handle their emotions and resolve practical problems in having a family member in jail (Behnke, 1999). Gender-specific prison programming, such as Canada's relocation of female federal prisoners into regional centers nearer their homes, is the place to start (Canadian Association of Elizabeth Fry Societies, 2007). Beyond that, advocacy is needed for pregnant inmates to receive proper medical care to ensure their health and the health of the baby, including the right to an abortion if desired. Kentucky law forbids using public funds for abortions; in one case an inmate begging for an abortion was forced to carry the baby to term because of this law ("State Won't Pay for Prisoner to Have Abortion," 1999).

The Bedford Hills Correctional Facility in New York State helps inmates maintain family ties by encouraging overnight family visits. Families stay with their inmates for 48-hour intervals in trailers on prison grounds. In the summer, the facility even runs weeklong programs for inmates' children, who are housed with local families. At other times children are bused in together; transportation is provided for them to visit their mothers (van Wormer & Bartollas, 2010). The Nebraska prison nursery program began in 1994 and has been pronounced a qualified success in that the presence of the infants has not been disturbing to other inmates, and the advantages for the mothers who bond with the child and learn parenting skills are many.

Other states with prison nursery programs are Ohio, California, and Washington with West Virginia pending ("State Considering Prison Nurseries," 2007). The recidivism rate of mothers who are afforded this privilege is far less than that among the general prison population. Feedback from prison officials indicates that caring for a baby is a civilizing experience and breaks down norms of criminality; the mother and child receive medical and nutritional care superior to what they would get outside; and the mothers better themselves by preparing for careers and taking courses on child care and development.

Pro-prisoner activism and advocacy in Canada are very strong, thanks to more humane policies, a lower crime rate, and well-funded, well-staffed, and highly respected prison reform groups, such as the Elizabeth Fry and John Howard societies. Unfortunately, as the official papers of the Canadian Association of the Elizabeth Fry Societies (2007) make clear, the vision of housing women in conflict with the law in halfway houses and minimum security regional facilities has not become a reality. Canadian female inmates are still all too often confined in isolation from the community; women with mental health problems are the most likely to be perceived as dangerous and classified as high risk. The Elizabeth Fry Society continues to advocate for an end to the gender-neutral assessment risk based on women's offenses because it does not capture the situational circumstances of women's violence. Minnesota's Shakopee facility and Australia's Emu Plains Institution, unfenced prisons that provide meaningful employment and educational opportunities, are seen as models. Instead of focusing on bringing women's children with them behind prison walls, the prison reform movement in Canada focuses on keeping the women in conflict with the law out of prison altogether so they do not relinquish their family roles. Nevertheless, several Canadian provinces provide the opportunity for mothers of children up to age 4 to have their children in full-time residence and up to age 12 in part-time residence (Alejos, 2005).

In many countries, it is taken for granted that young children stay with their mothers, even when the women are imprisoned. The Swedish arrangement is to house women in sections of men's prisons near their homes. There, mothers with babies can keep them up to the age of 2. In Singapore, inmate mothers keep them up to age 3 in the same room with them, and in Spain and Pakistan, up to age 6 (Joo Lin, 2008). Babies in prison are often kept in special nurseries cared for by professional child care workers. In Australia, however, unlike England and most countries, mothers might share a room with their child, although this varies by state (Farrell, 1998). Farrell makes a strong argument for policies that are more family-friendly and support the inmate as mother. French mothers in prison can keep their babies up to 18 months of age (Alejos, 2005).

LIFE AFTER PRISON

Returning to the community can be a dream come true for many inmates and especially for mothers of young children, but many problems arise for which the women are unprepared. The men in their lives have often bonded with other women, and children have grown and changed in their mothers' absence. Parents of teenagers typically will find their children have little respect for the authority of elders who have engaged in heavy drug use or other illegal activities. Others who have lost custody of their children have to deal with feelings of grief and loss. Compared to male ex-convicts, women have three strikes against them: the lack of a partner or spouse who has dutifully waited for their return, immediate child care responsibilities, and the need to overcome the stigma that faces a woman and especially a mother who has broken the law.

Because a key determinant of a child's adjustment to an incarcerated parent is regular contact, prison visits should be encouraged as much as possible. Children who visit their parents often and who visit under homelike visiting conditions (such as in the private trailers available at Bedford Hills Correctional Facility) exhibit fewer adjustment problems than children who are shielded from prison visits altogether (Petersilia, 2003). Maintaining ties through telephone conversations is important as well. Unfortunately, as Petersilia indicates, inmates often are allowed only to make collect calls home or to make calls at highly inflated prices. Some prisons earn millions of dollars on phone call kickbacks. Were these practices ended and telephone contacts encouraged, family communication would be enhanced for the good of the inmate and the family.

Keep in mind the fact that in addition to these obstacles, many released women have major health problems and backgrounds of addiction. Referral to treatment services on the outside, such as health clinics and self-help groups, for ongoing problems is therefore vital.

Economically, the road to stability and self-sufficiency can be bumpy. Since women's work records were inclined to have been poor before imprisonment, their prospects for rewarding work are apt to be dim following incarceration (Brooker, 2007; Talvi, 2007). Restrictions on receiving welfare benefits and student aid on individuals who have been convicted drug users close off resources that might be badly needed as bridges to independence.

Psychologically, reentry to society brings many challenges. First of all, it entails a major transition in behavior from that of inmate, in which every aspect of life is taken care of and any signs of independence or organizing are punished, to displaying the expected qualities of a fully independent and responsible adult. In resuming life in "the free world," the very type of initiative that has been suppressed for years is now essential to find suitable employment, stay clean and sober, and resume caretaking responsibilities. Depending on the number of years of confinement and degree of institutionalization, this transition from passive prisoner in captivity to active and mature member of society can carry a high risk of failure.

Moreover, there are social barriers to consider, such as the scarcity of living-wage jobs and affordable housing and society's prejudice against ex-convicts. Research shows that ex-convicts with the fewest problems are those who had once earned their living from legal sources and who, accordingly, have marketable skills and stronger support systems to which to return (Brooker, 2007). Poor, unskilled, and uneducated women have fewer resources on which to draw. But for all women who have been incarcerated, the journey to productive citizenship is fraught with challenges related to their personal histories of trauma, emotional problems, and addictive tendencies. Many of the women have been retraumatized within prison walls. In the absence of much-needed reentry services and economic help, it is no wonder that the majority of women eventually are reincarcerated—sometimes just a few weeks after their release.

A GLOBAL PERSPECTIVE

Viewed internationally, the United States can be considered a generally punitive nation, one that does not treat men or women who have broken the law with compassion. To discover other approaches to women convicted of serious crime, journalist Silva Talvi (2007) visited prisons in Canada, Finland, and the United Kingdom. One theme that emerged from her visits was that everywhere she traveled, she found a disproportionately high rate of incarceration among minorities. In Canada, it was Aboriginal women; in Finland, Roma women; and in the United Kingdom, people of color including non-criminal immigrants. Another observation was that, in contrast to the U.S. situation, smoking was omnipresent at institutions in all three countries.

In terms of actual living conditions, Talvi found that those in other countries were far superior to those in the United States; the grounds were more accessible and comfortable, and the atmosphere was more compassionate. In the United Kingdom, for example, there was no such thing as a life sentence without parole. The historic Holloway prison is located on a busy city street, is not surrounded by barbed wire, and has a predominantly female staff. Talvi appreciated the fact that inmates could wear their own clothes and can use makeup and jewelry. She also was favorably impressed with standards at the medically supervised detoxification unit and with the cheerful atmosphere in the mother and baby unit.

A report by Baroness Jean Corston of the British Home Office (2007) presents a less optimistic view of the treatment of women in British prisons. According to the Corston Report, women in prison live in crowded cells, with unhygienic sharing of facilities. Access to bathing facilities was restrictive; showers were often dirty. Corston was dismayed to find toilets without lids, sometimes not screened at all. The report's recommendation was to reduce strip-searching to the absolute minimum, to use scan machines for drug searches. There needs to be, according to the report, "a radical new approach, treating women both holistically and individually—a woman-centered approach" (p. 2). Women offenders should be referred to secure units in the community. The government has not fully endorsed the report's recommendations; doing so would amount to a revolution in how female offenders are treated (Morris, 2007). In the meantime, the evidence suggests that women in trouble with the criminal justice system are harshly treated by a system designed for men. Women are inflicting harm and killing themselves in prison as a result. Corston (2007) eloquently expressed her understanding of the need for gender-sensitive treatment of women in these terms: "The new gender equality duty means that men and women should be treated with equivalent respect according to need" (p. 3).

Canadian prisons, similarly, mainly employ female officers who, according to Talvi (2007), chat amiably with inmates. She had criticisms, however. The mother-baby unit at Alouette Correctional Centre in British Columbia, for example, was rather drab. Little treatment was provided to women with hepatitis C and a shortage of medical and mental health counseling staff was a concern. On the positive side, First Nation peoples had their own sweat lodge, a place that was never subject to inspection.

Talvi's description of Finland's only enclosed women's prison provides a glimpse of Scandinavian progressivism. Inmates enjoy highly nutritious meals. Men are never allowed within the housing units. Women and men take educational classes together. There is one intensive drug rehabilitation unit that is self-contained. As at Holloway, no prisoner is addressed by number or last name. Women are allowed to stay in solitary cells for a maximum of 5 days; mentally ill inmates are sent to a mental hospital. Finally, as in the rest of Scandinavia, inmates are sent home on vacations periodically to rest up from the prison experience and to reconnect with the community.

There are, of course, parts of the world where women sentenced to prison receive far worse treatment than in the United States. Such cases rarely reach the international news. A recent report from *The New York Times* (Barrionuevo, 2007), however, documents cases of torture of girls and women in the Brazil prison system. At Abaetuba, a 15-year-old girl arrested for petty theft was placed in a cell with 34 male inmates. She was repeatedly raped and tortured by the men while the police turned their backs. According to the report, female prisoners were being illegally placed with men across the country.

The European Network for Children of Imprisoned Parents (Eurochips) advocates that attention be paid to the needs of children in maintaining ties with their incarcerated parents. The Swedish Prison and Probation Service ordered for all prisons in Sweden:

- Special leave will be granted for important events concerning children.
- Children should be allowed to telephone and speak directly to the parent. (In the past, children could only leave a message and ask the parent to call back, which frequently occurred several hours later.)
- Each new prisoner should be asked about his or her children.
- Flexible visiting hours for children need to be provided (Eurochips, 2008, p. 22).

In western Europe, except for Norway (a country that makes extensive use of long-term foster care), children are kept at the prison for up to several years. Germany has, perhaps, the most outstanding prison nursery system. In this program, teachers and social workers help mothers learn how to be good parents. According to a BBC broadcast (2001), mothers of small children who have been sentenced to prison can keep their children until the children are six years old. The facility at Frondenberg in northwest Germany has no bars in the windows; the mothers can go outside and play with the children and can visit the town. The mothers go to work after the child is two years old, and they can go on leave from the grounds for 21 days of vacation per year. The children attend a regular nursery school and kindergarten. It has been found that mothers in this program have a much lower reoffending rate than a comparable group of mothers who do not have their children with them. A California state program allows female prisoners with small children a chance to move to one of seven homes in the state where they can live with their children and take parenting classes. Several hundred women, only a fraction of the mothers in California's prison system, have graduated from this program.

In Spain, in reaction to the old, brutal system during the Franco dictatorship, since 1979, extremely progressive penitentiary policies have been in force. A luxurious prison opened its gates near Madrid in 1998. It includes swimming pools, squash courts, paid work, and liberal, mixed-sex regimes that allow prisoners to spend all day outside their cells. The majority of female applicants to this new prison are members of the Roma (Gypsy) minority group serving time for drug trafficking, the men for theft (Fraerman, 2007). Inmate parents may leave their children at the prison nursery—complete with its own swimming pool—during the day while they work or study (Webster, 1998).

Other family programs involve conjugal rights for prisoners and their spouses. Russian women are entitled to a couple of three-day visits a year with their husbands. In the United States, apart from New York State and California, few states allow conjugal visits. California allows conjugal visits for lesbians as long as both partners are not prisoners and partnerships existed before the woman was imprisoned.

Many of the issues dealt with in this discussion of prison conditions are the same internationally. Idealistic goals are expressed but not achieved in practice. For example, the Canadian Task Force on Federally Sentenced Women produced a set of guidelines for gender-based correctional programming that still stands as one of the best templates of feminist correctional philosophy in existence. According to the report, *Creating Choices* (Correctional Service of Canada, 1990/2007), all aspects of the correctional system, from architecture to staff recruitment and training, were to reflect women's special needs (Hannah-Moffat & Shaw, 2003). That these idealistic plans were not implemented, however, was revealed, shockingly, in a televised exposé in 1994 of violent strip searches of emotionally distraught female prisoners in Canada. Spurred by the public outcry that ensued at the SWAT team–like attack on the screaming women, the government commissioned a special inquiry with recommendations for change (Faith, 2004). Again, the impetus for reform was short-lived. One innovative development, however, was the opening of a Healing Lodge for 30 First Nation women. In the end, however, the Correctional Service of Canada showed itself reluctant to relinquish the vestiges of older models that were designed to deal with hardened male offenders. So instead of the woman-centered focus that was promised, security concerns took over. Today, there is a strong reliance on surveillance technologies and the construction of double chain-linked fences topped with razor wire. Paralleling these developments, in the treatment area, a paradigm shift has occurred away from a feminist orientation toward principles that were developed for the control of antisocial male inmates. This approach, similar to that which predominates south of the border, is built on a patriarchal ideology and the premise that a general criminal personality characterizes all offenders (Dell, Fillmore, & Kilty, 2009; Kendall & Pollack, 2003).

As in the United States, Canada is sending persons with serious mental disorders into the prison system. In her comparison of U.S. and Canadian correctional systems, Talvi (2007) acknowledged that, on the surface, they are the same and that minorities (First Nations People) are disproportionately incarcerated, yet in her visit to one prison in British Columbia, she found the atmosphere very different: No one was held in solitary confinement, encouragement of inmate business enterprises, and an easy relationship between inmates and the staff. (Canadian researchers Dell et al., however, do note instances of use of segregation of self-harming prisoners.) Unfortunately, political pressures are mounting in Canada to build new, bigger prisons and to raise the standards for parole (Harper Index, 2007). What remains to be seen is whether Canada, in keeping with *Creating Choices,* can reclaim and redefine the assessment of women offenders as women first and whether women's corrections can develop a truly woman-centered alternative (Hannah-Moffat & Shaw, 2003).

SUMMARY

In this chapter, we have seen the circumstances for women in prison come full circle—from confinement in overcrowded, male-run prisons, to removal into maternal reformatories focusing on inmates' moral development, to confinement once again in overcrowded, punitive prisons run by a predominantly male staff. We have turned our attention to two developments in the administration of women's institutions since the 1970s: the rise of prisoners' litigation and the replacement of matrons with male officers. The scandals of today that center around sexual abuse and the exploitation of female inmates echo the scandals of days gone by when females were originally placed under male authority.

The challenge to social workers, counselors, and other noncustodial workers is to work at the policy level of alternatives to prison for nondangerous offenders and for affordable and accessible substance abuse treatment as an important measure that would prevent a large proportion of crimes in the first place. For workers within the system, knowledge of the psychological dynamics of victimization from early childhood and of the political and social context within which crime occurs is crucial. As advocates, we need to promote funding for a return of mental health facilities to take care of the nation's people who cannot function in society.

Psychiatric breakdowns are not a justification for imprisonment, for being locked up in solitary confinement, and, when the inmates crack, for overwhelming show of force and use of painful restraints.

How to promote strengths in women locked in a setting the very structure of which is designed to intimidate and control: this is one of the imponderables of the counseling professions. The surprising fact is that despite the hindrances, so much innovative and gender-sensitive programming does take place. The ultimate strengths approach, clearly, would be to close the prisons down.

Chapter 5

GENDER-SENSITIVE PROGRAMMING WITHIN INSTITUTIONAL SETTINGS

No hay mal que por bien no venga.
(There is nothing so bad that good cannot come of it.)
                                        —**Popular Mexican Saying**

As suggested in previous chapters in this book, the three strongest arguments for gender-specific programming are women's unique biology, cultural role expectations and vulnerabilities, and gendered pathways into crime. A recognition of the close connection between an individual's marginalized status (on the basis of poverty, abuse, sex, and sometimes race or ethnicity) and her criminal activity is integral to gender-sensitive treatment. Recall from Chapters 2 and 3 the common pattern by which girls and women get into trouble with the law: the path that extends from early and long-term childhood victimization to use of drugs for self-medication, to falling into bad company, and involvement in abusive relationships and crime. To break this pattern and undo this damage, these unique life experiences must be addressed. This is what gender-specific programming in women's institutions is all about.

139

CHALLENGES OF PROGRESSIVE
WORK IN A TOTAL INSTITUTION

The helping professions share a commitment to identify the best, empirically based practices at the micro and macro levels and to advocate for these as opposed to traditional, punitive approaches that have been shown to be ineffective or downright harmful (Miller & Carroll, 2006). In correctional as well as substance abuse treatment, the need, as expressed by Ann Abbott (2003), is for a multifaceted approach that encompasses primary prevention and intervention and a coupling of research and practice.

A Rift in the Correctional Treatment Field

For girls and women in the criminal justice system, gender-responsive policy provides effective interventions that address intersecting issues of substance use, trauma, mental health, and economic oppression (Bloom, Owen, & Covington, 2003). This fact is not always acknowledged, however. The what-works crime and delinquency prevention literature asserts that the core principles of treatment effectiveness apply to males and females alike and that such principles are research based (Hubbard & Matthews, 2008). The cognitive-behavioral approach designed to target errors in thinking is the favored model of the what-works researchers.

The result of the flawed emphasis on identical programming for males and females in conjunction with a punitive ethos has resulted in an across the board use of what I will call a criminal thinking model. The focus of this approach is on the putative criminal belief systems of the client that need to be corrected by attacking these dishonest and uncaring values. Euphemistically called a cognitive-behavioral approach, this model was adopted from work with antisocial men and is the dominant treatment framework used with correctional populations. This approach is widely used in both the substance abuse treatment field and throughout the correctional systems in the United States and Canada. Note that it is not the cognitive model I am challenging here, geared toward instances of irrational thinking and the thinking-feeling nexus. What I am challenging is the decidedly negative form that this model has assumed in working with mandated clients in the criminal justice system. Instilling hope is a fundamental principle of effective counseling; a positive approach that builds on client strengths rather than their deficiencies is essential to this goal. Strengths-based approaches are designed for work with clients of both genders but have a special resonance for work with girls and women.

Empirical support for the gender-specific female-oriented approach is in its infancy but is forthcoming. The Ohio Department of Rehabilitation and Correction has singled out several programs of proven effectiveness in reducing recidivism in female offenders. (See the description of the Forever Free program in the section titled "Programming for Reentry into the Society.") A comprehensive gender-specific case management model utilizes a best practices treatment design that is yet to be evaluated (Pettway, 2006).

Treatment versus Control Issues

Not only are there philosophical differences among treatment staff members; between treatment and custodial staff, the rift is even more pronounced. Prisons are carefully controlled environments where security issues take precedence over everything else. Custodial staff often resent correctional counselors whom they rightly see as more interested in their clients' welfare than in being firm but fair to all inmates and in the smooth running of the institution. As far as advocacy is concerned, the correctional staff, subject to almost constant manipulation by a hostile and resentful criminal element, develop a code of loyalty for their own protection. If counseling staff, therefore, speak out publicly or advocate for their clients without taking into account institutional concerns, they often find themselves in trouble with authorities.

The empirically validated strategies that are used for the control of juvenile delinquents, according to Hubbard and Matthews (2007), were developed on White male samples, and they place the sole responsibility for the criminal activity on the individual by ignoring macro-level factors such as poverty, sexism, and racism, not to mention mental health issues. For working with girls, gender-responsive theorists support therapeutic approaches that are based on a relational model and provide treatment for past victimization. Hubbard and Matthews call for an integrated approach that is research based and directs cognitive strategies toward girls' "self-debasing distortions" (p. 249) and internalized victimization. To meet delinquent girls' special needs, Hubbard and Matthews recommend a focus on career development, vocational training, women's issues, life skills, assertiveness, and empowering activities.

Prisons are places designed to confine and control and generally are not conducive to therapeutic programming (Kubiac & Rose, 2007). The prison environment, in short, is not the natural domain of mental health professionals or religious counselors. All higher-level positions, in fact, are apt to be filled by mainstream correctional staff, often with military backgrounds and conservative political affiliations. Ethical issues arise when inmates disclose information about abusive situations within the institution. This might put the counselor in a dilemma about whether to report this behavior by correctional personnel and to whom to report it (Kubiak & Rose, 2007).

Unlike involuntary clients on the outside, often resentful of having to travel to appointments at inconvenient times, prison inmates are inclined to be grateful for the help they receive. The problem here arises when expectations are too high to be realistic, when an inmate expects the counselor, for example, to be able to pull strings with the authorities for the client's benefit. Another problem occurs when clients really open up and share personal aspects of their lives, then later become paranoid about the secrets shared. The more punitive the institution, the less trusting the inmate will be.

In progressive institutions where correctional officers and inmates have more chance of developing close bonds, mental health workers will experience little conflict as open, friendly relationships develop across professional lines. In situations of hostility and racism, however, when inmates observe camaraderie between officer and therapist, a kind of paranoia can set in; the fear is that secrets are being shared.

Many prisons and jails today, as a cost-saving measure, subcontract with substance abuse treatment centers and mental health professionals for the provision of counseling services. From the perspective of substance abuse counselors, this approach provides greater freedom to speak one's mind about programming and psychologically harmful institutional practices than would be the case if these professionals were employed directly by the correctional authorities. Moreover, workers from outside agencies may build alliances with offenders more readily than staff members who answer to the prison establishment. Whatever the administrative arrangements, treatment providers are badly needed for women who, if they needed help before they got in trouble with the law, need help even more now.

Kubiak (2009) studied what she calls hybrid models of substance abuse treatment within male and female correctional settings. These hybrid models are staffed by both criminal justice and treatment professionals in a joint program. Kubiak's research goal was to assess whether the dissonance created by merging two divergent staff groups within a prison setting would be detrimental to the formation of a therapeutic environment. Perceptions of male and female inmates were examined in over 700 therapeutic units and over 300 nontherapeutic units. She found that the hybrid programming functioned well, did not detract from corrections staff authority with inmates, and, overall, staff in the treatment programs were rated more positively on personality items than were staff in the nontreatment programs. Female inmates consistently were more positive than were male inmates, a fact that, as Kubiak concludes, may reflect and underscore the relevance of gender-specific treatment for incarcerated women.

Although custodial staff could benefit by utilizing the counseling services of treatment providers who can help subdue volatile situations, clinicians should never underestimate the knowledge or capabilities of the front-line workers. Social workers and counselors must rely on correctional officers for their own personal safety as well as for gaining access to their clients. In many settings, correctional officers have similar educational backgrounds as counseling staff; yet their loyalties and responsibilities are otherwise—to seek out any break in the routine or potential source of trouble. Their training prepares them to distrust first and only let down their guard later, if ever; the counselor's tendency is to do just the opposite, to err on the side of trust until that trust is violated. And yet the mental health practitioner who works within the rigid constructs of the correctional bureaucracy can learn from Sister Helen Prejean (1994), spiritual advisor to death row inmates, the importance of respecting the humanity of all representatives of the system for effective teamwork.

Still, ethical dilemmas sometimes arise. Psychologist Louis Rothenstein, who worked for six years in the women's federal prison in Dublin, California, later commented on the code of silence that within the prison industry shields it from public scrutiny. The fact that guards went into women's cells for sex was ignored. "You would be blackballed if you were thought of as an advocate for the inmates," he explained (cited in Stein, 1996). Prison chaplains, such as one I interviewed for this book, are reluctant to be quoted about prison conditions because of threatened job loss.

Counselors, social workers, psychologists, and of course chaplains all subscribe to codes of ethics that place client needs ahead of their own professional or personal needs (see van Wormer & Bartollas, 2010). Even to be a witness on behalf of a client at a disciplinary hearing or in a lawsuit can make the counselor feel torn between ethics and risking his or her personal career. Sometimes compromise with an oppressive system is no longer possible. We learned of the next example from a former medical assistant who was interviewed anonymously for the California Coalition of Women Prisoners' newsletter (Fadem, 2006):

> B. was employed as a medical assistant by KT Staffing [a company contracted to provide services to the California Dispute Resolution Council (CDRC)]. She was assigned to chart activities every 15 minutes of women being held under a suicide watch at the infirmary. B. immediately experienced hostility from COs [correctional officers]

in the unit.... As well, B. soon saw a disturbing level of cruel and inhumane treatment toward women prisoners by COs. Some COs deliberately provoked women who were ill. B. told about how an older woman who appeared to be suffering from a severe case of dementia—was continually taunted and harassed by staff members who then laughed at the inmate as she became more and more agitated.

B. said, "I found this very degrading and very unnecessary. I was also told by more than one inmate that you could get privileges (such as extra towels) for trading sexual favors." Less than a month later, B. was dismissed from her job. As one CO said to B. in a very threatening and aggressive way, "You have nothing to say to the inmates, do you understand?"

Generally, when the counselor is under the supervision of a substance abuse or mental health treatment center instead of the correctional institution itself, there is more job security when problems with prison authorities or inmates arise. This is because services provided to the jail or prison are external to the jail and prison itself. Besides, the worker often can be transferred elsewhere within the agency. This was not the case for the medical worker just described, however. Still, it is always worth remembering, and as we can learn from the medical assistant's example, between losing your soul and getting fired, getting fired is better. Sometimes compromise is possible between system norms and professional values. We see this regarding classifying and assessing inmates for security priorities and treatment needs.

PUTTING GENDER-BASED PRINCIPLES INTO PRACTICE

Progressive interventions are being designed to reduce recidivism in adult female offenders and to enhance the lives of these women. The most prominent of these is the Women Offender Case Management Model (WOCMM). Developed by the National Institute of Corrections (NIC) (2008), this model is based on the gender-responsive approach of Bloom et al.'s (2003) formulation.

Participating women must be assessed at a high risk and needs level and must have at least 18 months left on supervision. Extensive staff training is provided before the program is implemented. A special gender-responsive assessment helps practitioners with specific case planning needs. Unique to this project, protective factors and strengths are emphasized in addition to risks.

WOCMM (National Institute of Corrections, 2008) builds on five principles of gender-responsive treatment. As described on the Web site (http:// community.nicic.org/blogs/nic/2008_28_5_WOCMM_RFA.pdf), the five core concepts are:

1. Relational: Work with women in a relational way to promote mutual respect and empathy.... WOCMM model promotes the importance of connections throughout the case management process.
2. Strengths-based: Recognize that all women have strengths that can be mobilized. WOCMM is based on the underlying premise that all women entering the criminal justice system have strengths and resources that can be mobilized to address challenges and mediate the impact of risk.
3. Trauma-informed: Recognize that history and context play an important role in how women respond to services. An overwhelming majority of women entering WOCMM have experienced or witnessed sexual, emotional, and physical abuse. Trauma-informed practice is critical to this model because the language and approach we use can either trigger females or help them to feel safe and thus more engaged and motivated in their work with us.
4. Holistic: Provide a comprehensive Case Management Model that addresses the complex and multiple needs of women in conflict with the law.... Therefore, a critical element of the WOCMM model is to ensure that services are designed to help women build personal resources as well social capital. Services may include information, advice, treatment, assessment, brokerage, and referral across an array of need areas including, vocational, family/social, personal, and life needs.
5. Culturally Competent: Women entering WOCMM are from diverse cultural backgrounds. Practitioners must be sensitive to the messages and values that are shaped by culture and which impact on the lives of women (pp. 9–10).

CLASSIFICATION AND ASSESSMENT

Classification

In the context of corrections, *classification* refers to the systematic scoring and assessment of inmates on items related to security, medical treatment, and educational needs. Usually all new inmates are tested for a week or so at a special classification center before being sent to a residential center. Offender classification serves several purposes, ranging from security placement, to treatment planning, release decision making, and supervision requirements (Blanchette & Brown, 2006). Standard classification devices and other instruments that are used to assess for security risk are empirically validated only in research on male offenders and are not apt to be very helpful in predicting women's adjustment to prison. Instruments used fail to take into account the fact that women who have been sentenced to prison have life histories that are unique to their gender; in addition, they often have serious psychological problems that may affect their adjustment to prison. And since within the state systems, a major purpose of classification is to determine which institutional setting is most appropriate (e.g., medium or maximum security), for women in the criminal justice system who have few options, classification is of less significance than it is for men for whom there are many possibilities. Classification can be used, however, to predict postprison outcomes and to determine which if any treatment or educational options would be desirable or relevant.

The developers of the Level of Service Inventory—Revised (LSI-R) argue that this instrument and the theoretical foundation on which it is based are gender neutral. Therefore, the LSI-R is widely used to classify women for programming and/or to predict women's risk of reoffending. In their evaluation of 41 studies on the performance of the LSI-R for samples of men and women, Holtfreter and Cupp (2007) found this instrument to be an effective predictor of behavior for women whose backgrounds and crimes were more like men's but to be invalid for predictions for women whose lives followed gendered pathways to crime. Generally, women in prison are overclassified when tools designed for men are applied to them (Blanchette & Brown, 2006; Van Voorhis, 2005). This is because their crimes occur in a different context from that of male convicts, and they are not the security risk to society that male prisoners are. A significant research finding from a Canadian study is that family contact is a variable that is particularly salient for the prediction of a woman's conduct in the institution and of her risk of reoffending (Blanchette & Brown, 2006). The Federal Bureau of Prisons uses a separate classification scheme for females in the system to reflect the fact of their lower rate of violence and less likelihood of escape compared to male inmates.

Assessment

In contrast to classification, assessment is less focused on risk from the administrative viewpoint than on treatment needs. Assessment typically is performed by mental health professionals who rely on testing based on medical diagnoses of mental and substance disorders. Compared to the initial classification process, assessment is more comprehensive (Springer, McNeece, & Arnold, 2003).

Female-centered assessment is an ongoing, individualized process; the information obtained may relate to the client's attitude, readiness to change, and/or past history of abuse (Wallace, 2005). Treatment goals should be revisited over time as well.

Cowger, Anderson, and Snively (2006) provide us with guidelines for a strengths assessment with special relevance to working with women. To elicit client strengths, the therapist listens to the client's story and draws attention to instances of strengths in the story. Blaming and negative labels are avoided. Together through collaboration, therapist and client reach a mutual agreement on the treatment plan. Asking questions concerning the client's highest level of functioning is one way to help the practitioner discover strengths that he or she can draw on over time.

Correctional counselors are often required to administer standardized assessment instruments and screening devices that are neither strengths based nor gender sensitive. Even so, as Wallace (2005) advises, the counselor can ask about goals at end of screening if not included and should respond positively to begin the process of building a therapeutic alliance.

The WOCMM pilot program taps gender-responsive needs and strengths (National Institute of Corrections, 2008) and is currently being used experimentally across the United States. The Orbis Partners of Canada produced the Women Offender Case Management Model to be used in the United States by the National Institute of Corrections. This holistic assessment addresses issues of special concern to women as women rather than as offenders. Significantly, the term *offender* is not used anywhere in the document; the less judgmental term *woman in conflict with the law* is used instead.

The NIC/University of Cincinnati Women's Risk/Needs Assessment is a complete risk/needs assessment for adult women offenders. The WOCMM (National Institute of Corrections, 2008) assessment is comprehensive. Central to this approach is the discussion of the results with the woman. After reviewing the strengths and challenges, the case manager asks the woman to prioritize issues and set goals to work on. Among the issues are:

- Relationship dysfunction
- Anger/hostility
- History of mental illness
- Symptoms of depression/anxiety
- Symptoms of psychosis
- Parental stress

- History of child abuse and adult victimization
- Self-efficacy
- Substance use
- Family support

More traditional offender risk factors, such as antisocial attitudes, antisocial friends, substance abuse, education, employment, and others, are also assessed. By focusing on motivational factors within the assessment, the case manager can prepare for the future work of debriefing with the woman and engaging her in the case planning process.

The assessment process involves administration of a 40-minute interview (administered by a correctional practitioner), followed by a 35-minute pencil-and-paper survey that is completed by the offender. The NIC Women's Risk/ Needs Assessment is available in separate forms for probationers, parolees, and inmates. Case planning guidelines are available. Among the forms that are used are a checklist of support systems that ask questions such as "Who can you trust?" and an ecomap (a visual representation of one's self in the center surrounded by support systems such as church, school, work, family, etc.). These forms are available to download at the WOCMM Web site at http://nicic.org/Downloads/PDF/Library/021814.pdf.

According to the WOCMM Web site, the team approach to case management is essential to the delivery of this model. Team members consist of the woman and possibly family members, who work in conjunction with available representatives from a variety of disciplines that might include correctional, health professionals, clergy, and other supports. Professionals on the WOCMM teams will be trained to use a gender-responsive approach when interacting with the woman. This means that the delivery of WOCMM is defined by the five core concepts listed earlier, which include: using a relational approach and being strengths based, trauma informed, holistic, and culturally competent.

This women's assessment is in the public domain and may be used free of charge by correctional agencies and researchers, but not for commercial purposes. The assessments hold copyrights through the University of Cincinnati at www.uc.edu/corrections. Users will provide assurances that interviewers are being trained in five areas:

1. Evidence-based practices
2. Gender-responsive principles and practices
3. An overview of the tool
4. Motivational interviewing and skills of good listening
5. Gender-responsive case planning

Assessment for posttraumatic stress disorder (PTSD) is an important part of the process to determine treatment needs. Flashbacks, hypervigilance, and avoidance are the characteristic symptoms (American Psychiatric Association, 2000). Experiencing victimization does not necessarily mean a person is experiencing symptoms of PTSD, however. To distinguish this disorder from other anxiety disorders, professional training is required (Kubiak & Rose, 2007). Without appropriate intervention and supports, chronic mental disorders such as PTSD contribute to decreased functioning and substance use, which in turn are associated with increased recidivism (Salina, Lesondak, Razzano, & Weilbaecher, 2008).

TREATMENT OF CO-OCCURRING DISORDERS

The lack of nationalized healthcare in the United States undoubtedly is a reason so many persons with serious mental and substance disorders end up being arrested for crimes (van Wormer & Bartollas, 2010). Alcohol, cannabis, and cocaine, in that order, are the most commonly used substances by persons with severe mental illness (Mueser, Noordsy, Drake, & Fox, 2003). The rate of reported mental health disorders in the state prison population is five times greater (56.2%) than in the general adult population (11%) (Bureau of Justice Statistics [BJS], 2006). The rate is higher among White than of minority inmates.

Statistics on Co-Occurring Disorders

From the BJS (2006), we learn these facts:

- Three-quarters of female inmates in state prisons who had a mental health problem met the criteria for substance dependence or abuse. (This is compared to 55% of men.)
- Female state prisoners who had a mental health problem were more likely than those without to:
  - Meet criteria for substance dependence or abuse (74% compared to 54%).
  - Have a current or past violent offense (40% compared to 32%).
  - Have used cocaine or crack in the month before arrest (34% compared to 24%).
  - Have been homeless in the year before arrest (17% compared to 9%).

They were also more likely to report:

- Three or more prior sentences to probation or incarceration (36% compared to 29%).

- Past physical or sexual abuse (68% compared to 44%).
- Parental abuse of alcohol or drugs (47% compared to 29%).
- A physical or verbal assault charge since admission (17% compared to 6%). (BJS, 2006, p. 8)

Treatment Issues

As the Substance Abuse and Mental Health Services Administration (SAMHSA) (2005) informs us, offenders are far more willing to admit to their criminal activity and substance abuse problems than to discuss their mental disorders. Yet since these problems are interrelated, the assessment needs to screen for both problems at one time rather than to conduct separate assessments.

Although jails and prisons have become the new mental institutions in today's world, these institutions are not set up to provide adequate mental health services; as a result, inmates are left undertreated or not treated at all. The convention in correctional psychiatry is to identify as serious mental illness only bipolar disorder, major depression, and schizophrenia and to limit treatment to prisoners with these disorders only (Human Rights Watch, 2003). Antipsychotic medication and medication for mood disorders typically are administered, with the result that many inmates wander around like zombies. But we need to recognize that medications for severe mentally ill persons may not work or only partially, and thus are not a cure-all (O'Hanlon & Rowan, 2003). Across the United States, prisoners with mental health problems face a shortage of qualified staff, lack of facilities, and prison rules that interfere with treatment.

Because of the close correlation between early childhood trauma and substance abuse as a way of self-medication and the correlation between childhood abuse and self-mutilation and other self-destructive behaviors, long-term, in-depth treatment is required to alleviate problems that are all interconnected in one way or the other (see Chapter 7). Yet the next description from prison inmate Barrilee Bannister is typical (cited in van Wormer, 2001, p. 284).

> The only counseling we have is amongst ourselves. When one of us feels cheap, dirty, or cheated due to what occurred—she knows that there's always one of us available to cry with, to bitch with, to seek justice with and when all else fails, we do what the old saying says is the best medicine—we find reason to laugh by knowing that we survived and have become stronger individuals.

Oregon Department of Corrections refuses to give us professional counseling, however, which we really do need. Our counseling amongst one another often leads to fantasies of revenge by getting out of prison and castrating our abusers.... That can't possibly be healthy.

Biological Research

Traditionally, the most common approach to treating clients with dual or multiple disorders has been to identify one disorder as "primary" and the other as "secondary" (Mueser et al., 2003). This ideological conflict concerning which disorder came first has now receded from the public view as we have learned from advanced technologies such as the magnetic resonance imaging about diseases of the brain and cravings related to addiction and relapse.

Recent biological research has helped solve the riddle that has plagued the treatment field for some time: Why do mental illness and drug addiction so often crop up in the same person? The American Psychological Association (2007) provides some clues with recent research on the brains of rodents. When one part of the rat brain — the amygdala (the emotion control center) — was damaged under experimental conditions, the rats grew up with little response to stimuli and, compared to normal rats, they got hooked on cocaine very rapidly. This finding tells us that brain conditions may increase the susceptibility to addiction. In humans, physical and emotional trauma may be the cause of such disturbances. Studies on trauma in childhood bear this out, as early childhood trauma and addiction problems are closely linked (see Chapter 3 and Salina et al., 2008). The close correlation between PTSD and substance abuse disorder is generally explained in terms of a response to victimization that involves use of various substances to cope with the feelings of depression and anxiety that accompany exposure to traumatic events. Changes in the brain may occur through traumatization as well, changes that can have long-lasting consequences.

Treatment Programming Needs

Despite the fact that substance and mental health disorders do not come singly but tend to occur together, treatment programming within prison rarely is set up to treat both disorders at once (Kubiak & Rose, 2007). And substance abuse counselors often fear that addressing past trauma will open a Pandora's box, contributing to increased psychological symptoms. Killeen, Hien et al. (2008) conducted a large-scale clinical trial that integrated trauma therapy with substance abuse treatment for one group and found there were no adverse consequences from this approach. This is an important finding because inattention to coexisting disorders, such as PTSD, may negate the success of substance abuse treatment. Women need help to heal from their wounds to enhance their overall life adjustment.

Prisoners with serious mental health conditions find it difficult to adhere to prison rules and to cope with the stresses of confinement. The prevalence of childhood and later sexual abuse histories among incarcerated women leaves them at high risk for being retraumatized by the invasive body searches and violations of bathroom or other personal privacy that occur routinely in the prison setting. Yet rarely is trauma discussed in relation to the incarceration experience itself (Kubiak & Rose, 2007). A Texas prison inmate with whom I am in private correspondence has a serious problem with anger and has been diagnosed with bipolar disorder. In her correspondence of September 17, 2009, she writes:

> Sometimes we all feel like saying "to heck with it." My life in here's okay. I feel great being drug-free and God letting me have another chance to live. When I was out there I overdosed on drugs. And luckily my friends were there to revive me and to get me stabilized again....I just finished anger class Thursday. The class is Go Ahead. My other groups I attend are Stop Chaos and Grow Ahead. I'm signing up for all of them through the Psy Center. I have a very bad anger problem. Stop the Chaos is talking about sexual abuse in your life. I was molested by my mom's boyfriend as a child. He raped me when I was 12 years old. And ruined my insides. And when I was 19, he beat me up when I was pregnant with my second daughter. When I had her, I almost bled to death....I have so much anger built up in me through my years of growing up. I was beat on as a child. I've tried over the years to let go but it's so hard. (pp. 2–3 of letter)

We do not know the extent of prison traumatization, but we do know that women with mental disorders have serious adjustment problems within the prison environment. This fact is verified in the BJS (2006) report's finding that 58% of state prisoners with such problems have been charged with violating prison rules compared to 43% without mental health problems. Charges of verbal and physical assaults on staff are commonly reported in this population.

Human Rights Watch (2003) found that mental health treatment in women's prisons is inferior to that in men's institutions, despite the fact that a higher percentage of female inmates have mental health problems. Many of the women's prison systems lack specialized mental health units.

Once inside the jail or prison, the inmate who is seriously mentally ill often fails to obey orders and ends up in solitary confinement. In Vermont, for example, where the investigator found a caring mental health staff, the resources were simply not there to provide anything other than solitary confinement to women who engaged in constant head banging and other acts of self-mutilation.

Over the past decade or two, we have seen the criminalization of emotionally disturbed youth into the criminal justice system. At least one out of five within this system has a serious mental disorder (Landsberg & Rees, 2007). Children are locked up because adequate help in the community is rare. Few beds are available in the mental health system for intensive treatment.

Often girls suffering from PTSD are given the negative label borderline. *Borderline personality disorder* (BPD) is a catchall term used by mental health practitioners and paraprofessionals for highly manipulative and troublesome clients. Many of these girls who have been abused early in life commit self-destructive acts such as self-mutilation. (For criticism of this term, see research by O'Hanlon & Rowan, 2003.)

BPD is a more useful term if it is viewed in terms of the various dimensions that are its defining criteria. As delineated by Harriette Johnson (2004), these are: fluctuating moods, impulsive behavior, interpersonal stress, and self-injury. This division is useful because different neurobiological structures probably underpin each of the dimensions. Medication management with selective serotonin reuptake inhibitors in conjunction with skills training is often helpful in reducing aggression and impulsive behavior. Johnson recommends providing education about the biological aspects of the symptoms so that women with this diagnosis can understand their own internal reactions and behaviors.

Exemplary Programs

Cusack, Morrissey, and Ellis (2008) examined the impact of integrated intervention with almost 3,000 women with dual diagnoses. Improvements were especially dramatic for women with severe mental disorders. In the community, mental health professionals now are joining forces with substance abuse treatment specialists to treat clients simultaneously for substance and mental disorders (van Wormer & Davis, 2008). The realization that an integrated approach is the preferred treatment modality is slowly making inroads in the correctional system. The Cook County Sheriff's Department in Illinois, for example, has developed an integrated treatment program for women inmates (Salina et al., 2008).

The features that distinguish a co-occurring treatment program from other criminal justice substance abuse treatment programs are:

- An integrated treatment approach
- Treatment of both disorders as primary
- Comprehensive services that are flexible and individualized
- Small caseloads
- Educational approaches
- Staff expertise in treating both mental and substance use disorders (SAMHSA, 2005)

For the substance abuse component of integrated treatment, motivational strategies as defined in Chapter 7 are of proven effectiveness when tailored to the individual client's attitudes and readiness to change. Motivational strategies, in fact, can operate as a bridge to unite substance abuse and mental health treatment modalities (van Wormer & Davis, 2008). Kassebaum (1999) suggests that the health benefits from successful substance abuse treatment for court-ordered women clients are many. Preventing new cases of HIV/AIDS, prevention of fetal alcohol syndrome, and reducing welfare costs and foster care costs are among the benefits.

One of the most progressive institutions for women is the Bedford Hills Correctional Facility in New York. Among its well-known programs are the Puppies behind Bars to train seeing eye dogs, a family violence program, and special housing for whole-family visitation. A well-staffed mental health unit offers an integrated treatment format since 80% of the women on the mental health caseload have had a substance abuse problem. The annual report on its mental health services, however, points to some serious deficiencies (Correctional Association of New York, 2007). Among the concerns are: shortage of qualified mental health staff; the heavy use of solitary confinement for rule breaking; and the "the lack of a gender-specific, culturally sensitive, and trauma-informed approach to Bedford's mental health-related programming and services" (p. 5). We have to give some credit, nevertheless, to the state of New York for providing this annual report on the mental health programming.

Landsberg and Rees (2007) recommend as an alternative to residential treatment wraparound services that bring mental health treatment directly into the home. The success of such a program, however, depends on the involvement of responsible adults in the family. Good news for adult offenders from California is that, due to prison overcrowding, persons involved in criminal activities related to substance abuse will now be sentenced to treatment instead of to prison (Gordon, 2008). Among the proposed initiatives:

- Placing parole violators in treatment programs instead of sending them back to prison
- Having some low-risk offenders serve their time in county jail or on probation instead of state lockup
- Electronic monitoring
- Offering inmates who successfully complete drug treatment, vocational training, and educational programs in state prison credit for good conduct that could reduce their sentences

(For further description of treatment of co-occurring disorders, see the SAMHSA/CSAT Treatment Improvement Protocol [TIP 42] on Substance Abuse Treatment for Persons with Co-Occurring Disorders, found on the Internet at: www.ncbi.nlm.nih.gov/books/bv.fcgi?rid=hstat5.section.74165.)

Self-Mutilation and Suicide Attempts

The Human Rights Watch (2003) investigation into the treatment of prisoners with mental illness determined that suicide attempts and instances of self-harm were rampant. Prisoners have swallowed pins, bitten chunks of flesh from their arms, and slashed and gashed themselves, according to the report. Such episodes of self-harm violate prison rules; the mind-set in corrections is that there is a price to pay for self-mutilation, or else it is feared that inmates would deliberately commit such acts in hopes of a transfer to better living quarters. The general attitude that investigators found by corrections staff was that the prisoners were simply "bad" rather than "mad." Staff discounted the mental health significance of the behaviors. One example given was at Taycheedah prison in Wisconsin where a woman who slit her throat was sentenced to 180 days in segregation; when she repeated her act, she was given another 180 days. I have personally visited this prison, the name of which is the American Indian term for home. I can confirm that the environment of this prison is highly militaristic and anything but homelike.

In the *Diagnostic and Statistical Manual of Mental Disorders—Text Revision (DSM-TR)* (4th ed.) (2000), self-injury such as cutting oneself is listed as associated with eating disorders, childhood sexual abuse, and subsequent trauma. It is also included as a symptom of borderline personality disorder. It is estimated that 70% to 80% of people diagnosed with BPD engage in some form of self-injury or attempted suicide. Most of the episodes of self-mutilation are not related to suicide attempts but are rooted in reactions to a history of chronic childhood abuse and trauma (Kress & Hoffman, 2008). Biological research indicates that decreased serotonin levels are associated with impulsive behavior, aggression, and self-injury. The best explanation for this seemingly strange behavior is, according to Kress and Hoffman, that some individuals who have grown up in abusive families often experience constant emotional dysregulation and cannot handle strong emotions and attack themselves. These authors recommend using strategies to help motivate clients to change, avoiding confrontation, and helping promote their sense of confidence.

When women are housed in single cells, as they are in the United Kingdom, and in solitary confinement in the United States, the rate of self-harm and suicidal attempts goes up (Kruttschnitt & Vuolo, 2007). Having a roommate is apparently helpful in preventing some self-destructive acts in women who are prone to abuse themselves. The housing of suicidal inmates in solitary confinement is not only dangerous to their mental health but, according to Human Rights Watch (2003), a violation of the American with Disabilities Act of 1990, which bans discrimination against persons with disabilities. This inhumane treatment is also a violation of the U.S. Constitution's stipulation against cruel and unusual punishment. The disciplinary facilities in which prisoners are locked provide only a few break periods for exercise a few days a week; typically, little or no mental health treatment is provided.

Suicide Prevention

When people are mired in their problems, as is the case with many female offenders, they often have difficulty seeing beyond their immediate circumstances. Assessment for suicide risk is therefore important. Most effective institutional suicide prevention programs provide staff training in identification of suicide risk at intake, sharing of information among all staff members, and safe housing options for suicidal inmates (Springer et al., 2003). From a strengths perspective, Corcoran (2005) provides a checklist that includes questions such as: Have you had thoughts about hurting yourself now or in the past? What did you do to get past that point? How did you stop things from getting even worse? These questions can get at suicide risk while attempting to elicit positive responses. This is important because mental health therapists sometimes, in the way they word questions, leave clients feeling more depressed than before and even full of self-pity.

Writing in the California Coalition for Women Prisoners' newsletter, Block (2008) tells of six attempted suicides over 18 months, four of which were successful. At least one of the women who killed herself was turned away from the mental health professional. According to Block, factors contributing to the increasing suicide rate are the drastic overcrowding in the facility, the longer sentences women are serving that deprives them of hope, and increasing denial of services and medication to inmates with psychiatric problems. After two suicides occurred in the York Correctional Institution, the education staff reached out to the community for help. The prison school broadened its curriculum to include year-round workshops on women's health and healing, and volunteers were recruited: poets, journalists, dancers, musicians, and Buddhist monks. Through such activities, the women were able to discover a certain joy in living and realize that they too had a contribution to make.

Gender-Based Curriculum

Within women's correctional institutions, all studies consulted support rehabilitative programs—education, job training, parenting education, and mental health treatment. In a comparison study of two HIV-risk prevention programs, one behavioral-cognitive, the other gender based, the gender-based intervention resulted in greater improvement in safe-sex practices (Pomeroy, Roundtree & Parrish, 2006). Conceptualizing substance abuse as a criminal justice problem rather than a healthcare issue has led to severe overcrowding and sentences so long as to remove all hopes of a brighter future. Because even though the therapeutic services provided by the prison can be helpful, the creation of real choices for women lies in developing genuine alternatives to incarceration.

When imprisonment is necessary, however, we can consider the German example of how the prison and social worlds may connect. In Germany, rehabilitation is actively promoted in these ways: lengthy home leaves even for "lifers," conjugal visits, and work release programs. The children of the inmates attend a regular nursery school in town (Quaker Council for European Affairs, 2007; van Wormer & Bartollas, 2010). In accordance with the Prison Act of 1976, rehabilitation is the dominant philosophy, and assimilation from a life within prison walls to an independent life outside prison is the fundamental theme. Inmates live alone and enjoy the privacy usually accorded to adults; staff members knock on their cell doors before entering.

In Canada, regionalization to keep incarcerated women near their home communities was the key recommendation of a government report (Hannah-Moffat & Shaw, 2003). The report, *Creating Choices* (Correctional Services of Canada, 1990/2007), spelled out five feminist principles on which all future developments were to be based:

1. *Empowerment* to help women overcome the inequalities they have experienced in terms of violence, poverty and racism.
2. *Meaningful choices* to provide realistic and meaningful opportunities to develop one's potential.
3. *Respect and dignity* especially for those with racial and cultural differences—a circular healing lodge was developed for Native women.
4. A *supportive environment* to include nutritious food, fresh air, space, and privacy.
5. *Shared responsibility* between the prison and community for the women's personal growth

Note that the focus of this scheme is correctly on women's special needs rather than a pure equality model, which would entail a re-creation of the male prison model. A major criticism of the woman-centered philosophy as a blueprint for corrections, however, as Shaw (1996) concedes, is that the government can use this "feminism" to continue the expansion of women's prisons when the use of imprisonment itself for so many women needs to be rethought.

With the dramatic increase in the number of women offenders under correctional supervision, U.S. researchers and advocates are calling for correctional strategies that are gender specific as well. A gender-specific curriculum for correctional personnel is offered by Idaho and other states (B. Miller, 1998). The goal is to break down prejudice within the state correctional system against male correctional officers who work with women and to offer extensive gender-based training. But as Miller suggests, most training for correctional officers is focused on working with men, and there is resistance within correctional systems to adjusting to the different requirements of women. The continuing perception that female offenders are "more difficult" than male offenders prevents many criminal justice professionals from capitalizing on many of the advantages of working with women offenders. Gender-specific training for officers would do a lot, according to Miller, to reduce the incidents of sexual, physical, and emotional abuse of female offenders.

Programming for Group Work

Helpful educational interventions that can and should be offered to female inmates from high-risk backgrounds include education about HIV/AIDS and venereal disease risk and the risk of sharing dirty needles in drug use, sharing information on harm reduction practices including needle exchanges and condom use after release, and where to locate community public health resources. Because of the direct association of substance abuse with other high-risk and self-destructive behaviors, substance abuse treatment is obviously the greatest preventive measure. And in light of the high rate of abuse in the background of female inmates and awareness of the need for help in dealing with the aftermath of abuse, domestic violence group sessions are a popular program in jails and prison.

The socially empowering group, even within the confines of the stark prison setting, can be individually transformative, the more so among women who have been removed from and punished by society, estranged from loved ones, and forced into lockstep with institutional demands. The actively working, fun-loving group can thus represent a strange and powerful anomaly given where it is and the personal history of its members. Such a group can serve as a bridge to the cultural and social milieu of the larger society.

The hallmark of the effective group leader is enthusiasm and unshakable confidence in the women's latent talents and abilities. The leader's role, as described by Gutiérrez and Suarez (1999), should be that of consultant and facilitator rather than instructor, so as not to reinforce the sense of powerlessness that these women need to overcome.

Small groups, according to these authors, have special relevance for empowerment practice with Latinas because they offer an effective means for raising consciousness, and because it is in keeping with the Latinas' history of working with one another to provide mutual aid (Center for Substance Abuse Treatment [CSAT], 2004). African American culture is similarly oriented more toward family and community systems than toward individual achievement. Adopting a bureaucratic approach with members of these minority groups will doom the therapist to failure; the personal relationship and respect are primary. An Afrocentric framework goes beyond cultural competence to incorporate key elements of spirituality that are so essential to addiction and mental health treatment (Springer et al., 2003). Respect for tradition and for one's elders, for the community and the teachings of the church are emphasized. Native American teachings based on the medicine wheel and circle of life, and a sense of oneness with nature have been widely used in Canadian institutions to good effect (van Wormer & Davis, 2008). Refer to the CSAT *Substance Abuse Treatment and Family Therapy* and McGoldrick, Giordano, and Garcia-Petro (2005) for general guidelines for working with multicultural and other specific populations.

Despite the notorious treatment of men and women in the criminal justice system starting with harsh sentencing laws, there is some innovative programming, especially in women's prisons, that meets the criteria for empowerment therapy. Among examples of innovative, gender-specific programming are an art therapy program at the Kingston prison in Canada that provides incarcerated women with a voice to deal with trauma, the indigenously based Sycamore Tree project that follows the principle of restorative justice in helping female inmates in New Zealand reintegrate with the community, and a bereavement and loss group in an English women's prison for those who needed to mourn the death of a loved one (see van Wormer, 2001). The importance of such group work for all participants is that gaining competency in one area—writing poetry, drawing, parenting—leads to skills in performing adult roles valued by society. Such creative expression can foster a freedom of the mind. As we hear from Michelle Jessamy (2003), incarcerated at York prison in Connecticut:

> The prison environment causes you to shut down and distrust other people but writing has the opposite effect....By exploring my past through autobiographical fiction and sharing it with others, I am learning how to come to terms with the "whys" of my past actions and how to release my spirit from *its* prison. (p. 265)

Expression through art can be empowering as well. As another York inmate, Tabatha Rowley (2003) whose artwork is highlighted beside her story, tells us:

> In prison, I detoxed from a ten-year binge, entered recovery, and little by little began to understand who I was beneath all those bad habits and bad decisions. My art helped me do that—I rediscovered myself in memoir, in songwriting and performance, and in drawing. (p. 98)

Counselors can draw on artwork as a powerful means of helping clients work on their feelings. Art therapy emphasizes collaborative work in which the client becomes the expert on his or her own life and interpretations of the drawings (Corcoran, 2005). The use of artwork in treatment is effective because it offers insights while helping to build a relationship between client and therapist. Group work can be tremendously enhanced as drawings are shared and interpreted by members. Central to all these creative initiatives is the theme of personal empowerment, empowerment through self-expression of a fulfilling yet enjoyable sort. The learning of life skills, such as parenting, can flow naturally and spontaneously through involvement in mutual aid or support groups focused on a common, all-absorbing task or project. Read Box 5.1 for an example of empowering teaching within the total institutional environment.

BOX 5.1

Empowerment Behind the Wire

Ardyth Krause, Ph.D.

City Council Member, Eau Claire, Wisconsin

Even though I am a social worker by profession, the women I work with do not think of me as a social worker. Instead, I am known by the titles of "director" and "professor." Conversely, my students are not solely students to me. Since the university program in which I administer and teach is in a state prison for women, I must also view my students as "offenders."

A metal fence topped with circles of electrical barbed wire surrounds my students and me. Even though I am lucky enough to go home each night, my students and I are still literally and figuratively behind this wire together when it comes to our freedoms. My students have certain limitations on their basic freedoms of speech and action. For example, they cannot refuse the orders of authority figures, and there are strict limitations on what they can do, wear, or own. I, too, am limited by the procedural requirements of the prison in both my power to make educationally focused decisions in my formal university roles and in my ability to incorporate social work principles and values in my work with the students. For example, I am required to place "security" as the highest priority in my educational programming. Although crucial to prevent escapes and maintain order for the thousand plus people living and working within the prison, security is also in direct opposition with one of the most cherished social work principles, that of self-determination. Thus, if a student is planning a class presentation or research paper, I must restrict her from certain topic choices that might in any way promote prison violence, a proclivity toward gang activity, or facilitate an escape or a prison uprising. Or, if a student would rather miss class and sleep-in with a scratchy throat on a blustery morning, unless she has been formally "laid in" by the medical department, I must "call out" that student and insist that she come to class immediately.

(continued)

With these limitations notwithstanding, I still manage to insert social work principles into my work insofar as it is possible. Drawing on Wilson and Anderson's (1997) five dimensions of empowerment (educational, economic, personal, social, and political), I will briefly show how I shape my instruction and programming, accordingly.

Educational and economic empowerment come into play as my students work toward the goal of earning a college degree. Often on graduation day, the students shed the tears of a very special joy. One student seemed to speak for many when she said: "I'm so happy! I have finally done something right!" When she said this, I realized that walking down that aisle of the prison chapel to "Pomp and Circumstance" might be the first time ever for some of the women to achieve societal accolades for an accomplishment.

In my role of instructor in courses on psychology and sociology, I have multiple opportunities to facilitate *personal empowerment*. Keep in mind that these inmates, battered as they have been by life's cruelties and, any regrets they may feel at their own behavior, typically have low self-esteem. The degrading treatment they receive as prisoners compounds this phenomenon. This low self-esteem is evidenced in inmate writings for class assignments. Whether due to earlier substance abuse or personal trauma or poor education, many of the writings are strikingly superficial. In my psychology class, one strategy to help students realize they are special is to have them choose from a list of adjectives to describe their individual interests, views and characteristics.

A second strategy is to elicit group affirmation. For example, if we are discussing group membership and a student says: "I tend to keep to myself until I know people pretty well," I might ask the class something like: "Why might that be a good idea?" If another student then pipes up and says: "I'm different—I like to ask lots of questions to get to know people on my own," I might then ask the class: "How is asking questions another good way to fit into a group?" Finally, I try to further reinforce the students' sense of competence (as well as the value of individuality) by observing: "Isn't it neat how we can have two entirely different styles, and yet both of them are equally effective ways to relate?"

As both a teacher and an administrator in this environment, I try to provide as many choice-making opportunities as are practical. I do not just say, "It is your choice," when I present these opportunities. Instead, I advise the student that a part of the process of deciding whether or not to drop a class, for example, put extra work into a research paper for example, involves a careful consideration of the pros and cons of all options, plus acknowledging the potential short and long term consequences of a choice.

The fourth form of empowerment identified by Wilson and Anderson (1997), *social empowerment*, involves a sense of group identity as a platform from which to impact upon mezzo and macro systems. Group identity is already well developed within the walls of a prison. The women are very cognizant of their common identity as "offenders." Even though this label seems at first blush to be kinder than the older terms of "prisoner" or "inmate," in my opinion, it is more abhorrent. Being called an "offender" is being told that you continually offend. Most of the women are painfully aware of how they have harmed society with their criminal offenses, or rather how they have "offended." Accordingly, I refer to the women, simply, as students.

My favorite method of social empowerment is therefore to insert content from feminist and women's studies literature into my course content whenever appropriate. Helping these women to develop a group identity as women serves two purposes. First, as opposed to their group identity as offenders, being "women" places them in membership of a group that is in many ways viewed positively by society. Second, women as a group also share oppression as a commonality with offenders. By creating an awareness of the meaning, impact and coping strategies for the social injustices experienced by women as a minority, I hope to simultaneously instruct them in ways to deal with their other minority group status, or that of "offenders."

The final type of empowerment is *political empowerment*. This type is actualized by knowledge of and participation in the democratic system. My senior seminar, a course which prepares students for life "outside the wire," includes material on the major political parties. I tell my students that I would like them to understand the political system so that when they get out, they can have an impact on it. I impart my desire that when they are legally able, at the very least, that they will vote. (Our state—Indiana—is one of a limited number that eventually allows ex-felons to resume this right.)

(continued)

A second way that I attempt to facilitate power is to give the students an opportunity to participate in an actual democratic system. Recently, we held an election for a Student Advisory Committee. The students voted for which self-selected candidate they wanted to represent their degree program. The function of this committee is to advise our university program in the self-study that we are doing for accreditation purposes. We are hopeful that if successful, this committee will become an ongoing opportunity for our students to have a voice in their educational experience.

In summary, it is true that the wire boundary that reduces the liberty of the ones who I serve, also partially incarcerates the social worker in me. But what I tell my students, and what I remind myself daily, is that a fence is only a fence. Once we have tapped into the power of our internal wings, we are free to soar together to the remarkable heights of our own potentials.

REFERENCE

Wilson, M. K., & Anderson, S. C. (1997). Empowering female offenders: Removing barriers to community. *Affilia: Journal of Women and Social Work, 12*, 342–369.

Printed with permission of Ardyth Krause, who at the time of this writing was a teacher at the woman's penitentiary in Indiana.

Girl Scout Visitation Programming

To help break the mother-daughter lawbreaking cycle and to help prepare inmate mothers to eventually return to their mothering roles, social workers have been actively involved in a program in collaboration with the Girl Scouts of the USA (Pace, 2006). Originating in Maryland in 1992, with funding from the National Institute of Justice, the Girl Scouts Beyond Bars Program has grown to involve around 800 girls and 400 mothers nationwide (Acosta, 2005). The Austin-based Girl Scout Troop 1500 has been in the spotlight because of a PBS documentary called Troop 1500 that filmed activities from the program. All the girls in the program have mothers in prison, on probation, or engaged in another release program. The film, however, focused on the small group of girls whose mothers were incarcerated at the prison in Gatesville, about 90 miles away (Acosta, 2005).

Since its inception, the Texas Lone Star Council has broadened the scope of help by having counselors meet with each girl involved in the program twice a month, usually at the girl's school (Pace, 2006). When the girls meet with their mothers once a month at the prison in Gatesville, an art therapist from the Austin YWCA joins them to coordinate activities for the girls and their mothers. Through these activities the girls have an opportunity to share their anger and express their feelings. But they also get a chance to avoid the pitfalls that may lead to similar paths that their mothers followed: In addition to their therapy, they attend workshops and lectures on how to better their lives. Possibly most important, the social workers help devise a plan for after the mothers serve out their sentences.

PROGRAMMING FOR OLDER FEMALE INMATES

Within Prison Walls

A comprehensive survey of the Federal Bureau of Prisons system and Department of Corrections nationwide revealed striking differences in programming for male and female older adult inmates (Williams & Rikard, 2004). Of the 40 state officials who completed an interview, only 2 states (Alabama and Ohio) had specific age-specific policies for female inmates compared to 23 for males. The federal system, similarly, had no gender-specific services for older inmates. Alabama's program at the Julia Tutwiler Correctional Institution (where coincidentally the second author conducted research on prison conditions) is basically a hospice program that hires inmates to attend to the needs of dying residents. The Ohio Reformatory for Women has developed an assisted living unit that offers recreation activities, special programs, and a centrally located dining hall expressly for meeting the needs of geriatric inmates (Williams & Rikard, 2004). Those with severe medical problems are teamed with a H.O.T. (Helping Others Together) partner. H.O.T. partners are other inmates who serve in staff positions and who perform any activity that assists with the geriatric inmate's daily living needs. Older Resourceful Women (O.R.W.) provide the more able-bodied residents with opportunities to make quilts and other craft projects to finance the unit's various programs. The Central Ohio Area Agency on Aging sponsors a series of 14 educational programs on a variety of topics relating to age. The Meridian Garden Club offers an opportunity for inmates to care for plants on the grounds and within the facility's greenhouse. Additionally, there is a five-day a week recreational program that is designed specifically for the needs of all the facility's aging inmates.

Decarceration of Older Prisoners

Several states have enacted emergency release programs to deal with prison overcrowding, and there is a renewed interest in using scarce and costly prison space for the high-risk offender—a practice know as selective incarceration (Reuter & Bushway, 2007). The reverse side of selective incarceration is selective decarceration—or the early release of inmates considered to be of less risk to society. One such group of inmates consists of older adult offenders. On average it costs three times more to maintain older adult inmates compared to their younger counterparts (Williams & Rikard, 2004). These costs relate to the complex, chronic, and serious nature of health problems that are often so debilitating that geriatric offenders are no longer considered a security risk. Thus prison administrators are increasingly considering transferring their low-risk older adult inmates to less expensive community-based programs, such as state nursing homes, group homes, or congregate care facilities.

Yet it is has been observed that community-based programs often are unwilling to accept older multiproblem inmates with health-related limitations (Curran, 2000). This situation requires the need of trained social workers who can broker the needed resources and placements for decarcerated older adult inmates. Numerous legislative acts, such as the Older Americans Act of 1965, can be utilized by social workers to dismantle discriminatory procedures and policies that create barriers that prevent decarcerated older adults from receiving community services.

Funded by a U.S. Department of Justice grant, a reentry program has begun at the Nebraska Center for Women to teach better cognitive skills and practical facts about renting an apartment and paying bills. Because some of the elderly inmates have been removed from society for some time and become institutionalized, the teaching of decision-making skills is crucial to help prepare inmates for a return to "the free world" (Mabin, 2007).

DIVERSIONARY PROGRAMS

Case Management of Drug Court Clients

One of the most promising developments in recent years is an alternative to prison that was first launched in Florida in the late 1980s: the drug court. The success of these new courts, which divert nonviolent drug offenders from the prison system into treatment, are not your ordinary adversarial courts.

Intensive case management services are provided, mental health disorders are treated simultaneously with drug treatment, and medication is prescribed where appropriate (Deschenes, Ireland, & Kleinpeter, 2009).

As of December 2008, about 1,950 drug courts were operating in the United States: 1,215 adult courts, 475 juvenile courts, 235 family courts, and 25 combination adult/juvenile/family drug courts. Of these, 80 were drug courts within Indian country, called Tribal Healing to Wellness courts (National Institute of Justice, 2008). Federally funded drug courts have been set up in Kentucky, Hawaii, and in the midwestern states especially to deal with the meth crisis. SAMHSA's Center for Substance Abuse Treatment funds 62 drug courts that help adult and juvenile offenders stay out of prison, and parents at risk of losing custody of their children break the cycle of substance dependency (SAMHSA, 2006a).

Is such an investment in a relatively small number of individuals (the Waterloo, Iowa, court has a caseload of 20) with serious addiction and legal problems worth the effort? The evidence is encouraging. An extensive review of the literature, conducted by Belenko, Patapis, and French (2005) and Deschenes et al. (2009), concluded that the cost savings are substantial. The studies examined typically compared the recidivism rates of graduates of drug court with a matched sample of offenders who completed standard probation or jail time. Cost savings went beyond the correctional costs of confinement to include savings through the prevention of criminal activity, unemployment, Medicaid, health and mental health services, rearrests, reconvictions, criminal victimization of others, and the drug exposure of infants. Significantly, the research that included data over a four-year period showed far higher cost benefit ratios than did studies limited to one-year follow-up periods. The National Institute of Justice (2008) estimates the cost savings at almost $7,000 per participant.

Do methamphetamine users have as successful treatment rates through drug courts as do users of other drugs? This is the question Listwan, Shaffer, and Hartman (2008) explored. Their literature review seemed to indicate that meth users were more likely to be heavy substance abusers and to use a variety of substances but that they were less involved in other crimes, such as robbery, than were other drug users. As a result, their recidivism rates were generally lower, especially compared to participants who identified crack as their drug of choice. In their own empirically based study on hundreds of drug court participants, Listwan et al. found that drug courts had a similar impact on all the participants, regardless of drugs of choice. Women were more likely to be meth than crack users; if they dropped out, it was because of relapse rather than involvement in criminal activity.

Case management provided by a collaborative team is the organizing scheme of drug courts. Generally the team is composed of a judge, probation officer, substance abuse treatment counselor, prosecutor, and other representatives from the community. A focus is placed on obtaining employment and/or vocational training. Clients report once a week to the court, often with their family members, to review their progress. The positive results of such close monitoring as provided by drug courts are realized through the individual attention to persons while reinforcing their positive social networks. Also, such programs are cost effective to society in allowing people to obtain treatment while maintaining their work and family roles (Springer et al., 2003). For women, the courts' effectiveness is enhanced because of the continuum of services provided and the close partnerships with community-based organizations. Attention to family support systems is another factor of special meaning in women's recovery. From the harm reduction perspective, drug courts have been criticized because they are built on the principle of total abstinence and lack of trust (van Wormer & Davis, 2008). Extensive urinalysis testing is done to determine whether the individual is taking drugs. Nevertheless, compared to the restrictions of prison life, and within the context of America's war on drugs, we must see this intensive supervision in the community as a welcome improvement over the alternative.

Because many women offenders are mothers, correctional programs delivered in the community are particularly important for women who have young children. Community centers that house mothers together with their children are especially valuable, as they can provide counselors who model appropriate parenting skills as issues arise spontaneously in the common living situation. Knowing that jail time awaits them if they begin abusing drugs again offers women a strong incentive to change. By the same token, without help and the educational and vocational skills necessary to survive on their own, some women continue their patterns of destructive behavior and involvement in destructive relationships.

When offenders enter the program, an entire team is working with the judge. Case managers help participants tackle other problems in their lives, including emotional and health problems. Such programs can be viewed as a feasible and more effective alternative to adversarial procedures to combat nationwide drug problems. Such programs offer extensive, long-term treatment at little cost to the offender; many opportunities exist for professionally trained counselors to find employment with such diversionary, community-based programs.

According to a recent review of the research findings on drug court effectiveness by the National Institute of Justice (2006), many drug court graduates succeed, but others who are terminated from the program return to drug use and a criminal lifestyle. Retention could be improved, according to this document, through the employment of sufficient numbers of case managers for close supervision, the hiring of more minority counselors, a curriculum built on cognitive-behavioral techniques rather than a mixed approach, and inclusion of family members in counseling sessions.

From the liberal perspective, critics of the U.S. drug courts say both that they are too punitive and do not go far enough. Curley (2004) has noted a rift between less traditional treatment advocates and drug court practitioners as a result (Curley, 2004). The requirement for absolute sobriety and the punitive response to relapse as a failure prevent many participants from succeeding. The constant urinalysis testing for drug use is hardly consistent with the principles of the strengths perspective. For heroin addicts and other addicted persons, sometimes medical prescriptions for methadone and related drugs to reduce cravings are not encouraged.

In short, drug courts are a big step forward, because they stress rehabilitation over punishment and positives over negatives. The Scottish design, however, goes even further in this direction in using a harm reduction model that can succeed with more clients inasmuch as the expectations of this design are more realistic. Perhaps the U.S. drug court movement is a first step in the journey from imprisonment of drug offenders to harm reduction. Let us look more closely at one program—the Black Hawk County Drug Court in northeastern Iowa.

Only about two years old, the Black Hawk County Drug Court has as its primary goal to reduce drug-related crimes in the community (Steele, 2008). Using a team approach, the process draws on the services of a wide array of law enforcement, judicial, and treatment personnel. Family members are also welcome to attend the weekly drug court proceedings, where participants tell the court and the team what has been going on in their lives over the past week.

Up to 25 drug felons can take part, but only those with nonviolent offenses are admitted into the program. Phase I of the drug court is a minimum 90 days, with weekly court sessions and frequent and random drug testing. Phase II is designed as a 150-day period, where the offender attends drug court weekly sessions, maintains the substance abuse treatment program, works on his or her self-awareness and repairing personal relationships, and still undergoes random drug testing. Phase III lasts around 120 days, as the offender continues to recover from the life of drug addiction and performs community service work.

In just two years, the drug court has saved taxpayers in Black Hawk County almost $400,000. The cost is calculated, according to Judge Thomas Bower, who presides over this court, by taking into account the cost, per day, per client, in the program versus the cost, per day, per client, in prison (Reinitz, 2006). Social worker Renée Barbu wrote the description of this drug court in operation presented in Box 5.2 for this book.

BOX 5.2

Observation of Drug Court, January 23, 2008

Judge Bower was pleased to share his thoughts on the drug court program. "In a traditional courtroom all I would get to see is a person failing," he explained. "What I like about drug court, I get to see the participants progress, I encourage them, I try to match them with additional services, and in the end I get to share in their success and the joy of their family."

From my observation the program highlights visible and measurable objectives. The participants go to the podium and answer Judge Bower's questions such as: How many days have you been clean? How is the job? How are your relationships? Are you dressed appropriately for court?

This question is asked especially if the client is wearing jeans. Jeans are not to be worn to court. Even when a client answers all the judge's questions positively the participants will not get the reward of a week off from drug court if they are wearing jeans.

Looks are highly stressed as evidence that a participant is successful in the program. Before-and-after pictures are taken of the participants. The before picture is given to participants at the graduation ceremony as a reminder that they should never want to fall back into the old lifestyle.

Judge Bower believes in the reinforcement power of seeing a great transformation. He has even connected several participants with his personal dentist to fix teeth at a reduced cost that have been destroyed by methamphetamines. He gives the participants the contact information with instructions that they are to pay the dentist for the work in monthly payments.

One lady who graduated from the program the day I was there said that she was thankful to all involved in supporting her into recovery—her family that attended with her each week, her substance abuse counselor, and her probation officer. Finally, she expressed loads of gratitude to Judge Bower.

Printed with permission of Renée Barbu, MSW.

Child Welfare Programming

Project Safe is an Illinois state-wide program through the Departments of Children and Family Services and Alcoholism and Substance Abuse directed at mothers of young children who have been arrested often for drug possession and who have been found to be neglectful of their children due to drug use (Chestnut Health Systems, 2002). Most of the women are unemployed at the time of admission into the program. Gender-specific addiction treatment services are provided to the women while child care workers take care of the children. At the heart of the program is aggressive outreach for women reluctant to participate. Outreach workers build supportive relationships with these clients and through showing compassion and persistence somehow get them motivated for help. Aggressive case management is a critical part of Project Safe. Parenting skills are taught along with relapse prevention, a flexible approach to treatment compliance, and work on early childhood victimization. Follow-up studies show that of the 81% who complete the program, clients experienced improved emotional health and increased self-esteem.

Restorative Justice Strategies

Here is a definition of the strengths-restorative approach in a nutshell: From the strengths perspective, now making inroads (belatedly) in the social work profession, comes a focus on client strengths rather than weaknesses, assessment of capabilities other than liabilities. From religious teachings, indigenous people's traditions, and the writings of criminologists from around the world come the philosophy of an approach of restoration as opposed to retribution. The direct goals of restorative justice are geared toward the needs of the victim, the offender, and the community. The typical process is for the offender to make amends to the victim and be restored to the community.

Restorative justice, unlike the strengths approach, originates at the macro level and works downward to include professionals, victims, offenders, and the families of both. Restorative justice defines how the social institutions of justice are set up and the specific procedures that apply to achieving justice. The value system on which restorative justice is based, however, is directly compatible with the strengths approach to treatment. Restorative justice is about helping rather than hurting people, building on the good in men and women rather than focusing on the bad, working toward the future instead of dwelling on the past, listening not dictating—all the underlying principles of a strengths perspective as well.

Increasingly, restorative justice initiatives are being introduced into women's prisons. Minnesota, for example, has infused gender-specific programming within its juvenile and adult institutions, programming that is built on restorative justice principles. Meetings held at Shakopee Prison, for example, include victim-offender conferencing, panels, and healing circles (Minnesota Department of Corrections, 2007). A restorative justice committee comprised of inmates arranges for activities. Among the activities are collective restitution to the community, such as the donation of hair to cancer patients, the making of quilts for women's shelters, healing circles for offenders to meet with crime victims from the community, and arranging for victim-offender dialoguing in individual cases.

The transition from a punitive to a restorative ethos requires a radical transformation in our thinking about the nature of crime, victimization, and so-called corrections. The development of new forms of administering justice, in turn, further transforms our thinking about crime and justice while it gives voice to women's concerns. This more humanistic approach does not derive, as the adversarial approach does, from trial by combat. Following Gilligan's (1982) delineation of femininity (focus on relationships, empathy, and caring), the restorative approach, at its core, can be considered to be on the feminine rather than the masculine side of the continuum. Like women operating from the standpoint of an ethics of care, restorative justice assumes that human beings are interconnected and that relationships are central to repairing the harm caused by crime (Failinger, 2006).

Elsewhere I have introduced a strengths-restorative approach to meet the needs of girls and women who have committed a wrong and want to make restitution or who have suffered victimization themselves and wish to communicate their feelings about it within a safe and supportive setting (van Wormer, 2001). The strengths-restorative approach combines a strengths-based feminist perspective within a restorative framework.

Restorative justice exists in several forms, some operating at the level of the whole society, such as after mass victimization (e.g., genocide or apartheid) in order to make peace and provide reparations for the harm that was done. Others operate in small-group settings, such as a school or church. Our concern here is with the form known as victim-offender dialogue or conferencing.

Consider the typical case behind prison walls: After she has served about one year of her sentence, an inmate who killed a pedestrian or other driver when she was highly intoxicated is notified by her victim's family that they desire a meeting with her. They want to learn more details about the accident, but mostly they want to see the person who killed their loved one as a human being, and they want to reveal the extent of their suffering to this person so she will straighten out her life. After many months of counseling to prepare inmate and victims for the meeting, they are brought together in the presence of a staff representative and restorative justice expert to communicate their feelings about what took place. The meeting is highly emotional but ends with an apology by the inmate and a recognition by the victim's family of the inmate's remorse. Some degree of healing generally follows for all the participants.

But how about situations where the homicide was intentional? We can learn of cases of such magnitude from social work professor Marilyn Armour (2002), who has worked directly with the victims' families in pursuing a restorative justice process. Armour has found that victim-offender dialogue, when well planned and monitored, can be beneficial for the homicide survivors. The restorative process accords the survivors the recognition they were previously denied in the more formal judicial proceedings. Moreover, the process is affirming in offering the survivors the opportunity to tell the offender how the crime affected them.

Increasingly today, in the United States and Canada, victims and offenders meet for restorative processes in prisons. The restorative approach finds victory in the moment when an offender acknowledges, with remorse, what harm she has done (Failinger, 2006).This process is not recommended in cases in which the offender feels no remorse or suffers from a personality disorder, such as antisocial personality. True remorse is not possible in some cases; assessment should be done to screen out persons who cannot accept responsibility for what they have done or who are otherwise cognitively or socially deficient in ways that might hinder true dialogue.

Because so many of the women in prison have been victimized earlier and later in life by family members and partners, I would like to see the restorative justice process brought within prison walls for the perpetrator to engage in conferencing with the victim. For a battered woman or a survivor of child abuse or incest who is working on issues of past victimization, such a chance to confront her victimizer and, it is hoped, to receive an apology can be conducive to psychological healing.

In all these situations, victim-offender dialoguing offers a number of advantages. Advantages to the victims are:

- The restoration of a sense of safety and control of their lives
- The opportunity to speak their minds and confront the person who has harmed them
- Getting answers to often-haunting questions about the crime itself
- Hearing a confession
- Through such a ritual involving community support, beginning the journey toward healing and closure

To the offender, the advantages are:

- Having a way to begin to make amends for the harm done
- The chance to ask for forgiveness
- A chance to reveal his or her humanness

In cases of serious crime, such a process of reconciliation is of course not a substitute for punishment; the process here is an end in itself. A recent innovation is the use of restorative circles to help prepare women who are about to be released from prison for community life and to help prepare the community for the women's return.

PROGRAMMING FOR REENTRY INTO THE SOCIETY

Women as ex-convicts return to society to face the problems they left behind in addition to new ones: the stigma of the ex-prisoner status, the lack of vocational skills and recent job references, and the difficulty of resuming interrupted parenting roles. Many of the problems connected with a successful return to society and with female criminality, as O'Brien and Young (2006) inform us, are structural in nature. Meeting basic needs and having an income are key considerations. To help women restart their lives, access to support services is a necessity. The obstacles are many, especially when the individual has spent many years locked away. For parolees, the stringent post-prison supervision requirements have become the leading cause of return to prison for former inmates in many states.

According to a long-term study by the Bureau of Justice Statistics (2002) on two-thirds of all prisoners released during a three-year period, 67.5% were rearrested at the end of three years. The women's rate at 39.9% is much lower than the male rate but still unnecessarily high. Happily, a movement is afoot today at the highest levels of government to address this problem proactively.

The issue of offender reentry, according to Lemieux (2008), "has been jettisoned into the national spotlight, launching practice innovations, research projects, and policy conversations about the specific family functions that are associated with successful reintegration" (p. 187). The National Institute of Corrections (2008), for example, is providing funding for gender-responsive initiatives in the hopes of reducing women's repeat criminal behavior. So far the Connecticut Court Services Division for women on probation and the Utah Department of Corrections for women in transition from prison to the community have been selected to implement intensive case management services for women. These pilot programs will utilize a relational approach, be strengths based, trauma informed, holistic, and culturally competent. To ensure consistency across the board, all members of the case management team will be cross-trained to use a gender-responsive approach. Motivational interviewing strategies will be used throughout the program from assessment to treatment. Such community programs are of special importance because many women, in contrast to men, may experience returning to their community as reentering a traumatic environment (Kubiac & Rose, 2007).

For the offender with serious mental disorders, parole presents a major challenge. To meet this challenge, the Iowa Department of Corrections requires a prearranged parole plan that includes wraparound services and intensive community supervision. Persons with co-occurring disorders must follow through on mental health and substance abuse treatment programs (Brimeyer, 2003).

From a restorative justice perspective, Bazemore and Boba (2007) highly recommend community service engagement by former offenders as a way to ease their transition into the law-abiding, prosocial segments of society. An additional function is that through such community service work, the former inmate often improves her self image. Working for an organization such as Habitat for Humanity is suggested as a suitable community-building, action-oriented project. In this way, formerly incarcerated persons can be seen as resources in the community rather than liabilities.

Lovins, Lowenkamp, Latessa, and Smith (2007) found that intensive residential treatment was effective in preventing recidivism in a large sample of recently released female inmates who were judged to be at high risk to reoffend. Comparison was made to a control group who did not receive case management and counseling services. Risk was determined on the basis of substance abuse, mental health, education, young age, previous employment status, and criminal history. Interestingly, intensive treatment provided to women at low risk to reoffend was counterproductive, especially in residential treatment, and seemed to promote the chance of rearrest. These findings confirm the importance of individualized programming for women who need it.

Central to relational, gender-sensitive theory is a focus on the quality of relationships. Relationships are, of course, important to men as well as to women, but regarding rehabilitation the effects may be different. Marriage, for example, has been found to be helpful for men at reentry but not necessarily so for women whose relationships with criminally involved men may have led to their incarceration in the first place. Bearing these facts in mind, Leverentz (2006) interviewed over the course of a year 49 female halfway house residents straight from prison about their romantic and sexual relationships. She found that women who were linked to law-abiding men did well at reentry, as did women involved with ex-convicts in recovery. Women who were from crime-ridden neighborhoods fared the worst due to their contacts with criminally involved men.

Case Management for Drug-Abusing Offenders

To help ex-convicts reintegrate into the community and prepare for independent living, parole officers increasingly are encouraged to provide case management services. Sometimes an independent agency, such as the Treatment Accountability for Safer Communities identifies clients in need of substance abuse treatment and monitors client progress and compliance with conditions of release (Prendergast, 2009).

In addition to substance abuse treatment, parolees may need assistance with housing, employment, transportation, family issues, medical and mental health problems, and obtaining documentation, such as Social Security cards. Case managers assist clients in acquiring the skills and resources they need to help them overcome barriers in their community. The smaller the caseload, the more intensive the supervision can be. For women, help in finding suitable housing in a low-crime neighborhood may be the most important function of the case manager to help the woman get started on a path to a new life. Another consideration is the need for mothers to provide a healthy environment for their children.

The Forever Free Substance Abuse Program at the California Institute for Women is a demonstration project for inmates with substance abuse problems. The purpose is to reduce the reincarceration rate following release from prison. The curriculum offered within the institution emphasizes relapse prevention, 12 Step treatment, and work on specific women's issues, such as posttraumatic stress disorder. Following imprisonment, in order to measure treatment effectiveness, one group entered a community-based residential treatment program while another group did not. Evaluation studies at one-year follow-up showed that the women in the residential program had lower self-reported drug use and better employment outcomes than did the control group (Pettway, 2006). This experimental program is built on research that has verified the need for aftercare services to continue the progress made through in-prison drug treatment programs.

Similar effectiveness was obtained in the Delaware Key/Crest drug treatment and reentry program that used a modified (for women) therapeutic community rehabilitation format with an aftercare component. Although the format differed from that of Freedom Forever, the aftercare portion of the program seems to have accounted for program success in helping ex-convicts refrain from criminal involvement (Wells & Bright, 2005). Both these aftercare programs met women's needs and linked them to vocational and educational services to enhance their prospects for employment.

Treatment planning for women with alcohol and other drug problems should include education to prevent and treat chronic medical conditions such as HIV/AIDS, hepatitis C, and tuberculosis. Because many of the women have engaged in prostitution and trading of sex for drugs, the National Institute on Drug Abuse (NIDA) recommends education about sexually transmitted diseases as a part of treatment for criminal justice populations. For useful treatment guidelines, see NIDA's (2006) booklet, *Principles of Drug Abuse Treatment for Criminal Justice Populations.*

In addition to addiction treatment, parenting is another issue that needs to be addressed at an early stage well before release. Because the majority of women imprisoned in jails or prisons are parents, some programs are adding parenting workshops to their agendas (SAMHSA, 2005). Research suggests it is in the best interests of both mothers and their children to have continuing interaction while the mothers are incarcerated. Children of inmates who have maintained ties with their parents have been found to have increased cognitive skills and higher self-esteem than children who are denied such contact. The parents' benefit is shown in reduced recidivism rates when prison visits are provided on a regular basis. Lemieux (2008) is optimistic that the revival of the rehabilitation model and the increasing national emphasis on preparing inmates for reentry will force corrections professionals to bolster family programming. Involvement of family members, as Lemieux suggests, should be viewed as the cornerstone of successful reentry policies and practices.

Restorative Circles for Community Integration

A focus on the family is also central to the restorative justice circle format described by Walker, Sakai, and Brady (2006), who have developed a process to help inmates prepare to be reintegrated into society. Consistent with Hawaiian Native customs, restorative circles are meeting grounds for decision making for helping individuals take responsibility for their past behavior while making practical arrangements for living in the "free world." Present in the circle are family members; victims who have been wronged; and members of the prison staff chosen by the inmate to describe his or her successes, strengths, and work toward rehabilitation while in prison. In response to my invitation, Lorenn Walker agreed to write, especially for this book, a description of her work with restorative circles. Walker is the former deputy attorney general of the state of Hawaii and currently a public health educator and restorative justice trainer. Her contribution in Box 5.3 dramatically concludes this chapter.

BOX 5.3

You're Gonna Make It

Reentry Planning at a Hawaii Women's Prison

by Lorenn Walker

"I've been clean for over four years, and I quit smoking two and a half years ago," says Penny, her eyes looking up, off to the left corner, with a furrowed forehead. She is trying to remember all the things she has accomplished since being in prison this time around. "Oh, yeah, I made amends with my oldest daughter and have a good relationship with my youngest one now," she adds with a confident smile.

Penny is around 35 years old. She is *hapa*, part Hawaiian and part Portuguese. Her family is from the Wai'anae Coast of Oahu, which is 51% Hawaiian and the most economically depressed area on Oahu (U.S. Census Bureau, 2000).

Penny's black shiny hair is neatly pulled into a tight ponytail. She could pass for a grown-up cheerleader except for the home-made tattoos on her hands. She is dressed in clean blue hospital scrubs, the required uniform at the prison where she has been incarcerated for the last four years. She is in prison for selling drugs, an occupation mainly used to support her former drug habit.

Penny sits in a circle of 12 other incarcerated women who are participating in her Modified Restorative Circle (Walker, in press). The circle is a group reentry planning process designed in Hawaii for an incarcerated individual to make a transition plan for successful reintegration back into the community. The Modified Restorative Circle process is slightly different from the Restorative Circle process developed in 2005 in Hawaii (Walker, Sakai, & Brady, 2006).

In the original Restorative Circle, loved ones are invited and attend the group meeting, while the Modified Circle is for people whose loved ones are unable or unwilling to attend. Instead, other incarcerated people attend the Modified Circles as supporters.

The Modified Circle grew out of providing a Restorative and Solution-Focused Problem Solving Training program for incarcerated people (Walker & Sakai, 2006). It was developed to demonstrate restorative justice and the power of reconciliation to people in the training program.

Since the first Modified Restorative Circle in 2006, 30 more, including Penny's, have been provided for both women and men. Currently, the Hawaii prison system allows the Modified Circles for demonstration purposes only during the training program. The Modified Circle process, however, is a positive alternative to the Restorative Circle process and it is hoped that it will eventually be allowed by Hawaii's prison administration.

The original Restorative Circle and the Modified Restorative Circle (circles) give individual imprisoned people the opportunity to explore what is needed for them to live a healthy and happy life. For most imprisoned people in Hawaii, as elsewhere in the United States, this includes a drug-free life.

The incarcerated individual who discusses, makes decisions, and plans for her life, after gaining information generated by a group of caring supporters, drives the circle process. Both types of circles meet criteria necessary for promoting *desistance* (Walker, 2009).

Desistance is the phenomenon where most people who commit crime naturally and eventually stop doing it later in life (Maruna, 2006; Rumgay, 2004). Desistance is an ongoing process, and "sustained desistance most likely requires a fundamental and intentional shift in a person's sense of self" (Maruna, 2006, p. 17).

The circles use solution-focused brief therapy language skills that identify a person's abilities to create peaceful and happy lives and helps people set goals for themselves (Walker, 2008). The circles provide the elements that can successfully assist incarcerated people in rescripting their life stories, including assisting them in reconciling with loved ones and the community. The circles help imprisoned people find ways to meet their needs for reintegration into the community (Walker, in press). These positive results promote desistance by helping shift a person's image and sense of self.

Restorative Circles address an incarcerated person's needs, and the first need considered is the need for reconciliation. Here reconciliation does not require that any repaired or continued

(continued)

relationships be achieved. Reconciliation can merely be "the process of making consistent or compatible" (Dictionary.com, 2007), and coming to terms with the fact the person is in prison, had a drug problem, lost custody of her children to child welfare, and so on.

The major difference between the two circles' processes is that the reconciliation piece is much richer when loved ones participate because they explain how they were affected and what can be done to repair the harm that they suffered. Without loved ones participating, incarcerated people having a Modified Circle can only speculate about how they have harmed others and what they might do to repair that harm. This critical thinking, while done in a group, however, can be meaningful.

Usually in the Modified Circles, the incarcerated people decide that "walking the talk" and living a "clean and sober life" where they are independent is a step toward reconciliation, which they can take regardless of others participating.

During a Modified Circle, some incarcerated people address their need for reconciling with themselves and what they need to do to forgive themselves. Often they decide that walking the talk also works for reconciling with and forgiving themselves.

Sometimes if they believe it will not upset victims, they write apology letters asking what they might do to repair the harm. In some cases where others have custody of their children, they may write a letter and say that it is sent in good faith for the sake of the children. In these cases often their prison counselor reviews and signs the letter indicating this is true.

The incarcerated people in this program are quick to recognize that they have created trust problems with others and that only they have the power to rebuild the situation. Writing a letter as a result of a Modified Circle in at least one case led to an incarcerated person being restored into the family; the inmate's mother contacted him in response to a letter he wrote his former girlfriend's grandmother. The grandmother contacted his mother in praise of the man writing her and thanking her for all she had done for him previously. His mother was moved by his newly found gratitude and contacted him.

Penny has waited 12 weeks to have her Modified Circle. Two other women who wanted one cannot because the training program is ending.

After Penny lists what she is most proud of having accomplished, each woman supporting her in the circle says what she likes most about Penny and what her strengths are. The list of positive attributes eventually grows to 63 items including: "Honest, speaks up, loving, giving, productive, determined, creative, willing, visionary, humble."

The circle is a moving experience. Not only is Penny hearing what other people like about her for the first time, but her incarcerated friends are emotionally touched too. Some have tears in their eyes, including one who says, "You're determined and loving. I know you're gonna make it."

The circles generate inspiration, positive thoughts and emotions, something that the current system fails at providing because it focuses almost exclusively on deficits and what is wrong with people.

People need positive emotional experiences to change (Kast, 1994). The circles are a welcome and needed intervention. We are requesting another grant to continue the Restorative and Solution-Focused Problem-Solving Training because the women strongly advocated for it, saying they "learned things in it to help keep me out of prison."

We have also been successful in gaining state legislative support for the Restorative Circle program (Brady & Walker, 2008). Although the current governor has refused to fund it, we are confident that eventually we can get the Modified Circles institutionalized in Hawaii.

REFERENCES

Brady, K., & Walker, L. (2008, Summer). Restorative justice is a mandated component of Hawaii's reentry system. *Justice Connections, 6*.

Dictionary.com Unabridged (v 1.1). Retrieved December 27, 2007, from Dictionary.com Web site: http://dictionary.reference.com/browse/reconciliation.

Kast, V. (1994). *Joy, inspiration, and hope.* New York: Fromm International Publishing Company.

(continued)

Maruna, S. (2006). *Making good: How ex-convicts reform and rebuild their lives.* Washington, DC: American Psychology Association.

Rumgay, J. (2004). Scripts for safer survival: Pathways out of female crime. *Howard Journal of Criminal Justice, 43,* 405–419.

U.S. Bureau of the Census. (2000). Washington, DC: U.S. Census Bureau.

Walker, L. (2008). "Implementation of solution-focused skills in a Hawaii prison," In Dejong and Berg, *Interviewing for solutions.* CA: Cengage.

Walker, L. (2009). Modified restorative circles: A reintegration group planning process that promotes desistance. *Contemporary Justice Review, 12*(4), 419–431.

Walker, L., & Sakai, T. (2006). A gift of listening for Hawaii's inmates. *Corrections Today,* http://findarticles.com/p/articles/mi_hb6399/is_7_68/ai_n29318719 (last visited March 14, 2009).

Walker, L., Sakai, T., & Brady, K. (2006). Restorative circles: A reentry planning process for Hawaii inmates, *Federal Probation Journal, 70* (1): 33–37, http://www.uscourts.gov/fedprob/June_2006/circles.html (last visited June 1, 2008).

Printed with the permission of Lorenn Walker, J.D.

SUMMARY

It is a clear understatement to say that the empowering rehabilitative goals discussed in this chapter are not the goals of most correctional systems or penal institutions in which social workers and other correctional counselors are employed. Correctional mental health practitioners can do one of three things:

1. Uphold professional values of self-determination by refusing to work in an authoritarian, politically driven system and stay away.
2. Knuckle under to the demands of the system and adopt a distrustful, pathology-based approach to the criminal population.
3. Work within the system to help alleviate individual suffering while attempting to change the system and through counseling to help change individuals within the system.

Professionals, who like ourselves harbor strong moral objections to the incarceration mania that is gripping this country, can resolve like Quakers to "be in the world without being totally of the world."

Happily, times are changing. Witness the innovative woman-centered programming described in this chapter. The reentry projects that help women become reintegrated into the community, the restorative justice projects that promote healing, and the drug courts that keep women in the community are promising developments that are due to expand in the future. Empirical research lends support to these projects in enhancing rehabilitation for women in the criminal justice system. Successful programs are those that are evidence based, integrated for mental health and substance use disorders, and gender sensitive.

Listening to the voices of females inside the system, we can learn of their desire for programming that is relevant to their parenting function, training skills, and skills-based work. It is hoped that this analysis of the context will prepare us (as helpers, researchers, and catalysts for change) for the challenges of actually doing therapy with female offenders, challenges to which we now turn our attention in the next chapter.

Part IV

SKILLS FOR CORRECTIONAL COUNSELING

Chapter 6

COUNSELING THE FEMALE OFFENDER

How could anyone ever tell you
You were anything less than beautiful?
How could anyone ever tell you
You were less than whole?
How could anyone fail to notice
That your loving is a miracle?
How deeply you're connected to my soul?
> —**Libby Roderick**, "If You See a Dream," 1988

Chapter 4 described a female prison environment from the viewpoint of inmates and staff, whereas Chapter 5 focused on correctional programming within prison walls. Having delved into facts concerning women's victimization, criminalization, and institutionalization, now we explore the fundamentals of correctional counseling from an empowerment perspective. *Correctional counselor* is the generic term I will be using to refer to those persons involved in both institutionally based and community-based programs for offenders. This term encompasses social workers, probation and parole officers, and substance abuse counselors. Much of what applies to these practitioners applies to prison chaplains, correctional officers, and psychologists as well. From the treatment standpoint, the counseling goal with offenders is to help people turn their lives around.

This chapter is predicated on the belief that as women develop a deeper awareness of their own strengths, they will take greater control over their own lives. This in turn will help them as they strive to reclaim some of their dignity even in the most degrading of circumstances. I am talking here of empowerment, paradoxically, in environments (correctional) that undoubtedly are restrictive in one way or another, whether the client is living in a halfway house or under probation or parole supervision.

Advocates of gender-sensitive treatment for women involved in the criminal justice system have suggested that women can be more appropriately treated within the community than in jails and prisons. In fact, the overwhelming majority of female offenders (around 85%) are in the community, on either probation or parole sentences (Kubiak & Arfken, 2006). Even for offenses involving illicit drugs, a large majority are sentenced to probation with conditions that include substance abuse treatment and sometimes treatment for mental disorders. As a result, over one-third of all admissions into publicly funded substance abuse treatment programs have been referred by the courts or officers of the court (SAMHSA, 2005).

High-risk factors for offenders (presumably male) are antisocial attitudes, lack of vocational and educational interest, substance abuse, and association with other criminals. A great deal more research needs to be done, especially regarding effective interventions for female offenders, given their special needs.

What are female offenders' special needs? As we learned from the national survey of prison administrators described in Chapter 4, the areas of urgent treatment need are, in order of concern, substance abuse counseling, anger management, and issues related to victimization. Trends that the administrators expect to see stressed more in the future are: substance abuse treatment, parenting education, motivational enhancement, and restorative justice programming. These themes gel well with the topics covered in this and the next chapter.

The purpose of this chapter is to integrate principles from strengths-based theory and motivational enhancement treatment with therapy for work with women in trouble with themselves and the law.

For specialized work with female offenders, this discussion extends the descriptions of gendered work with juveniles as provided in Chapter 2 to adult populations.

Starting with the treatment relationship, we proceed to an investigation into the use of the language of effective communication. Strengths-based dialogue is built on a language of affirmation. What to say and how to say it-these are the themes of this chapter. Practice illustrations and role-plays are derived from direct correctional and victim assistance work. This empowerment model, as we will see, is in sharp contrast to the traditional correctional model that has been dominant since the late 1970s and that often is more punitive than correctional. Both approaches are geared toward helping clients to change their thinking patterns and stay out of trouble. An empowerment or strengths-based approach, however, strives to bring out the good rather than to target the bad.

Because of the close fit between motivational interviewing (as first articulated by William Miller and his associates (1998)) and the theory and practice of a strengths-based approach, we are introducing a scheme for intervention with women offenders that combines the twin qualities of motivation and strength. Motivational interviewing, due to its seemingly laid-back style and its close attention to client readiness to pursue change, offers exciting possibilities for work with this population.

INTRODUCTION TO THE GENDER-BASED EMPOWERMENT SCHEME

For heuristic and organizational purposes, I am proposing a five-stage gender-based empowerment scheme. The scheme is built on a composite of activities in which clients progress from total absorption in their own stories, feelings, and addictions to self-understanding to making a contribution to others. The theory behind the phase approach is that a course of treatment, like life, is a journey, and that progress, if it occurs, is an outgrowth of identifiable, although overlapping, processes. The five identified processes from the therapist's perspective are:

1. Building a therapeutic relationship
2. Enhancing motivation
3. Teaching coping skills
4. Promoting healing
5. Enhancing generativity

In other words, as told to the client: relate, absorb, work, heal, and reach out to others.

The gender-based empowerment scheme is the organizing framework for this chapter and the one that follows. This chapter covers the first two components: relationship building and motivation enhancement. Chapter 7 takes us more specifically into the areas of feeling and skills work, healing and generativity.

These processes, which extend from development of a working relationship to generativity, are roughly comparable to the stages of change of Prochaska and DiClemente (1983). Like the first five stages of change—precontemplation to maintenance—they are about positive change, and they are progressive. Unlike the stages of change, however, they are not circular and do not include a sixth stage of relapse. Nor are they focused solely on substance abuse and addiction. A major assumption of this empowerment scheme is that offenders' needs will vary and that their capabilities will vary as time passes. Realistically speaking, many will never embark on the journey; some will make only a little progress; and many others will stumble along the way. But still others will make major life adjustments, altering their lifestyles and reaching out to a new set of friends. This is why we who work with offenders do what we do—because it matters.

And because a few miracles go a long way.

Correctional counselors work with people who basically are coerced into treatment, especially those with a jail or prison term hanging over their heads. Their motivation is strictly external. Such clients typically need to change not just one aspect of their lives but every aspect, including their alcohol/drug use and whom they hang around with; often they must change their whole outlook on life. On top of this, there is a natural human resistance to pressure to change. For work with such an involuntary but needy clientele, motivational interviewing techniques have been found to be highly effective for reaching people (Miller & Carroll, 2006). A digest of motivational strategies is presented in this chapter. Motivational interviewing is a model ideally suited for empowerment counseling; it really concerns how you go about asking the right questions at the right time and in the right way. Later we consider some sample questions relevant to work with female offenders.

Often referred to unaffectionately as the "dregs of society," these women, as a unit, are poorly educated, occupationally disadvantaged, and of low socio-economic status. The men and other family members in their lives are often crisis-prone as well and sometimes abusive. A task for correctional counselors is to help these women somehow get beyond their backgrounds, or at least that part that is destructive. To do so, the women need to acquire the tools—educational, vocational, and psychological—for independence. Women's crime, as we will remember, is closely related to their economic position in society and their involvement with some unsavory human beings.

Sometimes court-ordered surveillance is what is required as an impetus to change.

DOMINANT TREATMENT PARADIGM

The dominant treatment paradigm used by most correctional workers in the United States and Canada is a model based on the notion that offenders get into trouble because they have a criminal personality. Using what is termed a cognitive-behavioral approach, these programs are designed to counter criminal thought patterns and restructure offenders' ways of thinking. Within this framework, systemic factors such as race, class, and gender inequalities are considered to have little to do with criminal behavior (Comack & Brickey, 2007).

What Gendreau and Ross (1980) heralded as the cognitive revolution in corrections was inspired by Yochelson and Samenow's *The Criminal Personality* (1976) by Samenow's *Inside the Criminal Mind* (1984, 2004), and voluminous writings and popular workshops on the so-called criminal personality. Based on Samenow's earlier work with male antisocial offenders at St. Elizabeth's Hospital for the criminally insane in Washington, DC, the "revolutionary" framework was designed to tear down criminals' defenses—the tendency, for example, for rapists and robbers to blame their victims for the crimes inflicted upon them.

Basic to this deficit-based model are two beliefs:

1. The roots of criminality lie in the way people think and make their decisions.
2. Criminals think and act differently from other people, even from a very young age.

One goal of what Bayse (1996) terms the moral-cognitive approach is to encourage inmates' awareness of how they described their victims so as to arouse feelings of guilt and "self-disgust." Similarly, inspired by the criminal mind theory, Elliott (2006) made this observation:

> Throughout the course of my 31-year career as a correctional mental health professional, I have worked with countless prison inmates, both male and female, whose sole mission in life appeared to be the domination, exploitation, and/or humiliation of staff members. The tactics employed by inmates in the service of these objectives have ranged from the primitive and overt to the sophisticated and subtle. (p. 45)

In a major textbook on corrections, Van Voorhis, Braswell, and Lester (2000) praise Yochelson and Samenow's work as especially useful to counselors and custodial staff in correcting inmates' errors in thinking. Institutional staff, as Van Voorhis et al. state, are taught these correctional techniques:

- Accept no excuses for irresponsible attitudes or behaviors.
- Point out ways in which the offender may be refusing to accept responsibility.

- Call attention to, and do not accept "power thrusts."
- Teach offenders that trust must be earned, and call attention to other instances when the offender is betraying the trust of others. (pp. 173–174)

But times have changed. Since 2000, when these instructions were found acceptable, Van Voorhis (2005) has been influential in conducting research for the federal government and in promoting gender-responsive treatment programming and specialized classification systems for female offenders.

The treatment has not yet caught up with the theory, however. The tenets of the criminal personality formulation are used with offenders incarcerated for driving while intoxicated across the nation. Even in the Canadian women's prisons, where this approach is termed "cognitive behavioral programming," counseling is designed to counter criminal thought patterns in the women. The aim is to change the behavior of women's "manipulative and criminogenic selves" (S. Pollack, 2005, p. 75). This program actually encourages "participants to adopt the criminal personality story line" and to promote the internalization of a "criminal identity."

Note that critics like myself are not finding fault with the cognitive base on which the criminal personality theory rests but with the negativism and the one-size-fits-all generalizations on which it is based. As a treatment modality, the cognitive approach is of proven effectiveness in helping people cope with many forms of mental and psychological problems (Miller & Carroll, 2006; Project MATCH, 1993). (See Chapter 7 for a positive use of cognitive principles to help women develop images of themselves as survivors rather than victims, as good, caring people rather than as criminals.)

Use of Samenow's confrontational strategies may be warranted for work with the type of person for whom they were designed—the diagnosable psychopath or man without a conscience, now called the person with antisocial personality. Many men in trouble with the law, however, are nonviolent offenders, and even many of the violent offenders are putting on an act of bravado for survival within prison walls. Psychological testing, such as the Minnesota Multiphasic Personality Inventory, can fairly effectively differentiate among various types of criminal mentalities. See Table 6.1 for a comparison of traditional and strengths-based approaches to correctional treatment.

Table 6.1.   Comparative Approaches to Correctional Treatment

Traditional Counseling Approach	Strengths-Based Therapy
Biological	**Biological**
Looks to the individual for specific causes of offending, disease	Stress on multiple, interactive levels of influence
Focuses on pathology	Focuses on the whole person
Dichotomizes reality, e.g., alcoholic versus nonalcoholic	Mental and addictive behaviors are seen as existing along a continuum
Psychological	**Psychological**
Encourages self-concept as criminal identity	Encourages self-concept as a resilient, rational being
Problem focused	Strengths focused, looks to possibilities
Readily uses labels such as borderline, alcoholic, codependent, offender	Tries to avoid use of negative labels
Seeks to motivate through negative reinforcement, threats	Motivates through building therapeutic relationship
Assesses problems and losses	Assesses and builds on strengths
Client typically seen as resistant, in denial, manipulating	Client seen as active participant in a collaborative, health-seeking effort
Client motivation unimportant	Intervention geared to level of client motivation to change
Focus to prevent recidivism	Focus to maintain a sense of fulfillment, well-being
Expulsion from treatment program for breaking rules or relapse	Client self-determination stressed; meet the client where he or she is
Confrontation used to elicit change, break denial	Rolls with the resistance; redefine resistance as a challenge
One size fits all	Individualized treatment; client choice is stressed
Social	**Social**
Identifies deficits in the environment	Identifies assets and resources in the social environment while viewing
External factors viewed as just an excuse for bad behavior	Structural factors recognized as criminogenic
Offender, convict identity is stressed	Holistic approach, reframes identity as worthwhile human being
Focus on following rules, such as rules for parolees	Focus on showing initiative for community living
Looks for codependency in family members	Family perceived as potential resource
Success measured in absence of recidivism	Success measured in moral development and success in daily living

A GENDER-BASED STRENGTHS PERSPECTIVE

Within social work practice and literature, a focus on client strengths has received increasing attention in recent years. *The Strengths Perspective in Social Work Practice* edited by Dennis Saleebey (2006) is an anthology describing how a strengths approach can be incorporated through every phase of the helping process and in all areas of social work. Take the assessment, for example. Shaped by a framework of empowerment, the therapy process may begin with an assessment of the person's assets and resources and of the strengths in family and community.

The biblical injunction "Seek and ye shall find" (Matthew 7:7) succinctly sums up the strengths approach. The view of humanity underlying this approach is a belief in human potential—strengths—that can be mobilized in times of crisis. This strengths approach promotes personal power in people—victims as well as offenders—whose lives have been circumscribed to various degrees and in various ways by crime. From a strengths perspective, the therapist goes to great pains to help the client tap into his or her inner resources. When people are down because of personal hardship or their own foolish behavior, there is no therapeutic benefit in making them feel worse.

From the perspective of the client, being able to grasp one's potential contributes not only to helping in the immediate situation but also in offsetting future difficulties. From the point of view of the worker, tapping into the client's strengths and support systems helps build rapport and even appreciation in contrast to a more traditional, problem-centered approach, which may tend to provoke resistance.

In the criminal justice system, clients often find their very selfhood defined by their crimes. Correctional counseling geared toward the negative and what went wrong in one's life can have devastating consequences.

Concerning Diagnosis

Cowger, Anderson, and Snively (2006) warn us against the reliance on deficit and disease in mental health practice and the emphasis on negative diagnostic labels. These authors recognize that use of a deficit-oriented classification system as provided in the American Psychiatric Association's (2000) *Diagnostic and Statistical Manual*, 4th ed. text revision (*DSM-IV-TR*) is often necessary to fulfill the requirements of managed care for reimbursement. But the use of negative, catchall labels included in the *DSM*, such as antisocial and borderline personality, should be avoided. Another problematic label often used to refer to women whose drug-related crimes stemmed from a dysfunctional relationship with the man in their lives is *codependency*.

This pejorative term, which was originally coined to refer to partners of drug dependents, has come to be considered a disease in its own right (see van Wormer & Davis, 2008). Accordingly, the term *codependency* has come to be associated with woman blaming, victim blaming, and self-blaming, and its use has been assailed by feminists both within and without the social work profession. This is not to say, however, that diagnosis does not have its uses.

The secret is in how the diagnosis is used. As in the traditional saying, knowledge is power, the knowledge of one's medical condition, if accurate and meaningful, can bring tremendous relief. A leading psychiatrist, John Ratey (1997), for example, describes what an eye-opener it was for him to understand why he is as he is:

> A diagnosis by itself can change a life. Instead of thinking of myself as having a character flaw, a family legacy, or some potentially omi-nous "difference" between me and other people, I could see myself in terms of having a unique brain biology. This understanding freed me emotionally. In fact, I would much rather have ADD than not have it, since I love the positive qualities that go along with it—cre-ativity, energy, and unpredictability. (p. 76)

Since many offenders share this diagnosis, this example is highly relevant to correctional work. The bulk of strengths literature, in the tradition of client-centered therapy, it should be pointed out, is highly critical of the use of diag-noses and other labels for understandable reasons.

Strengths Perspective as a Method

Throughout the criminal justice system, there is a preoccupation with failure. Recidivism rather than success reintegration into society is the focus. In statis-tics that list recidivism rates rather than successes, in the media that focus on horrendous repeat offenses, and in the work that correctional staff members do, failure is a constant. Yet former inmates who "make it" on the outside are rarely heard from again.

Rarely is the strengths or empowerment perspective articulated as such in the U.S. criminal justice literature. A computer search of the criminal justice abstracts index (as of May 2008) reveals only seven listings for articles under the headings "strengths approach" or "strengths perspective." This is seven more, however, than appeared in the decade before. The empowerment con-cept, however, does appear to be widely used as a descriptive term for progressive work with juveniles, female victims, and occasionally female offenders, according to the computer index.

For correctional clients, whose views of therapy and of all authority figures are apt to be decidedly negative, a positive approach is essential to establish the one crucial ingredient of effective treatment: trust. Sometimes one encounter or one supportive relationship—whether with a teacher, social worker, or member of the clergy—can offer a turning point in a life of crime.

There is nothing very new about this theory; the parallels with the self-fulfilling concept and the-power-of positive-thinking dogma are obvious. And yet, as a framework for treatment intervention, the strengths approach can offer a mental map to operate as a reminder when we as therapists get off course. In corrections, for example, viewing clients solely through the lens of the crimes they have committed can obscure our vision and impede treatment progress.

The strengths approach is not only a model but also a method as well. This framework, which is the predominant perspective in social work, has as its counterpart in psychology: the school of positive psychology. The challenge is to find themes of hope and courage and in so naming to reinforce them. Using a little imagination, one can discover qualities of goodness even in a life otherwise defined by crime and optimism in expressions of despair. Within the constraints of the coercive bureaucracy, a little goes a long way, and minor accomplishments can be seen as major triumphs. It is all a question of perspective and expectations.

A practice approach that has perhaps paid the greatest attention to working with client strengths is *solution-focused therapy*. This form of therapy seeks to discover positive exceptions to clients' problematic patterns and zero in on solutions that have worked for them in the past (Sharry, Darmody, & Madden, 2002). Asking the question, "What if a miracle would happen?" is the hallmark of this approach. Instead of problems, the focus here is on solutions. O'Hanlon and Rowan (2003), from a solution-focused perspective, recommend asking why the situation is not worse and having the client tell about a time when he or she did not experience the problem. This approach is geared to imparting hope, helping clients realize they are seen as people not equated with their illness or problems, and establishing rapport as the first step in developing a positive relationship.

Personal correspondence with Tinia (cited in van Wormer, 2001) captures a turning point in this inmate's life thanks to an empowering relationship. As she describes it:

Currently at Danbury, there is a program that assists female offenders who have a history of physical, emotional, or sexual abuse. Through this program, women are offered a safe haven within the confines of the prison system to realize their secrets. For the past two years, I underwent intense counseling sessions. Through these sessions, I have learned that I have a powerful voice, a voice which echoes through the shadow of pain. (p. 286)

From a strengths perspective, the aims of correctional counseling are to help people feel better about themselves, to enhance their coping with a life under some noxious form of supervision, and to engage them in decision making concerning such matters as their children, spouses or partners, employment possibilities, and living arrangements. To establish the kind of caring relationship essential for change, correctional counselors must move away from a context of hierarchy toward one of mutuality. But the heavy reliance by the state on imprisonment or threats of imprisonment compounds women's sense of social exclusion and makes later reintegration into society more difficult.

Helping female offenders be more than what their criminal labels indicate is the goal of the strengths approach and of those who believe in rehabilitation. We know that some offenders emerge from their encounter (if they emerge at all) with the criminal justice system redeemed and full of love for humanity while others become embittered and full of hate. Many prisoners become actively engaged in religious activities; the results can be life changing.

Substance abuse counselors and attendees of Alcoholics Anonymous and Narcotics Anonymous meetings are well aware of the many criminal lives turned around through sobriety coupled with 12 Step work. Many of the members, male and female, who were once in serious trouble with the law are now, as they put it, "in recovery."

ESTABLISHMENT OF A THERAPEUTIC RELATIONSHIP

Attempts to establish a therapeutic relationship will fail if there is an absence of trust and if the atmosphere is threatening in some way. Just as a negative approach by an "expert" can have a harmful impact, a positive approach can have the opposite result. The advantage of a feminist-based strengths approach is that it is realistic—acknowledging societal stress and a woman's resilience at the same time.

Psychologists such as Carol Gilligan (1982) and feminist legal scholars such as Marie Failinger (2006) stress the key role that personal relationships play in the making of a female offender. Especially if drug abuse is a factor, a woman's criminal behavior often derives from her connections with a male partner or spouse. Perhaps a meaningful relationship of another sort, therefore, could help such women turn their lives around and reclaim their souls. Once rapport has been established, worker and client can engage in a mutual search for alternative ways of coping with stress other than through violence or drug use or other illegal activities.

Historically speaking, among other qualities, it was the personal trust and caring that enabled Elizabeth Fry, a Bible-carrying Quaker, to organize the wretched inmates of England's notorious Newgate Prison. Her tendency to bring out the good in people defined her reform work with prisoners and politicians alike (Harris, 1988). In the United States, Dorothea Dix established the same kind of rapport with psychiatric patients and later with legislators on their behalf.

For practice with individuals involved in the criminal justice process (whether as victims or offenders or both), the starting point is the building of a trusting, collaborative relationship, a relationship that transcends differences in race, ethnicity, class, and power imbalances. Because empowerment methods initially were developed to address the needs and conditions of women and people of color, empowerment practice has always centered on the experiences of oppressed populations (Gutiérrez, Parsons, & Cox, 1997). Such an approach is designed to help build a relationship of trust even across the boundaries of professional status, race, and class.

Relationship, according to *The Social Work Dictionary* by Barker (2003), is "in social work, the mutual emotional exchange; dynamic interaction; and affective, cognitive, and behavioral connections that exist between the social worker and the client to create the working and helping atmosphere" (p. 365). Relationship is interactive; it is based on language but transcends language. Observed from the outside, a congenial relationship can be inferred in a certain meeting of eyes, smile reflecting smile, head nods in synchrony.

Often offenders and especially inmates, understandably, feel resentful of the seeming (and real) power authorities have over them regarding information kept in closed files. In their relationships with correctional counselors, clients are likely to project onto them some of their innermost feelings, especially the ones they find most unbearable and of which they are the least conscious. In their powerlessness before representatives of the criminal justice system, clients are apt to experience the interrelated phenomena of regression and transference. *Regression* occurs as the powerlessness one feels coupled with the real threat of punishment which conjures up childlike emotions from the past. *Transference*, similarly, takes place as the individual brings into a new relationship unresolved feelings from an earlier, primary relationship. Relating to one's psychiatrist or probation officer as if interacting with one's father or teacher are examples. These qualities of regression and transference at once inhibit therapy and give it real power, a chance to rework conflicts and to rewrite aspects of one's life from before.

Building on Assessment

If the counselor is administering tests, it should be at the request of the client, but, in any case, it should be a collaborative process. "How would you like us to go over your assessment?" is an effective starting point for building trust and arousing interest in an otherwise disinterested or passively resistant client. Such sharing of results obtained earlier is also a good way to dispel paranoia about test results kept in the offender's file.

Results of objective testing can be extremely helpful in defining personality characteristics and areas of concern that will impinge on the counseling relationship. Clients generally welcome feedback, especially when the testing is presented as helpful and interesting. A shortened version of the Myers Briggs personality classification test, for example, is used in this way at The Facility in Waterloo, Iowa, for sentenced repeat drinking and driving offenders. This condensed version draws on four rather than eight personality types. Each type is described on a colored card. Green is the scientific, independent thinker; gold is the highly organized, punctual person; blue goes with the nurturer drawn to the helping professions; while orange is the competitive risk taker. Clients are assigned a card of their color based on their scores on a brief questionnaire. Results have important implications for relationships across personality types and boost self-awareness among participants.

Miller and Rollnick (2002) recommend pretreatment testing such as addictions inventories, not only for screening purposes but also as a foundation for motivational counseling. Test results can be very helpful in mobilizing the client toward commitment for change. Results can be presented with a prefatory comment, as the authors recommend, that underlines the freedom of choice. An example of the recommended tentative wording would be something like "I don't know what you will make of this result but..." Any scare tactics or threatening tones are avoided. Finding the positive in test results gives a boost to an approach centered on uncovering client strengths. A cautionary reminder: Underplay the role of "expert"; the client and helper *collaborate* on figuring things out (Saleebey, 2006).

Correctional counselors, such as probation officers, for example, find themselves in a position of extreme power imbalance that, if handled incorrectly, can be the death knell of a therapeutic treatment relationship. Workers can minimize this imbalance, however, through such measures as arranging office furniture democratically, encouraging mutual use of first names, and paying close attention to the client's perceptions and meanings. To reflect the status of clients as active partners, traditional roles must be redefined insofar as it is possible (Miley, O'Melia, & DuBois, 2006). The long-standing social work principle, "Begin where the client is," has profound implications for the path that individual therapy will take. In partnership, workers and clients map out an area of where to go (the goals), how rough a road to travel (issues to address), and the means of getting there (intervention and exercises). Instead of a philosophy of the treatment guide as expert and teacher, the notion of this type of journey is simply that two heads are better than one to figure things out. Since clients are the ones who have been there, after all, they generally have some knowledge regarding their own situation. Treating the client as a companion in uncovering hidden truths and in search of solutions to seemingly insurmountable problems is revealed first and foremost in the way the therapist speaks to the client, in the words that are used.

Language of Strengths

Seek the positive in terms of people's coping skills and you will find it. This is the cardinal rule of strengths-based therapy, a general rule that helps guide one's choice of vocabulary and timing. Look beyond presenting symptoms and setbacks, and encourage clients to identify their talents, dreams, insights, and fortitude. Other rules pertinent to work with women in the criminal justice system are:

- Listen to the personal narrative with the focus on listening.
- Validate the pain.
- Do not dictate, collaborate.
- Draw on the best of your creative resources and imagination.

Much of this is conveyed through language.

Part of the training that professional counselors and social workers receive consists of learning to phrase comments in such a way that the meanings are clear and to use words skillfully to subdue resistance in the hostile or hard-to-reach client. Novice counselors make mistakes and often learn, as I did, through trial and error. A few of my early clients got offended and let me know. Between healing words and fighting words, as I learned the hard way, there is often a fine line.

Sometimes the problem is in advertently using a no-longer-acceptable term to refer to persons with disabilities or members of a minority group. Some lesbians may refer to themselves as lesbians; others may use the more generic term, gay. Some alcoholics refer to themselves as recovered, while most prefer the term "recovering." A useful strategy is to adopt the term that is used by the individual member of that group or simply to ask which is the preferred term.

Our professional diction, as Saleebey (2006) reminds us, has a profound effect on the way we view clients and the way they relate to us; words can "elevate or inspire or demoralize and destroy" (p. 10). The lexicon of strengths is constructed of positive words, such as capacities, resilience, promise, and possibility. Professional jargon must be avoided for good communication and sending a message of caring (Cournoyer, 2008). Experienced therapists have learned, over time, often through trial and error, the ways of putting things for best results. Yet even the most experienced therapists can stumble on occasion. Here are some basic guidelines:

- On greeting the client, the student social worker may say, "What is your problem?" The word *problem* has problematic connotations. Alternatively, the therapist might say, "I see by your note to me ..." or "What brings you here today?" Sometimes just a friendly introduction will put the client at ease: "Call me Pat."
- For the novice therapist, failure to follow through is common. The flow of the communication is rendered choppy through use of close-ended questions that change the focus abruptly. This example is typical:

  Client: "I just don't know what to do." (pause)
  Worker: "What are the ages of your children?"

- In response to a yelling probationer, the student trainee might say, "We need to calm down." Questions to ponder are: How does the word *we* used in this fashion make a client feel? Does this form of address seem patronizing? What does reference to *calming down* imply? Simply saying "Stop!" or "I'm going to interrupt at this point" might be more productive.
- To an elderly woman assaulted by a relative and deciding whether to prosecute, the worker says, "I understand how you feel." A common client reply is "How can you possibly at age 25 (or so) understand how I feel?" To avoid this reaction and to better reflect the client's feelings, we could say something like "This is a very difficult decision for you, or anyone" or "You're torn between the desire to get justice and teach your relative a lesson and your wish that all of this would just go away." Or "I can sense the pain you must be going through right now."
- In response to any given situation, the trainee might ask, "*Why* do you feel this way?" The client might snap, "If I knew why, I wouldn't be

here." Or, simply, "Why not?" Social workers often learn through painful experience not to ask *why* questions but to show through appropriate nonverbal responses, such as head nods, that their clients' feelings are genuine and understandable.

- The feeling words crop up over and over: "You look angry; You feel upset" are clear favorites. Words like *anger* and *upset* should be used sparingly as they may generate denial or resistance in the client. The client-centered approach, however, relies more on open observations, such as "Your head nodding seems to say 'This is not for me.'" Or "How do you feel when you hear your friend say these things?"

Language and Culture

Language must be adapted, to some extent, to time and place and, above all, to the vocabulary of the audience. Clients of limited education, for example, often complain of counselors who try to impress them by using big words. At the same time, they may be equally put off by counselors who are unfamiliar with their slang expressions and who do not bother to find out what these expressions mean.

For maximum effectiveness in the correctional field, counselors need to be fluent in the current legal jargon and the basic concepts from criminology but, above all, in street language. Over time, the counselor who is not streetwise can master the language with the help of the offender as teacher. Being streetwise is of course a requisite of survival on the streets and a knowledge that middle-class practitioners often lack.

Just as culture is reflected in language, so does language reflect the culture. With humanists of whatever nationality, the color-blind, gender-blind approach to therapy carries much weight. "Treat everybody the same"; "I see no differences—people are people" are typical comments. Yet persons from the mainstream culture need to be prepared, as Bhatti-Sinclair (1994) correctly argues, to understand norms and values of their clientele. The differences among people must be valued as well as the similarities.

Because of European American culture's emphasis on the nuclear family and on families "headed" by a male, social workers from these backgrounds often offend their clients who may think in terms of an extended support network. Whites in the northern United States for example, often convey the message that grandparents are not members of the family. In working with Vietnamese and Latino families, this limited conceptualization can be erroneous.

A further issue relevant to correctional counseling is the heterosexist bias in both language and culture. Practitioners need to be made aware of the bias inherent in assessment forms that speak of spouse or married couple rather than partner. As heterosexuals talk about this issue, they often use words such as *normal* or *natural* for heterosexual, and they should be made aware of the implications of such terminology. More obviously, fag, sissy, or queer are names that can inflict irreparable harm.

The belief of the empowerment approach is that personal growth, when it comes, will come from within but that the catalyst may well be a synergistic relationship, a relationship that instills a sense of "together we can." To be effective, such a relationship is based on the three cardinal principles enunciated so memorably by Carl Rogers (1951): genuineness, empathy, and nonpossessive warmth.

Genuineness

Genuineness is the quality of being sincere, of responding to the client truthfully rather than giving personal encouragement to the person's face and then writing up something altogether different for the files, for example. Because this kind of thing has happened to offenders so often in the past, they are slow to trust correctional workers. If the agency or institution allows clients to see their files or if the worker reads out notes as they are written, this can help clear up any misunderstanding and keep the worker honest. Genuineness sometimes entails telling the client what he or she does not want to hear. Genuineness is illustrated in these counselor's statements:

> As I think about it now, I'm aware that sometimes I'm walking on eggshells with you.

Or:

> I feel angry when I think about all the time we spent looking for your job and now after just one week, you are ready to quit.

Empathy

Empathy is the second essential for good therapy work. *Empathy*, or putting oneself in the place of the client and viewing the world through his or her eyes, can be conveyed through good listening skills including head nodding, eye contact, and use of body language appropriate to the words expressed. If our relationship is to matter to the client, we must first enter his or her world. Use of one's imagination is helpful in achieving empathy. Imagining the temptations of drug abusing; fantasizing what being kicked out of your home is like; putting yourself in the place of a victim of domestic violence—all are examples of the use of this skill. Not only do counselors need it, but clients require it as well if they are to have any understanding of other people, if they are going to be able to forgive persons, such as their parents, who have wronged them. Sometimes they need to be helped through role-plays or telling their significant other's story in order to develop this skill. *Victim blaming*, very common among criminals, is the opposite of empathy. Victim blaming is a way of rationalizing another person's suffering so as to divorce ourselves emotionally from it (see van Wormer, 2007). As the client, whether receiving counseling as victim or offender (or both), gains a sense of her own power and experiences empowerment, she develops her ability to explain herself to others in the context of mutually empathic responses. Developing empathy is a process that evolves over time.

Nonpossessive Warmth

Nonpossessive warmth is the third quality integral to effective counseling. Nonpossessive warmth entails providing feedback in a nonjudgmental, nonpossessive way, but also with warmth. White counselors working with minority clients will want to be certain to send clear signals of respect and positive regard (see the American Psychological Association [APA], Guidelines on Multicultural Education, Training, Research, Practice, 2002). Offenders may be reluctant to trust authority figures, and racial and ethnic differences compound the problem. European American professionals tend to appear hurried and too task oriented to persons of diverse backgrounds. It is helpful to begin with small talk until the client is settled and to pay close attention to the client's definition of the situation.

Through nonpossessive warmth, the counselor communicates liking without dominating. This approach is vital so as not to lose clients who are alternately dependent on their therapist and fiercely independent as a counterreaction. The difficult task for the therapist is to be able to work with the discordant elements of clients without getting sucked in emotionally. Even the client who is rejecting can be helped to draw on her own inner resources to reconcile contradictory feelings so therapy can proceed. This process of responding warmly but nonpossessively is illustrated in this statement made to a confrontational client in a group setting: "I'm pleased you shared these feelings because I've noticed you've been quiet in our sessions and I wondered why.... I'd like to know more about you as a person. Maybe you can tell the group a little more about what you've been experiencing."

These three attributes of the seasoned therapist—genuineness, empathy, and nonpossessive warmth—are also fundamentals of motivational enhancement treatment.

ENHANCING MOTIVATION

We are all change-seeking creatures to the extent that we like to grow, learn, and produce. But perhaps even more so we are creatures of habit, doomed, many of us, to repeat our histories, and to resist change at all costs. If change comes, it is often as a result of crisis, a crisis that comes from without or within. Being caught up in the throes of the criminal justice system is a crisis that may offer at least an external incentive for change. The real challenge is to help the client be self-motivated for change.

Motivational interviewing is presented here as an alternative person-centered approach to the current dominant framework targeting criminal thinking patterns and as a much more sophisticated way of helping clients get more control over their lives than the treatment philosophies currently in vogue in corrections. Instead of *attacking* an individual's errors in thinking and by implication, the individual, empowerment practice guides, reinforces, and supports. Instead of problems, the empowering therapist seeks solutions; instead of weakness, strength; and instead of shame, pride.

Derived from work with problem drinkers, motivational enhancement therapy is a treatment strategy designed to produce rapid, internally motivated change. Treatment outcome research strongly supports this client-centered approach, which is based on a deceptively simple interviewing style. Counselors trained in this technique rely on a variety of listening skills to reinforce clients in their feelings of discomfort with current circumstances and in their desire to embark on an active program of change. Motivational precepts with a key emphasis on choice are compatible with the European American harm reduction model, a pragmatic approach to helping drug users reduce the harm that bad habits may cause them. Today, the model is being used in treatment centers across the United States because of its demonstrated effectiveness in motivating resistant clients to seek healthier lifestyles.

Motivational enhancement techniques are derived from truths from psychology and social psychology about how to help persuade people to take a certain course of action. Although these techniques usually are associated with substance abuse treatment, they are also of proven effectiveness in the fields of health, mental health, and child welfare. Motivational interviewing has been used successfully, for example, to promote medical compliance in the taking of antipsychotic medication (Wallace, 2005). It has possibilities in fields such as batterer education programming that are only beginning to be recognized.

This format is of proven effectiveness in substance abuse treatment (Project MATCH, 1993). Actually, the effectiveness of this model of person-centered counseling should come as no surprise; each of its basic principles is derived from strategies that have been shown to be effective in social psychology laboratory situations. The overall technique of eliciting a self-motivating statement from the client is perhaps the most basic of these scientific insights. We have filtered from one of the most popular books on social psychology—*The Social Animal* by Elliot Aronson (2007)—the basic principles of persuasion. The ones that most closely parallel the principles of motivational enhancement are these:

- If we are encouraged to state a position, we become motivated to defend that position (p. 85).
- When individuals commit themselves in a small way, the likelihood that they will commit themselves further is increased. The behavior needs to be justified so attitudes are changed (p. 158).
- People with high self-esteem are more likely to resist the temptation to commit immoral acts (p. 186).
- A person can become committed to a situation by making a decision, working hard to attain a goal (p. 186).
- Dissonance theory predicts that people will change their attitudes to bring them in line with the evidence (p. 189).
- Changing one's attitudes in order to justify one's behavior can initiate the processes that are persistent over time (p. 193).
- People desire dissonance-reducing behavior (p. 198).

Keep these teachings in mind in your study of motivational strategies and compare them with less scientific attempts to get people to break their bad habits and self-destructive behavior.

In their seven-part professional training videotape series, Miller, Rollnick, and Moyers (1998) provide guidance in the art and science of motivational enhancement. In this series, the don'ts are as revealing as the dos. According to this therapy team, the don'ts, or traps for therapists to avoid, are:

- A premature focus, such as on the addictive behavior
- The confrontational/denial round between therapist and client
- The labeling trap—forcing the individual to accept a label, such as alcoholic or addict
- The blaming trap, a fallacy that is especially pronounced in couples counseling

- The question/answer format, which is characterized by asking several questions in a row and reliance on closed yes-or-no responses, which exchange paves the way for the expert trap
- The expert trap, whereby the client is put down (the opposite of a collaborative exchange of information)

These precautions are especially relevant to work with teens, as is the motivational theorists' handling of client ambivalence about change. Specific strategies can be tailored for the individual's readiness to cooperate with the therapist and make the desired changes. The following four stages, Miller and Rollnick (2002) derived from the work of Prochaska and DiClemente (1983), who investigated the process by which cigarette smokers came to quit their habit.

Precontemplation Stage

At the *precontemplation* stage, the primary tasks for the therapist are to establish rapport, to ask rather than to tell, and to build trust. When there is resistance, as there inevitably will be with young substance abusers, Miller and Rollnick (2002) advise rolling with the resistance instead of fighting. The practitioner's role at this stage is educational; the goal is to build client awareness. Wallace (2005) presents the example of a parolee who when asked what his reason is for coming to treatment says it is to stay out of jail. In other words, the individual is concerned only with external coercion.

As he states in the videotape on motivational enhancement, Miller is uncomfortable with the concept of *resistance*; his preference is to think of clients as simply cautious in trusting the therapist. To establish this trust and enable the client to elicit the desired self-motivated or insightful statements, such as "I think I do have a problem," the skilled therapist relies on open and multifaceted questions, reflective listening, and purposeful summarizing of the client's story. Key to this process is the reframing of the client's story in the direction of decision making. A format such as "I sense that you are saying, on one hand, that smoking means a lot to you and, on the other hand, that you are beginning to have some health concerns about the damage that the smoking is causing you or may cause you in the future" provides helpful feedback to the reluctant client by reflecting back to him or her what is heard.

Contemplation Stage

During the *contemplation* stage, the client may show some movement in the direction of a more intrinsic motivation for treatment. For example, he or she might express a reason for being in treatment that is more intrinsic in nature, such as working on some areas of concern. If substance abuse is one such area, the counselor, in the hope of tipping the decision toward reduced drug/alcohol use, will emphasize the client's freedom of choice. "No one can make this decision for you" is a typical way to phrase this sentiment. Information is presented in a neutral, take-it-or-leave-it manner. Typical questions are: "What do you get out of drinking?" "What is the down side?" and (to elicit strengths) "What makes your sister believe in your ability to do this?"

Preparation and Action Stages

At the *preparation* and *action* stages for change, questions such as "What do you think will work for you?" will help guide the client forward without pushing too far too fast. Use of reflective summarizing statements is helpful—for example, "Let's see if I've got this right. You have a concern that I'm trying to get you to give up smoking and drinking all at once. We do seem to be moving along too fast. Why don't we look at some things people have done in this situation, some of the options you might want to consider?" Central to this whole treatment strategy is the belief that clients are amenable to change and that timing is crucial in persuading them to take the steps that will free them from harm.

The Substance Abuse and Mental Health Services Administration (1999) book *TIP 35: Enhancing Motivation for Change in Substance Abuse Treatment* is available online at www.ncbi.nlm.nih.gov/books/bv.fcgi?rid=hstat5 .chapter.61302. Chapter 6 of *TIP 35* contains William Miller's Change Plan Worksheet to guide the action plan at this last stage of the motivational process. The worksheet consists of a sheet of paper with these headings spaced a little over an inch apart:

The changes I want to make are

_____

The most important reasons why I want to make these changes are

_____

The steps I plan to take in changing are

_____

The ways other people can help me are

_____

I will know that my plan is working if

_____

Some things that could interfere with my plan are

_____

This worksheet can be used to guide the counselor during this treatment phase. It can be filled out through dialogue with the counselor or used in group work for members to fill out periodically and discuss in the group. The five basic principles of this model as enunciated by Miller and Rollnick (2002) are:

1. Roll with resistance.
2. Express empathy.
3. Avoid argumentation.
4. Develop discrepancy.
5. Support self-efficacy.

These tenets underlie the specific strategies that are used as part of the harm reduction approach in addictions counseling and as a part of a strengths approach in correctional counseling. We have discussed empathy earlier. Avoiding argumentation is obvious. Here we focus on the other three tenets: rolling with resistance, developing discrepancy, and supporting self-efficacy.

Roll with Resistance

Cowger et al. (2006) urge an understanding of client resistance as opposition to oppression rather than as a refusal to comply with a certain process of treatment. Sometimes, however, as they recognize, the resistant behaviors become maladaptive to the client's goals. This is especially true for the offender bent on achieving or maintaining freedom from the oppression of imprisonment. Positive forms of resistance to an abusive system can be suggested or reinforced.

The power of words, as we have seen, is evidenced in promoting or disarming hostility. Fighting words may entail unintentional put-downs or be explosive in themselves. Anger management workshops help participants to phrase their requests and needs through use of I statements. In contrast to you statements—for example, "You get on my nerves"—I statements allow for nonaccusatory feedback. An example from the therapist's perspective is provided in this statement given by a social worker who shares with a late-arriving client:

> When you did not show up for our scheduled appointment, I have to admit I felt annoyed and even put down because I got the feeling you didn't really care about continuing the work we were doing together.

In response to oppositional behavior, the motivational approach draws on good listening skills, empathy, and acceptance of the client as a person. It is hard to fight with someone who does not want to fight with you, who listens receptively to what you want to say, and who does not threaten you. In the same vein, the correctional counselor who describes a prison love relationship as lesbian may hit a brick wall. A safe approach is to use the word that the client uses—friend, girlfriend, partner, wife, for example.

Saleebey (2006) warns against use of negative labels, jargon, and bureaucratic language and judgmental statements in responding to client hostility. Joining the resistance by aligning yourself with the client's feelings about the system is a further recommended strategy for dispelling resistance. In correctional counseling, this is tricky, however. The counselor must be prepared to be quoted to the authorities. A hostile inmate very likely will report criticism of jail or prison administrators or of their rules to the front office. Working in the substance abuse field may require reporting to the court or the child welfare department any continued use of substances by the client. Sometimes clients must take routine urinalyses (van Wormer & Davis, 2008). Helping clients understand the reasons for some of the seemingly asinine rules may be the smartest strategy, under these circumstances.

Develop Discrepancy (or Challenging)

Sometimes positive reframing is insufficient to change behavior, and a more direct approach is required. Unfortunately, due to some overzealous use of this strategy in substance abuse treatment centers, the word *confrontation* has taken on a decidedly negative tone. In previous decades, this kind of confrontation, and especially in substance abuse treatment circles, was designed to break down defenses. Research has shown, however, that this type of harsh approach does not help the client recover

(Miller & Rollnick, 2002). The classic confrontation usually starts with phraseology such as:

> On one hand, you say you want to keep your friends, but on the other hand, you drank alcohol to the point of agitation and annoying your friend. What do you think of that? (Wallace, p. 213)

Or

> I sense you want to go deeper into explaining your relationship with your father, yet when the subject comes up you change the subject. I'm beginning to see a pattern here.

My preference is to use the term *challenge* rather than *confrontation*. This term is more consistent with the empowerment approach. One may challenge a client who is withdrawn to disclose more information about herself. I have used these challenges to seemingly nonresponsive clients with good effect:

- I sense you're a much more feeling person than you show on the surface.
- What was it like, Linda, when you were small and you wanted to show your feelings of anger?

This is a little like positive reframing discussed earlier in that it assumes the client wishes to express herself and will do so if given the chance.

Promoting Self-Efficacy

Self-efficacy is a person's belief or confidence in his or her ability to overcome barriers and carry out a given behavior successfully. Promoting self-efficacy is an important part in actually getting someone who is motivated to change to take some steps in that direction.

Female correctional clients often suffer from a low opinion of themselves; they feel rejected by society and tend to internalize this rejection. The correctional counselor can teach clients to refrain from the little put-downs that are likely to come up in conversation. "Say something positive about yourself" is a good response to such self-denigrating remarks.

Positive reframing relies on careful working to help a client reconceptualize events in a more positive light. Motivational treatment uses reframing as a technique to deal with client ambivalence by helping him or her move in the direction of the desired change. For instance, the shift from "I am a reformed drunk" to "I am a recovering alcoholic" involves a totally different framework for viewing oneself as a person who has a disease. Similar is the shift from

"I'm a criminal," to "I'm a person who did some things I shouldn't have done, but now I'm getting my life in order."

A supervisee is taught to rephrase the sentence "You seem to have difficulty talking" into something like "Today, you really opened up and expressed yourself." The strategy here is to reinforce the positive and therefore get a more positive response. In this way, the therapist can address a delicate issue without hitting the client when he or she is down.

"You think I'm crazy, don't you?" is a question commonly asked by those diagnosed as mentally ill. Taken off guard, the novice counselor may be stumped for an answer. And the wrong response (either yes *or* no) can be risky. The seasoned professional might answer:

> We prefer to call your problem a psychosis. Basically, you have a chemical imbalance which can be controlled through medication. The doctor can give you something that will stop those visions you've been having.

The counselor in this scenario is using language that is at once professional and simple while at the same time conveying hope and reducing the stigma of the condition. There are many opportunities to help women see themselves in a more positive light as they tell their stories.

Use of the Personal Narrative

As Saleebey (2006) states, "There is something liberating, for all parties involved, in connecting to clients' stories and narratives, their hopes and fears, their wherewithal and resources rather than trying to stuff them into the narrow confines of a diagnostic category or treatment protocol" (p. 18). This brings us to use of the personal narrative as the optimal device for building insights, for locating strength and possibility, and for client-counselor sharing. Use of the narrative is consistent with the definition of empowerment drawn from feminist therapy offered by GlenMaye (1997): "Empowerment is speaking the truth of one's life in one's own voice, and working collectively to create that possibility for all" (p. 35).

Whereas objective testing offers one thing (objective facts for placing the client in specific categories), the use of the narrative offers quite something else. This "something else" is the personal side of the individual's offending and revelations about the social conditions of the girl's or woman's life that got her into trouble. Narrative therapy is culturally sensitive. Bacon (2007) has found this approach to be successful as a counseling intervention in helping

Australian indigenous alcoholics curb their drinking problems. In its attending to ways in which gender, culture, and social context shape the client's worldview, both worker and client have their consciousness raised. Through empathy, the client's reality becomes the counselor's reality as well. For example, an offender from an immigrant background may reveal a truth of intergenerational trauma and marginalization that is a revelation to both the storyteller (who may gain new insights through the sharing) and her listener. The revelation may be built on later to indicate a linking of the personal and the political in a life story involving oppression. Such personal storytelling is a useful device for prison English teachers, including teachers of English as a second language.

Through entering the world of the storyteller, the practitioner comes to grasp the client's reality, the suffering and defeat, while at the same time attending to signs of initiative, hope, and frustration with past counterproductive behavior that can help the client move toward a healthier outlook on life. The strengths therapist, in continually reinforcing the positive, seeks to help the client move away from what Van Den Bergh (1995, p. xix) calls "paralyzing narratives." Counselors and group leaders can draw on women's narratives to help them reauthor their lives (Brown, 2007). Through careful questioning, the therapist introduces alternative ways of viewing reality and of providing hope thereby.

In narrative therapy, the woman tells her story, and together the client and therapist weave the fabric of meaning from themes in the story. Questions are introduced at key points to help the storyteller analyze events for alternative meanings. As people progress through the stages of personal growth, their narratives will change. During the initial stages of counseling, the woman's story will likely answer the question, "Who am I?" The therapist not only listens, therefore, but co-creates with the client a story that contains within it solutions as well as problems (Brown, 2007). Clients who like to write can do so between sessions and share their autobiographies, poems, and other creations with the therapist. The therapist will want to discourage criminal justice clients to get beyond the specifics of their court cases (e.g., "my lawyer told me") to reflect on the matters relevant to the task at hand.

Through an investigation the stories that women construct around the histories that brought them to prison, McQuaide and Ehrenreich (1998) discovered a distinctly gendered pattern. Whereas a man may have participated in a robbery for money, for example, a woman may have participated at the insistence of the man. Alternatively, a woman may have gotten involved in drugs as a form of escape or self-medication due to the trauma of past or current victimization. Thus, for the woman, the commission of a crime may be driven by an attempt to solve a problem that, on the face of it, bears no relation to the crime itself. And however nontherapeutic the correctional environment may be, McQuaide and Ehrenreich argue that for some women, their earlier lives may have been so harrowing that prison actually may provide a respite from a traumatizing and disempowering world. At the same time, the dehumanization of prison body searches and other intrusions may be retraumatizing to those with a history of sexual abuse. In any case, knowledge through the stories of the lives women led before prison is essential to understanding their relationship to the law and with those who work within the correctional system.

Listening to the personal narratives of women who have gotten into so much trouble and dealing with the effects of so much trauma and retraumatization in clients can lead to vicarious reactions by correctional counselors. In an article on the phenomenon of what is sometimes called "compassion fatigue" or "secondary trauma," Beaucar (1999) discusses the need for social workers to be able to share with their colleagues their feelings of being overwhelmed, especially when working in a milieu not conducive to resilience. She advises that kidding around with colleagues, doing fun things with clients, and using humor as a coping mechanism can help counter the inevitable feelings of disappointment in correctional work. On the bright side of institutional counseling, clients in the prison setting are highly motivated, often with time on their hands, and eager to talk to a professional.

A useful exercise is to have women tell or write about a major turning point in their lives. However the personal biography is presented, a cognitive approach is helpful to get clients to focus objectively on the whole of their lives and to identify any patterns that might be self-defeating. According to Corcoran (2005), cognitive therapy is the *why* and motivational interviewing is the *how*. A focus on personal cognitions directs attention toward unhealthy, fatalistic patterns of viewing the world. But many cognitive theorists (e.g., Ellis, 2001) force clients to listen to the therapists' analysis of client thinking errors. A gender-strengths approach, in contrast, espouses a collaborative method whereby the therapist guides the client through positive reinforcement as the client simultaneously guides the therapist through her life story.

The concept *suspension of disbelief* borrows from studies of ancient Greek literature and was adapted by Saleebey (2006) as one of the key concepts of the strengths perspective. It has special relevance for narrative work with offenders. In contradistinction to the usual practice in interviewing known liars, con artists, and thieves, which is to protect yourself from being used or manipulated, this approach would have the practitioner temporarily suspend skepticism or disbelief and enter the client's world as he or she presents it. To the extent that involuntary clients may "have us on," as Saleebey (2006) acknowledges, we should regard this as a reaction to their loss of freedom, a form of resistance that may be abandoned once trust is developed. A willingness to listen to the client's own explanations and perceptions ultimately encourages the emergence of the client's truth.

Goal Setting

As the woman tells her life story, she shares her pain, worries, and hopes for the future. Her narration also is apt to show instances of how she survived and helped others in times of great difficulty. From the difficulties and wishes revealed in the narrative, the process of setting goals can emerge quite naturally. Such goal setting is a typical requirement of most treatment plans. Most conventional treatment agencies require that a record be kept of client goals and that goals be individualized, tangible, and achievable and expanded over time (Corcoran, 2005). Assertiveness, developing healthier eating habits and other practices, making better use of leisure time, reducing feelings of depression, and reaching out to make friends are typical treatment goals in any setting. The typical case management treatment plan provides a client with a chart with these blank columns to be filled in: goals toward achievement, who takes responsibility, date to be accomplished, date accomplished, and comments.

Goals provide a structure and focus for therapy sessions; they provide a later measure of treatment effectiveness as well as a focus toward which clients might work between sessions; they help clients build on strengths toward definable ends. Empowerment goals include these and other psychosocial goals, such as learning to express oneself, developing a group consciousness, recovery from a background of personal oppression, and reducing self-blame.

De Jong and Berg (2002) offer some useful guidelines for helping clients set goals from a solution-based standpoint. In the typical session, clients talk about some seemingly insurmountable problem. A useful technique toward helping clients locate their own solution is to draw their attention to an exception to the problem, bad day, or bad feeling. This sample dialogue with a woman who is clearly overwhelmed shows how the client's attention can be refocused:

Worker: When was the last time you felt real good?
Client: I don't know; maybe one day three weeks ago.
Worker: What was different about that day? (p. 105)

The process is slow, but together practitioner and client discover how things might be better in an emphasis on *exceptions* to the malaise. A possible goal might be to develop greater confidence and feel less anxious about the future. Possible means to the end might be to work on replacing negative thoughts with positive thinking and to follow a definite program for tackling the situation that needs to be changed.

Note that the strengths perspective puts the emphasis on solutions rather than problems. Corcoran (2005), similarly, stresses the asking of questions such as, for example: "What's better about your life right now?" This approach increases the chances of uncovering exceptions (to pain and misery) and associated strengths on which to build future strengths.

Useful techniques for helping the client make the shift from a negative to a positive direction are paraphrasing what the client said in your own words, perhaps with an added emphasis, and summarizing the client's story by pulling together the themes at regular intervals. To illustrate a summary statement, let us use an example of summarizing for a prison inmate who was denied parole on the first try and who does not want to ever risk such disappointment again:

> "Not getting approved for parole is a real setback. I'm sensing that you're feeling discouraged enough not to want to plan to try again in the future. You took a major risk in coming up for parole at all, knowing how hurtful it would be if you were turned down. It sounds like you came really close to being successful. I'm wondering if you might be protecting yourself from more hurt when you say you're through getting your hopes up."

In the making of a therapist, techniques alone are necessary but not sufficient. One key ingredient that is missing in most discussions is what I call the therapeutic imagination. This term is roughly comparable to C. Wright Mills's (1959) concept of the sociological imagination. The *therapeutic imagination* refers to that combination of empathy, suspension of disbelief, insight, and resourcefulness that makes for a caring and productive therapy relationship. In working with female offenders, our role is often that of intermediaries between the institution and the individual in a mutual effort toward discovery. Drawing on our therapeutic imagination makes it possible to experience the beauty of relationship against the bureaucratic assaults in the search for purpose and meaning.

SUMMARY

In this chapter we have taken the female offender on a journey that started with building a therapeutic relationship, a relationship that helped women discover their strengths and resiliencies but also the risks they face. We have seen the power in storytelling. And we have examined the power of words in establishing rapport so essential to an empowering relationship. Well-chosen words, as we have seen, are powerful. They can heal, subdue, or provoke.

The challenge of this chapter has been to present an approach designed to women's special needs within a paternalistic system for hardened male convicts. For this purpose, I have taken an empowerment, strengths-based framework and adapted it for direct practice with the female correctional client. I have also freely drawn from the science of motivational interviewing (informed by a cognitive approach) and the art of person-centered counseling. To help motivate correctional clients for treatment and to establish a working relationship, the therapist needs to draw on the language and concepts of these women, hearing their pain and anguish in order to thereby enter their world.

The counseling process is at once a science and an art. We have presented the first two stages of a gender-sensitive five-stage model built on relationship and motivational theory in this chapter. Now we turn our attention to the feeling, healing, and generativity dimensions.

Chapter 7

TEACHING LIFE SKILLS AND PROMOTING HEALING

I was angry with my friend:
I told my wrath, my wrath did end.
I was angry with my foe:
I told it not, my wrath did grow.
                    —**William Blake**, "A Poison Tree," 1793

When thinking is out of whack, feelings are out of control as well. An essential aspect of any counseling work is to take a close look at the thinking/feeling relationship. For prison inmates, the possession of adaptive coping skills is crucial to prepare them for the crises, temptations, and parenting challenges they face in the institution and, later, release (Wallace, 2005). Otherwise they unwittingly may sabotage themselves and jeopardize their chances for freedom.

As we learned in Chapter 6, a focus on client cognitions is an essential part of motivational enhancement. This is because motivation and thinking are intertwined. Developed by Aaron Beck (1991), cognitive therapy is based on the theory that the way a person thinks determines how he or she feels and behaves. A person's depressed state of mind, for example, may be linked to recurring negative self-concepts. Self-defeating self-talk ("I will never be able to do it," "I am a born loser") inclines the individual toward depression characterized by a general flatness of affect. The utter pessimism and, in some cases, the hopelessness that are common symptoms of depression stand in the way of the development of a healthy lifestyle.

Think of this as the feeling and healing chapter. In the limits of space, only some of the major troubling feelings are discussed here—anger, grief and loss, guilt and shame, anxiety, depression. And love as well, which we might consider the source of our greatest joy and greatest sorrow. It is my experience that women can easily distinguish these emotions from each other but that some men who are in tune with their visceral response to anger require some remedial work in differentiating what we might call the finer emotions.

A discussion of these basic human feelings and the teaching of strategies to handle them in a mature fashion form the core of this chapter. These emotions are selected because of their special relevance for the lives and daily crises that female offenders face, whether they are serving time in prison or are on parole or probation in the community. Because of the close link between negative feelings and use of mood-altering substances, feeling work forms the basis of most substance abuse treatment programs. There is a correlation between strong feelings, such as anger, irrational hatreds, and jealousy, in outbursts of violence; for this reason, work in these areas is important in quelling such outbursts. A realization of the source of too-strong feelings can be helpful in controlling them. Practice in identifying and examining underlying assumptions and beliefs can help clients take responsibility for their own emotional responses to certain people and situations. Following the discussion of the science and art of feeling work, this chapter concludes with sections on healing and generativity.

COGNITIVE THERAPY

The popularity of cognitive therapy is based on its successful applications to a variety of clinical problems including depression, anxiety, relationship issues, personality disorders, and substance abuse, areas of key concern to female offenders. Didactic instead of dogmatic, the mode of cognitive-behavioral therapy is both egalitarian and educational in nature. Designated roles for the cognitive therapist are teacher, listener, clarifier, and coach.

Cognitive-oriented therapy assumes that it is often offenders' self-defeating thoughts, and resulting feelings and actions, that sabotage their lives. Uncontrolled depression may lead to a self-defeating pattern of behavior such as fighting and drug abuse. The legal or social problems that result, in turn, further distort thinking and can induce a sense of paranoia: "People are out to get me." Whether these distortions of reality originate in some underlying organic disorder, such as low serotonin levels in the brain, they still can be controlled to a large extent by careful monitoring (Beck, Rush, Shaw, & Emory, 1979; Schwartz & Begley, 2003). An intensive treatment program utilizing cognitive theory and techniques can offer a powerful mechanism for turning things around. Intervention in the cognitive realm is relatively easy to do, nonthreatening, and conducive to short-term, demonstrable results.

Clients who are motivated to work on their problems are often very receptive to the intellectual exercises involved in cognitive work. Although they sometimes balk when asked directly to work on their feelings, clients often will readily participate in work on thinking patterns and belief systems, especially when brief exercises and checklists are provided. The counselor can introduce such items to the client in a casual way, saying, for example, "How would you like to..." or "Here's something we might enjoy doing."

Showing clients a checklist of common irrational ideas believed at times by all of us is an effective way of eliciting self-disclosure while heightening insight. A sample list of illogical beliefs may include:

- All-or-nothing thinking
- Jumping to negative conclusions
- Overgeneralizing about others
- Making mountains out of molehills
- Putting down members of your own group (such as other women)
- Self-blaming
- I can't live without a certain person
- I must be perfect
- Everyone must like me
- If things do not go according to plan, it is a catastrophe
- I never forgive or forget a wrong
- People are either all good or all bad

Sometimes just the act of classifying certain thought patterns in terms of categories, such as "catastrophizing" or "all-or-nothing thinking," can bring about a major improvement in this area. In talking to a counselor who is non-judgmental and enthusiastic about analyzing thought processes we all share, women will begin to question and challenge many of their long-held assumptions and recognize that they can change the way they feel (depressed, anxious, guilty) by being more accepting of themselves and of others.

For easy-to-follow instructions for challenging common self-defeating thought patterns, see Albert Ellis's (2001) *Overcoming Destructive Beliefs, Feelings, and Behaviors*. The discussions of recovery from addiction and trauma are especially relevant to work with women who are in conflict with the law and with themselves. A cognitive exercise that can be used in either individual or group therapy is to write A, B, and C on a paper and leave spaces between each. A is the activating event that caused you pain; B stands for believing-emoting-behaving, or the interaction between the idea you had about this event and behavior; and C is for the consequences of your emotion or behavior.

A cognitive-behavioral therapy (CBT) approach has been found to be a highly effective component of substance abuse treatment. The National Institute on Drug Abuse (2008) offers details of a manual-driven, highly structured program for treating cocaine addiction. This manual follows the 20/20/20 rule: The first 20 minutes of the session is for open discussion and checking in; during the second 20 minutes the therapist presents the session topic and teaches a particular skill; the third 20 minutes is spent exploring the client's understanding and reactions to the training. Specific instructions for organizing this format and responding to client reactions are available at www.nida.nih.gov/TXManuals/CBT/CBT5.html. From a woman's and strengths-based perspective, this CBT format needs to be modified to be less confrontational and geared toward women's needs. The reliance on urine tests conducted by the clinician is not conducive to establishing rapport and a sense of mutual trust, in my opinion. My recommendation would be to include family sessions in treatment for validation of client progress in maintaining sobriety.

Ellis's (2001) CBT approach forms the basis of many of the exercise manuals widely used in the correctional system to help addicts and others work on their thinking errors. I have examined several of these manuals and found the questions to be overwhelmingly negative. Questions asked are apparently designed to elicit self-blaming responses and make participants feel bad about the losses associated with their addictive behaviors. Using the same cognitive principles, we can turn this focus around, however, and ask questions designed to elicit self-enhancing responses. Instead of asking, for example, "Tell about a time when you hurt someone because of your intoxication," we might ask, "Tell about a time when you wanted to drink more but controlled your drinking because of concern for another person." The point I am making is that a cognitive approach is flexible and, in the hands of a strengths-based therapist, can serve to help people with low self-esteem feel empowered by showing them they have more control over their lives than they realize. To help women turn their lives around, we first must help them realize they can do so.

Leukefeld et al. (2009) conducted a cognitively based intervention with soon-to-be-released female inmates in Kentucky to help them protect themselves from contracting or transmitting HIV/AIDS. Most of the participants were African American. The researchers focused on demolishing false beliefs that were found to be prevalent among these women, placing them at high risk. Among the myths accepted were: "Having sex without protection will strengthen my relationship," "I have to use sex to get what I want," and "I can use drugs and still make healthy decisions about sex" (p. 27). When compared to a group of women who received a video-only intervention, the women who received five sessions of activities to counter the thinking myths and build skills for promoting safe behaviors significantly reduced their risky behavior following release.

FEELING WORK

The starting point for behavior change is a collaborative analysis of the thinking/feeling dyad. It is not the situation, but our *view* of the situation, after all, that is at the heart of many emotional problems. Underlying most of the problems for which people seek counseling—whether for depression, addiction, anger, or uncontrollable violence—is an unbearable level of emotional pain. The challenge for the worker is to help the client separate the feelings from the thoughts and the thoughts from the actions as a first step toward alleviating the pain.

If we agree with cognitive therapist Aaron Beck that thinking and feeling are intertwined (see Beck et al., 1979; Beck, 1991), we probably would figure that behind much debilitating anger and depression is irrational thought. And like cognitive therapists, we would help people with emotional disturbances work on their underlying thought processes. In contrast to Yochelson and Samenow (1976), who targeted cognitive distortions as a way of knocking down criminals' defense mechanisms, the gender-sensitive therapist would challenge such distortions in the interests of empowerment. The cognitive approach, after all, can just as well be directed toward building one's sense of self-worth as combating criminal attitudes.

The starting point for working on feeling is often the teaching, perhaps in a lecture form, the four basic feelings: anger, sadness, fear, and happiness (Corcoran, 2005). Once the client has learned to identify these and dozens more, Corcoran recommends a journaling exercise in which the client, as homework, writes down several feelings per day with a brief explanation of what triggered them.

Anger

Many men in treatment are so alienated from all feelings except for anger that they have to begin by learning to label other feelings. Feelings such as hurt, jealousy, and even fear tend to be expressed as anger. Women, however, are more apt to have a wider range of emotional expressiveness, all except for feelings of anger, which may be suppressed (Sorbello, Eccleston, Ward, & Jones, 2002). Among offenders of both genders, anger may cause problems either in its inappropriate manifestation (such as in periodic explosions of rage) or in its suppression. Sometimes anger at one source (e.g., at the judicial system) is displaced onto another (the counselor or correctional officer).

Reports of gender-based anger management group work, although scarce, show that women participants benefit through becoming more aware of their anger, identifying stress causes of anger, and developing managing strategies (Sorbello et al., 2002). Knowledge of feeling and the thought processes connected with these feelings (I hate my mother, hate myself) will help clients work toward change. One useful exercise for helping clients get in touch with their feelings includes four steps:

1. Identify what you are thinking right now. How do these thoughts make you feel?
2. Listen to your self-talk. Look for extremes in thinking; avoid use of words such as *never, can't, always,* and *everybody.*
3. Examine objective reality. Once the facts are identified, relax, take a deep breath, and repeat them *out loud* three times. (For example, "I used drugs to escape from problems. I now have learned solid coping skills and I have been clean for two years. My children are proud of me. My life is not ruined."
4. Note how your feelings change.

The message should be truthful and realistic, given the client's abilities and situation, not insincere positive statements. Statements should be consistent with a healthy, moderate outlook on life, not of the order of Muhammad Ali's "I am the greatest" bravado.

In feeling work, the role of the therapist can be conceived of as a coach. The first step in feeling work is to assess the woman's awareness of her inner-body or visceral responses to different emotions and her ability to differentiate one from another. Clients can be encouraged, often in groups, to name a feeling, then to describe it in physical terms, providing a gut-level, *visceral* description. Rudimentary feelings of special relevance to offenders are: anger, guilt, depression, fear and anxiety, and love in its many manifestations.

Anger Management

Generally the anger management programs offered to women do not differ from those designed for men. This is a mistake. Gender differences in the awareness and expression of anger suggest the need for women-centered approaches here as elsewhere (Sorbello et al., 2002). Female clients (and students) typically describe these visceral responses to anger:

I'm told I feel the blood drain out of my body. (indicating readiness to fight)
I feel hot, I'm boiling over, and can hardly breathe.
My body tightens up.
I don't know what anger feels like.
I cry.

Women placed on probation and at risk of loss of their children harbor feelings of resentment and often see the authorities as messing up their lives. Women in confinement have many more sources of anger from the cruelties they have faced, but, above all, they are angry at themselves. Some let go of the anger rapidly and get into more trouble; others internalize their rage, letting it build to destructive levels. That there is a lower public acceptance of female expression of anger goes without saying. Middle-class women do not ordinarily fight with each other. But for lower-class, minority girls in the United States, especially those involved in criminal behavior, aggression and violent outbursts are more common (Centers for Disease Control and Prevention, 2006). Female inner-city gang members often fight each other, sometimes over a boyfriend.

There are many unproven assumptions about anger—that it does not exist at all as a primary emotion, that anger is really depression, or that depression is anger turned within. In *Mistakes Were Made (But Not by Me)*, Tavris and Aronson (2008), examine the scientific evidence or lack of evidence concerning anger, the misunderstood emotion. Myths pertaining to anger that they have demolished include that:

- Suppressing anger is dangerous to health
- Anger can be uprooted as if it were a turnip
- Anger invariably is the key factor in depression, hysteria, bad dreams, and so on

In fact, anger often builds on itself; ventilating anger is cathartic only if it restores your sense of control.

Of all the treatment modalities for addiction, motivational enhancement therapy has been found to be the most effective when applied to people who are hostile or angry. Establishing empathy with clients can get to the source of their anger and enable them to develop more understanding of other people's motives. If clients can understand the motivation for others' actions and learn not to take them personally, the irrational wave of anger should diminish.

Sometimes anger that surfaces, in fact, is a cover for another, deeper emotion, such as a feeling of betrayal or even insecurity. An intriguing question to ask the perpetually angry client is: "If you weren't feeling anger, what would you be feeling?" The answer may be a revelation to the client as well as to the therapist.

Programs for male offenders, such as batterers, often include anger management training to teach appropriate means of expressing anger. Women more often have difficulty labeling or expressing anger. They may feel angry on the inside but suppress it. Some become compulsive house-cleaners, energizing themselves in the endless war on dust and dirt. Such individuals need coaching to help them learn to absorb the angry feeling without fear and to mobilize that energy in more productive channels. Anger-avoiding individuals, in short, should work on expressing anger, while those who have difficulty containing their anger should work to master the deescalating techniques of anger management.

A phenomenon well noted among feminist writers is how often women turn their anger on other women. Often women condemn other women in competition over a man. Society, as reflected in media portrayals and the working world, often sets up women as tokens and rivals. In any case, women locked up together in prison tend to be female bashing. Women need to recognize where their resentment of other women is coming from and that their low opinion of women may be related to lack of pride in their own womanliness.

Correctional workers themselves sometimes are given to angry responses. The bureaucratic dictates would drive those with even the best temperaments up the walls. Clients sent for treatment by the criminal justice system are at times more captive than captivating. When the worker feels him- or herself reacting to an individual client with an inappropriately strong sense of anger or rage, it is helpful to explore the possibility of countertransference. The worker can ask: Who does this client remind me of? What does the situation represent to me? Putting him- or herself in the client's place is also helpful in dispelling destructive reactions and overreactions.

Anger management is a specific skills training program popular with prison populations and widely supported in women's prisons because officers believe female offenders to have major problems in this area. When men fight in prison, their fights are often covert; women fight openly and with a lot of yelling and screaming (J. M. Pollock, 1998). Programs teaching anger management are not only about prison discipline; they are empowering because they help give women more control over themselves and their lives, as Pollock suggests. When combined with assertiveness training, these programs teach women how to express themselves so as to have a greater impact on their surroundings and the treatment they receive.

Anger management training teaches where anger comes from, what triggers extreme anger and why, and that there is nothing wrong with having stormy feelings. Learning to express anger verbally, calmly—for example, to say "When you do… I feel insulted (or rejected, or annoyed)"—instead of lashing out physically or with cursing is the goal of the women in the program. Teaching people to be more self-aware of bodily cues such as a racing heart, the program at the institute helps people to protect themselves from chronic anger (Demaree, Harrison, & Rhodes, 2000).

Gundersen and Svartdal (2006) present the steps for a cognitively based program that has been successfully used in the United States and Norway with adolescents who have problems with self-control. Called Aggression Replacement Training, this five-part approach to anger management consists of these cognitive steps:

1. Identify events and internal statements that trigger strong emotions.
2. Recognize the physiological cues that alert learners to anger (e.g., tense jaw, flushed face, clenched hands).
3. Use self-talk to calm down, such as the command "cool down."
4. Employ strategies for keeping control (e.g., breathing deeply, counting, changing irrational thoughts, walking away, exercising).
5. Evaluate how well anger was controlled.

Persons who are hostile and prone to outbursts of anger, according to psychologist Steven Stosny (2008), the author of *Love without Hurt*, can control these feelings by learning empathy. Hostile and angry people such as batterers and child abusers seem incapable of putting themselves in the other person's shoes. (See also van Wormer and Roberts, *Death by Domestic Violence*, 2009.) From Stosny's perspective, clients with anger problems need to tap into their capacity for empathy with the persons who are the objects of their anger.

For overcoming problems related to anger, group exercises can be especially helpful. Clients can be encouraged to keep a daily log of events conducive to anger and the thoughts and feelings that are aroused. The purpose of the exercise is to provide data for the clients, group participants, and group leader to explore the triggers for the anger and to consider the possible root causes. A visualization exercise is recommended by Wallace (2005). In her counseling of clients with anger control problems, she uses a self-calming technique of repeating both aloud and then silently, "I am calm, centered, and balanced" (p. 225). Wallace has clients visualize themselves sitting in a safe place.

The learning of assertiveness skills can be invaluable in alleviating situations that are the cause of distress. Women in confinement living in very close proximity with other women from diverse backgrounds and forced to relate to corrections officers from positions of extreme powerlessness can benefit tremendously from work on communication skills. Girls in residential centers can avoid a lot of arguing and misunderstandings if they learn to communicate their needs in an inoffensive fashion. And female offenders in the community can be counseled individually or with their spouses and partners to enhance their relationship. These rules, as presented in Box 7.1, can be copied and shared with clients.

BOX 7.1

Rules for Resolving Conflict (Assertiveness Training)

Often the differences that arise between people can be understood in terms of a clash in cultural background and upbringing. These differences may not be personal at all. Some conflict in the home is inevitable in a pluralistic society such as the United States. In any case, everyday conflicts between partners can be alleviated or prevented by developing skills in communication techniques for resolving differences. Skills in conflict resolution can be learned and practiced with a teacher or social worker and applied in actual situations. These techniques have been found to be helpful in resolving conflict and restoring goodwill between opposing groups or factions as well as in subduing heated marital disputes.

Here is a step-by-step framework for resolving a problem with another individual. The theme of this approach is to bring about the most change while doing the least amount of harm.

Step 1. Formulating the Problem

Meaning of the Behavior

Before putting your concern into words, try to get at the root of what is really disturbing you. Do you object to the person's behavior because he or she reminds you of someone else? Is your own insecurity or intolerance causing distress? Think about what is bugging you, and be sure you are not being unreasonable, possessive or overly protective, or snooping. Sound out your complaint with trusted friends to make sure it is a reasonable one. Analyze the objectionable behavior in terms of possible cultural or class patterns in upbringing of both yourself and the other party. Consider the participant's family background and family situation (birth order).

Choose an area where the other person can make a change. An area such as a serious illness or a judicial sentencing would not be negotiable. In relationships, financial planning, division of labor, child rearing, sexual behavior, family traditions, sleeping patterns, and bathroom sharing are examples of negotiable areas. In the criminal justice system, rule enforcement would be a likely area of focus.

Feeling Aroused by the Behavior

Identify your overt feelings (e.g., anger) and underlying feelings (e.g., hurt, guilt). Try to identify where these feelings are coming from. Be specific.

Wrong	Better
"You're secretive with me."	"When you get word of a death in your family and don't share it with me, I feel left out."
	"I feel rejected when you don't tell me where you've been."
"You're messy."	"I'd like you to squeeze the toothpaste from the bottom, not the top."
"Your drinking is getting out of hand."	"Last night you threw the chair across the room; and now you don't remember."
	"Last night you drank six cans of beer."

(*continued*)

Step 2. Choose an Appropriate Time and Place

Don't approach a friend or partner who is tired or intoxicated (or in the bathroom). Choose a private time and place to say "I'd like to talk. If now isn't convenient, let's schedule a time later."

Step 3. Keep These Rules in Mind

- Attack the *behavior*, not the *person* or his or her background. Use a pleasant tone of voice; avoid yelling, hitting, cursing, or name-calling. Deal with one issue at a time—otherwise, the other party will likely counter with "Well, if you think I'm bad, you ought to see how you come across" or "When you get your act together, I'll think about it!"
- No mind reading. Don't say "You are jealous" or "You're just angry because you . . ."
- Narrow the problem down to a manageable size rather than focusing on vague wholes.
- No accusations and put-downs, such as "You're just like your father!"
- Do not rehash the past.

Step 4. Making the Request

Sentence 1: I'm feeling troubled about . . .

- . . . the way rules are being enforced around here.
- . . . the way the workload has been distributed around here.
- . . . hearing all these lies.
- . . . finding someone's been here while I'm gone.

Sentence 2: I want a change in the situation so it's more fair.
Sentence 3: I'd like your help.
Respondent: I'll try to . . .
Sentence 4: I'd like something more definite. What I would like from you is . . .
Respondent: I'll cook on Mondays and Wednesdays.
Sentence 5: That would help a lot.

Step 5. Use Active Listening Skills

When you discuss the matter with the other party, listen to the response. A good technique is to rephrase what the person said by beginning with "What you're saying is ..." or "What I hear you saying is ... " Ask your listener to play the request back to you to make sure he or she hears what you are asking.

Follow-up Questions

This "growth fight" was successful if:

1. You feel better now than you did about yourself and the other person.
2. Your relationship has been helped.
3. The behavior in question has improved.
4. There are no hard feelings.
5. You expressed your feelings.
6. There is greater trust in the relationship.

This fair-fighting scheme can be used for a variety of relationships, such as mother/son, colleague/colleague, husband/wife, inmate/inmate, and inmate/staff. When misunderstandings are cleared up early in a relationship, the bad feelings have less time to fester. It is unfair to yourself and others not to point out the things that can be changed.

And you can derive strength by saying the Serenity Prayer:

> God grant me the Serenity
> To accept the things I cannot change,
> Courage to change the things I can,
> And the wisdom to know the difference.

> —Niebuhr, orig. 1934, 1987

All-or-Nothing Thinking

Because it is so rampant among offenders, especially those with addictive problems, we will take a close look at polarized, or all-or-nothing, thought. The all-or-nothing thrust ("Give me liberty or give me death") involves an extremeness in word and deed. It is a caricature of the American obsession with being number one. "Whatever you do, be the best at it," the saying goes. Related to perfectionism, the all-or-nothing (Black or White, or dichotomous) syndrome is broader than perfectionism because it tells what you will have if you are less than perfect—nothing. The all-or-nothing perspective is a split into either/or as opposed to both/and: *either* I am the greatest *or* I might as well quit; you are *either* my best friend *or* my worst enemy. Note the extreme elements in these statements from former alcoholic clients:

- I'll stay in jail until my time is served. No probation for me. When I get out, I want to be completely free. Otherwise, forget it!
- I expect to get an A in any course I take. Otherwise I'll drop it. Or just plain fail.
- I never tolerate any dirt in the kitchen. I say if you are going to clean it up, make it spotless.
- When I drink it's not to get high. It's to get rolling-on-the-floor drunk. Or else why drink at all?
- What do you mean I haven't completed my hours of court-mandated therapy? Just send me to jail then!
- I said to my daughter, "Either you mind me or get out of this house."

The destructiveness that ensues from such polarized thinking is immortalized in ancient and modern drama and recorded in death notices of suicides and crime reports of homicide. Depending on an individual's tendency to internalize or externalize pain, the means to end it all may range from merely quitting a job or running away to the ominous extremes of suicide or murder. A pattern of escape from difficult situations is an early clue of possible untimely death. The seeming desire to bury oneself in substance abuse can be conceptualized as merely another avenue of escape into nothingness. Whatever form the escape mode takes, the danger to self and others can be immense.

Self-Talk and Positive Restructuring

By learning positive self-talk and cognitive restructuring, clients can be actively helped to replace unhealthy responses to disturbing and anger-provoking situations with healthy and productive ones. Positive self-talk is taught by the counselor's juxtaposition of the client's defeatist cognition—"I might as well quit"—with more encouraging pronouncements—"I can do it; I've done it before!" The client is trained to use the word *Stop* when the old words appear, then to very deliberately substitute new formulations for them. Often the client may have been previously unaware of the destructive nature of the thoughts that were going through her head as well as of their emotionally draining power.

Positive restructuring is a related strategy for inculcating in the client cognitive techniques for coping with difficult situations in the future. Criminal justice agencies are increasingly using restructuring groups in correctional programs because of their proven effectiveness in reducing violent reactions. By means of cognitive restructuring, the counselor reframes life events in terms of a challenge rather than as the beginning of the end or an evil omen. The fact that a client does not achieve the *all* in the all-or-nothing framework can be reinterpreted in light of what has been achieved rather than in terms of what has been lost. The occasion of a relapse provides a typical illustration. Through cognitive reframing, the recovering alcoholic will be encouraged to view the relapse not as failure but as a normal process in recovery. A review of the client's progress will be undertaken.

Grief and Loss

Whether on probation or in jail or prison, female offenders are commonly mourning the loss of loved ones, especially children, and of jobs, self-respect, and freedom. For women convicted of crimes, the sense of having failed can be overwhelming. For alcoholics and drug addicts who are forced into treatment, the loss of the drug is the loss of their coping mechanism. The love affair with the alcohol or cocaine is now suddenly over. In many cases booze has served as an alcoholic's best friend. With abstinence from the addictive substance or behavior (such as gambling) comes a recognition of all the losses that have accrued over the years related to the addiction. In working with women convicted of drug offenses, it is essential to help them fill this void and overcome the constant craving.

Prison chaplain Kay Kopatich (cited in van Wormer, 2001) of the Iowa women's prison sums up the situation facing the women with whom she works: "We squeeze 500 women in a space that is for 175 women. You have lost not only your belongings; you not only become a pauper and indigent, but then you have lost your psychic space, spiritual space. The losses don't end with the loss of freedom."

Grief is a constant companion of women locked up away from homes. The source of grieving for most of the women is the loss of their children and families. And earlier losses, such as the loss of children through miscarriage, stillbirth, adoption, or death, must be dealt with directly as soon as the women feel safe enough to grieve. An exploration of the impact of such issues on the developmental process of teenage mothers may provide an understanding of events that led to problematic behavior. Sharing the grief and understanding with an empathic listener can lessen the loneliness and help lighten the load.

Rushing in prematurely with false palliative remedies also breaks the flow of the interaction. Let us take the case of a young woman arrested on a drug abuse charge who expresses horror at the prospect of serving a lengthy sentence. These are typical gut-level responses:

> "Aren't you glad you got caught now before you got into more trouble?"
> "It will all work out for the best, you'll see. Your children will be fine."

We all need to be aware of a natural tendency to try to force people suffering from loss or grief to "look on the bright side." This overly positive approach helps us to feel less sorry for the victim or client, but it does nothing to acknowledge the magnitude of the other's suffering. Clients, like the rest of us, need their pain validated rather than denied. Positive elements can be elicited more effectively in other ways. For example, after attending closely to the client's narrative, the counselor could say: "The picture I get is really dismal. I wonder if anything good could come out of this whole thing." More specifically, the client who is required to attend a parenting or substance abuse program could be helped to see some personal advantages to be gained by such participation.

A rare find in the literature is the case study of a bereavement and loss group in a British women's prison. Jennifer Woolfenden (1997) describes how she as an insider, a counseling instructor, recruited inmates by putting up a poster for a group to meet to deal with the pain of grief and loss. "I never said goodbye" was the dramatic heading. The resulting group of five despondent mothers engaged in intense sharing over an eight-week period. Two African women who were arrested straight from the airport described their traditions of mourning. Another told of her refusal to attend her father's funeral in shackles. The English women talked of their estrangement from their loved ones, which marked a sharp contrast to the African women's own close-knit extended families. All in all, the bereavement group pulled together an unlikely combination of women for a joint focus on loss through death. The group experience enabled these women to mourn in a setting in which there had been no "space" to speak of their feelings of dislocation, numbness, unreality, anger, or sorrow following news of a death of a family member from the outside.

The clearest need of a majority of female offenders is for programs that can address the effects of prior painful loss. As women pour out their stories in therapy, the theme of victimization emerges. Here the loss is a loss of trust, trust in adults, trust in the world, and, above all, the loss of childhood innocence. Typically, the women's more recent loss was associated with a later pattern of seeking relief through some form of substance abuse, sometimes including compulsive overeating. Guilt feelings often arise from these experiences. Sexual victims may feel guilty because they have engaged in forbidden sex with an inappropriate person often under vile circumstances. The don't-tell-anybody advice compounds the sense of guilt, shame, and differentness. Then if they have reacted to the strong feelings through substance use, they feel guilty about that as well. Let us explore this complicated emotion in more depth.

Guilt

Instead of programs on anger management, women, as Baletka and Shearer (2005) suggest, tend to respond more positively to treatment that includes techniques to reduce feelings of guilt and self-blame and that promote self-esteem and self awareness.

Healthy in small doses, guilt feelings can be extremely damaging to an individual and to interpersonal relationships. In his classic study on prejudice, Gordon Allport (1954) defines the sense of guilt as "I blame myself for some misdeed." However, since blaming oneself can be unacceptable to the individual, guilt may be manifested as anger or depression (Stosny, 2008). As a feeling, guilt is hard to describe viscerally. When asked the question "How does your body tell you you're feeling guilty?" perceptive clients may describe a pain in the stomach or head, a feeling of being "down" yet nervous at the same time. The body may be described as feeling sort of slumped over.

People may feel guilty because they *are* guilty—because they have acted badly, deceived someone, or hurt others. This is the guilt of culpability. Most people recognize the feeling if they stop to analyze it. But in many people, guilt may come out as displaced anger, pathological grief, or compulsive denial of wrongdoing.

A prime example of underlying guilt occurs with loss and grief. In the grieving process, such as with the loss of a loved one, family members and friends often must deal with feelings that are disturbing and unfamiliar. In the bereavement literature, guilt is commonly mentioned as an underlying source of disturbance to families.

Apart from real guilt for crimes of commission or omission, especially surrounding neglect of a child, three types of guilt are common among women offenders. The first is the *guilt of contamination* just described. This is an outgrowth of the sense of defilement. This feeling may manifest itself in bitterness, depression, or extreme passivity. Women who mutilate themselves generally have a history of physical violation. In harming their own bodies, they compulsively are expressing rage and reenacting the trauma inflicted on them in childhood.

Because self-blame is so destructive, therapists would do well to recognize the signs either in the narrative or comments made by the client in the course of talking. Clients can be taught to replace negative self-statements with positive thoughts. Victims of physical or sexual violence, for example, can tell themselves something like "It was not my fault," "I did not deserve this," "I am no less whole or pure because of what happened to me."

Survivor guilt occurs when one person is spared death or a calamity and another or others are not. The one who is spared may go into a depression marked by obsessive thoughts. The "Why me?" syndrome of the victim has its counterpart in the "Why not me?" reaction of the survivor. The survivor, such as the person who lived through Hiroshima or a plane crash, may feel a need to justify his or her own survival. Underneath, there may be a feeling of unworthiness.

Parents who have lost children, children who have lost parents, and surviving siblings all experience their own version of survivor guilt. Women who have killed another person—an infant, a child, or a husband/partner—probably feel this sense of guilt many times over. Whatever the circumstances were, the women are alive and the others are not.

A more commonly experienced form of guilt affecting women offenders is *guilt due to helplessness and failure to protect*. Legal restrictions affect a woman's capacity to protect her loved ones, to carry out her family responsibilities. This reaction is well expressed by Barbara Lane (2003) who writes from her confinement at the York institution in New York State:

> My youngest child is floundering, reaching for the wrong things, and I am powerless to do anything but pray for God's mercy. I pray for His forgiveness too. My failure to escape an abusive marriage, my crime, my incarceration—for all of this I bear the guilt of having let go of my baby. (p. 240)

To incarcerated women, who have time to reflect on their failures as mothers in the context of substance abuse and crime, feelings of guilt can sometimes be redirected as anger toward correctional workers (Sorbello et al., 2002).

Ambivalence guilt applies to family members of the offender who love her on one hand but who also deeply resent all the trouble she has caused and the humiliation her criminal behavior has inflicted upon her relatives. What do the prisoner's children say about her whereabouts? If they lie, they feel guilty; if they tell the truth, embarrassed. When family members neglect their own people who are institutionalized, the inmates, in turn, suffer ambivalence toward them. Eventually, the love for their neglectful families turns to hatred. Being thus cut off from their main support system hinders women's rehabilitation possibilities.

Similarly, when women are accused by relatives or others of failing their children or spouses by their previous behavior, they can respond with something like "I'm not going to let you put me in a guilt trip." Responses such as these can be planned and rehearsed in individual and group therapy to great effect.

An inmate correspondent from Danbury, Connecticut, describes an innovative program for trauma survivors that helped turn her life around. Tinia writes:

> Many have been sexually abused as children. The counseling session is conducted in a group fashion. The number of women in one group ranges from 12–15 women. The common bond that we all share is we have endured abuse, and we have survived. I suffer from survivor's guilt. My only sibling died many years ago, and I had always felt like I was the one who should have died. He was the one who was never physically beaten, but he was the one who tried to ease my physical pain, and, in doing so, he endured great emotional pain. I never thanked him for being my brother. (quoted in van Wormer, 2001, pp. 339–340)

The antisocial type of criminal, needless to say, does not suffer from inner turmoil at causing others grief or public humiliation. Interventions aimed at the guilt ridden and grief stricken will be singularly ineffective in dealing with the con artist who is incapable of empathy and devoid of conscience. The vast majority of female offenders, however, can benefit from extensive therapy work to alter the deep-seated feelings about the self.

Feelings of guilt associated with early childhood sexual victimization and physical abuse also need to be addressed. *Beginning to Heal* by Bass and Davis (2003) is an excellent resource to help both men and women reframe their early life experiences. Clergy can play an invaluable role in helping offenders come to terms with themselves and with whatever wrongs they may have committed. Many persons in recovery derive a sense of self-forgiveness through prayer and through working the 12 Steps. The eighth and ninth steps cover listing all persons harmed and making amends where feasible.

Many of the self-esteem-boosting exercises done in groups, such as saying positive things about each other, are directed toward reducing feelings of guilt and achieving a more positive perspective on a person's life and experiences. Group support is found to be tremendously helpful in boosting a person's self-acceptance.

Shame

Whereas guilt is internalized, shame is experienced through being publicly stigmatized. Having gotten into trouble heightens the offender's sense of failure and shame. *Shame* can be defined as the public counterpart of guilt. That shame is a highly destructive emotion is revealed in scholarly research by Hosser, Windzio, and Greve (2008). In interviews with 1,243 offenders from six prisons for young offenders, these researchers examined to what extent feelings of shame and guilt experienced during a prison term influenced recidivism after release. Interestingly, they found that feelings of guilt at the beginning of a prison term correlated with lower rates of recidivism and feelings of shame correlated with higher rates. Results are discussed with regard to their implications for further research and the justice system.

According to Robbins, Chatterjee, and Canda (2006), shame is an emotion with special meaning for women and a preeminent cause of distress. Shame occurs because women are faced with numerous conflicting and competing sociocultural expectations related to sexuality and motherhood. Awareness of the impact of pressures from society is a starting point in helping reduce a woman's sense of shame. Women can increase their shame resilience through the development of empathy and a sense of connection with others. If ordinary women experience shame because they cannot live up to the ideals of society, how much more will women who are in trouble for breaking the law experience this emotion? The stigma attached to criminal justice involvement— particularly for women with children—leads to feelings of personal shame and perceptions of discrimination (Kubiak & Arfken, 2006).

Abrahams (1996) describes her healing work at a rape crisis center in Washington State. Participants were Latina and Anglo survivors. Volunteers at this center, often middle-aged women, achieved tremendous satisfaction in providing services that were not available to them when they were raped; they wanted both to heal from their experiences and to support other women, according to Abrahams. Defining rape as a social, and not a personal, problem, volunteers helped move rape out of the domestic realm into the realm of the state. Liaison work with law enforcement and medical care establishments and through a Latina outreach program provided a new level of community involvement for these women and channeled their anger in productive directions.

Anxiety

Women in trouble with the law and in jail or prison are in a state of near-constant stress. Whereas surveillance in the community may get on their nerves, the demands—the urinalysis tests, work requirements, enforced self-help group attendance—of living in an overcrowded, noisy, cagelike facility are infinitely more anxiety-laden. The excess of stimuli, visual and aural, can make solitude seem an attractive alternative. Sleeping, eating, and concentration problems abound. In many prisons, accordingly, inmates willingly let themselves be tranquilized for most of their stay.

"I'm so nervous, so afraid." This is a common reason that women seek out therapy. Viscerally, feelings of fear and anxiety are closely related. Fear is commonly experienced as a rush of energy as the body prepares itself for fight or flight. Physical strength and attractiveness are intensified. Some who have experienced fear can remember hearing and/or feeling a loud heartbeat and/or a stabbing sensation in the stomach. Outpourings of sweat, tightening of the throat, and irregular breathing are also reported.

With fear, however, the source of the feeling is clearly identified: the growling dog, the deep water, the about-to-crash car. With anxiety, in contrast, the source of the distress is often not clearly known or defined. The stress is less severe, perhaps, but more enduring. Anxiety is often chronic. Responses to anxiety are subject to much individual variation. There may be an inability to swallow and digest food (perhaps associated with dehydration). Binge eating also may be anxiety related. Physiologically, anxiety may be experienced in the stomach, throat, sweat glands, and breathing. In most people, an alcoholic beverage or tranquilizer "kills the worry," and the anxiety temporarily goes away. The trial is still pending, but you do not care. Eventually, the solution to the problem—use of chemicals—becomes the problem itself.

A highly useful process recommended by Cournoyer (2008) is called partializing. *Partializing* is the process of breaking down aspects of a crisis into small, manageable parts. To help the client in this regard, the counselor can simply explain the process and ask, "Which piece of this concerns you the most right now?" (p. 229). This strategy helps the individual in a crisis to keep from getting overwhelmed, taking one step at a time.

Stress Management

The perpetual nervousness that plagues some individuals can be readily reduced through cognitive therapy techniques. Worrying, anxiety-provoking self-talk ("My kids will hate me; my parents will never forgive me") can be replaced with new ways of thinking ("I'll do my best to explain things; they'll be happy to see how much healthier I am now that I'm sober").

Some commonly set goals in therapy pertaining to fear and anxiety are learning to handle fears, managing to face fears calmly, identifying what one is truly afraid of, and being emotionally prepared for likely outcomes. Imagining the worst possible thing that can happen is often helpful. Clients who have *phobias*, or irrational fears, can be helped to trace the origins of the phobias. Behavioral treatment provides for exposure to the feared source (e.g., a snake) in slow steps until the panic response is extinguished.

Through cutting down the use of stimulants, such as coffee and tea, physical anxiety can be reduced greatly. A drink of warm milk at any time can produce a quieting effect. When adrenaline is high, brisk exercise can aid in using up the excess energy and enhancing relaxation. The usefulness of physical exercise as a treatment intervention was verified in an empirically conducted study utilizing a control group (Lake, 2007). Results indicated a significant difference in post test scores on reduced levels of both anxiety and depression by virtue of the physical training provided.

Depression

Depression, organic and situational, is common among women offenders whether they are in detention or under community supervision. Even apart from having a mood disorder, loss of freedom gives one a lot to be depressed about. Depression and negative thinking go hand in hand. When you feel down, the world becomes a grim place. By the same token, if you view your life and the world negatively, your mood would sink to low depths.

The *Diagnostic and Statistical Manual of Mental Disorders* (4th ed.) Text Revision (American Psychiatric Association, 2000) characterizes a chronically depressed mood in terms of poor appetite or overeating, insomnia, low energy or fatigue, low self-esteem, poor concentration or difficulty making decisions, and feelings of hopelessness. Cognitive therapy alone or cognitive therapy plus antidepressant medication has been found to be enormously effective in alleviating such symptoms (Beck et al., 1979). As we learn more about the brain and the crucial role of serotonin levels in giving us a sense of well-being, the prescribing of effective medication (e.g., Prozac, Luvox) is becoming more of a science.

The sense of feeling good can be enhanced be the natural highs that come with exercise, by being in good company, and by engaging in hobbies that are fun. With guidance, clients can learn ways to avoid setting themselves up for disaster. Realistic and fulfilling goals can be set to replace grandiose or self-defeating ones. Energy-producing activities, such as taking a brisk walk or going swimming or even altering breathing patterns (to breathe high in the chest), can pick up one's spirits considerably.

Most of us will get restless and dispirited when bored. The sense of having no future and nothing to do but eat and watch television leads prisoners to feel that life is not worth living. Love and work, as Freud once proclaimed, are key ingredients in human happiness. Even small children like to feel helpful. In light of this basic human need, counselors should make referrals to vocational, educational, and physical exercise programs, or even provide for challenging homework assignments, especially in the absence of gratifying work or its equivalent.

A national survey of prison dog-training programs found that these initiatives, which are operating in men's and women's correctional institutions in the United States, Canada, and Australia, are producing beneficial results (Furst, 2006). In working closely with dogs and with other residents in the program, women benefit in receiving vocational experience while receiving a psychological boost in successfully training dogs to be companions for elderly and disabled persons. Research shows a low recidivism rate for these women, an increase in self-esteem, and a reduction in feelings of depression.

Love

Healthy love is nonobsessive, defined eloquently in the Bible as kind, nonenvious "not easily provoked, thinketh no evil, rejoiceth not in iniquity" (I Corinthians 13: 4–6). Healthy love is above all reciprocal; it is about giving and receiving both. The deepest love between partners depends on shared emotional resonance over features of life they both consider most significant. These partners often find common ground in their shared experiences of life.

A positive concept of love is offered in Erich Fromm's classic *The Art of Loving* (1956). True love is realized only when a man or woman has realized himself or herself to the point of being a whole and secure person. Mature love welcomes growth in the partner. Carol Gilligan (2002), in her book on love, *The Birth of Pleasure*, says it beautifully:

> Maybe love is like rain. Sometimes gentle, sometimes torrential, flooding eroding, quiet, steady, filling the earth, collecting in hidden springs. When it rains, when we love, new life grows (p. 3).

What does it take to make love work? Olson, Olson-Sigg, and Larson's (2008) research, which included a battery of questions administered to over

20,000 couples nationwide, helps provide an answer. Their Couple Checkup Inventory revealed key ingredients that make for a happy relationship even long after the initial chemistry has faded. These qualities emerged as strongly associated with relationship contentment: The partner:

- Is a good listener
- Is understanding of the person's feelings
- Has a balance in leisure time spent together and apart
- Is easy to talk to
- Is creative and agreeable in handling differences including finances
- Is sexually compatible

"A relationship fired by erotic passion," writes Gilligan (2002), "leads in the end to a relationship between a man and a woman that uproots its history in patriarchy, becoming no longer uneven" (p. 233). The laws of relationship that Gilligan came up with in her work with couples in crisis were these: "I will never lie to you, I will never leave you, I will never try to possess you" (p. 233). Wouldn't such a pledge define any close relationship—mother and daughter, lesbian and gay, that of best friends?

Obsessive Love

Irrational love is celebrated in our culture; it is a theme that has inspired literature since time immemorial and of course in modern times has provided the story line for many a tear-jerking movie. The mature person can enjoy the romanticism in our culture, cry at the opera, and disregard the implications of the message at the same time. Thus romantic fantasy can be an exciting and healthy escape from the drudgery and monotony of everyday life.

Hartman and Laird (1983) contrast the differentiated (independent) person from the one who is fused in a relationship that knows no boundaries:

> The well-differentiated person is provident, flexible, thoughtful, and autonomous in the face of considerable stress, while the less differentiated, more fused person is often trapped in a world of feeling, buffeted about by emotionality, disinclined to providence, inclined to rigidity, and susceptible to dysfunction when confronted with stress.... The differentiated person, interestingly, is the one who can risk genuine emotional closeness without undue anxiety. (p.78)

In my work with alcoholic families (Family Week in an inpatient setting), I found it helpful to include a session on love relationships. I found that as clients and their family members prepared to resume their relationships, they were often on a disaster course. Expectations of the relationship were too high. In my mind's eye is a picture of two cartoon characters—lovers in a boat—about to enter the Tunnel of Love. Ahead, out of the lovers' view, is a steep waterfall. This is my image of the posttreatment alcoholic couple blindly heading down life's course. Whether addicted to alcohol or to a newfound relationship, the potential for destructiveness is the same. Many a recovering client has returned abruptly to the treatment center after a slip or relapse precipitated by a disastrous, all-consuming love affair, often with a fellow recovering alcoholic client.

Irrational thought patterns that are culturally ingrained but that most mature people would not take literally include:

- I cannot live without you.
- You are the only person for me.
- I'm never going to get involved with anyone else again.
- We must agree on everything.
- We should be happy in each other's exclusive company.
- Everything that is yours is mine and everything that is mine is yours.
- (And among alcoholics) You keep me sober.

The extreme element inherent in this kind of logic corresponds to a certain frantic quality underlying any addiction. The love partner, like the source of any addiction, will be used to satisfy a deep aching need for some sort of escape. And although the initial euphoria may be long departed, the dependency prevails. According to Peele (1976) in his analysis of love and addiction, the addictive foundations of a dependency relationship are revealed when it ends in an abrupt, total, and vindictive breakup. "Because the involvement has been so total," declares Peele, "its ending must be violent. Out of love so powerful grows a hatred most vile" (p. 88).

Many female offenders, especially those with addiction problems, are involved in relationships with battering men, relationships that they seem emotionally unable to escape. Behind bars, they tend to romanticize these relationships and long for their partners. A technique recommended by Corcoran (2005) to help such women manage their longing is to prompt them to recall the negative consequences of such a relationship and to use realistic self-talk and images (perhaps of their bruises and black eyes) to extinguish these feelings. They can also be reassured that such a craving for a return to the love relationship, even a violent one, is a normal reaction, that absence does sometimes "make the heart grow fonder" even when the love object is undeserving and a threat to one's well-being. Women can be educated collectively, nonjudgmentally, about healthy relationships while their pain of separation from their loved ones is validated at the personal level.

Validating the Pain of Loss

Loss and pain and, in all probability, anger, are staples of the offender experience. Apart from relationship loss, other typical losses include loss of freedom to varying degrees, court sanctions, relationship adjustments, and forced abstention from alcohol and other drugs. Strengths-oriented treatment helps clients to grieve their losses and to achieve acceptance of things that cannot be changed. The therapy process engages girls and women in treatment and helps them pursue alternative ways of coping without resorting to use of chemicals or self-destructive behaviors. The focus is on enhancing the client's sense of control and reinforcing her efforts to find purpose and meaning in the present circumstances and to make realistic decisions for the future. Finding meaning in the present moment can do much to enhance recovery from the legacy of past injuries of oppression, neglect, and domination.

HEALING

Most of this chapter has been devoted to skills work, the third stage in the gender-sensitive empowerment scheme. Now we have covered the first three stages: therapeutic relationship, motivational enhancement (in Chapter 6), and life skills/feeling work. This brings us to the last two: healing and generativity.

Healing is defined by Saleebey (2006) as implying "both wholeness and the inborn facility of the body and the mind to regenerate and resist when faced with disorder, disease, and disruption" (p. 14). Healing also can refer to the inner change, the sense of peace that may result from therapy work in labeling feelings and controlling them through cognitive techniques, reframing of troubling events in one's life, and recognizing how past events influence present feelings, thoughts, and behavior. Reclaiming lost and damaged childhood selves may occur through the joint effort of the treatment relationship.

To "heal our wounds," as bell hooks (1993) tells us, "we must be able to critically examine our behavior and change" (p. 39). As the client begins to take responsibility for her life, the healing process can begin. Generally this involves a recognition of how past events influence present feelings, thoughts, and behavior. Women's (and men's) healing may involve a journey to childhood or early adulthood where trauma occurred; healing may require a working through of guilt feelings, whether those feelings are justified or not. Inner change often comes through identification of irrational thoughts and concomitant feelings and the reframing of unhealthy assumptions and beliefs.

Healing is often accompanied by inner change, the sense of peace that may result from therapy work in labeling feelings and controlling them through cognitive techniques, reframing troubling events in one's life, and recognizing how past events influence present feelings, thoughts, and behavior. Reclaiming lost and damaged childhood selves may occur through the joint effort embodied in the treatment relationship.

Healing often involves reclaiming what was lost either through drug addiction or in living in a family consumed with another's addiction. There is so much to reclaim: the fun in life, one's sense of peace and safety, one's spirituality, one's wholeness. In writing on Black women and self-recovery, hooks (1993) connects the struggle of people to "recover" from suffering and woundedness caused by political oppression/exploitation with the effort to break with addictive behavior. "Collectively, Black women will lead more life-affirming lives, " she writes, "as we break through denial, acknowledge our pain, express our grief, and let the mourning teach us how to rejoice and begin life anew" (p. 111).

Bonnie Foreshaw (2003), an inmate author who contributed her narrative to Lamb's (2003) anthology, found forgiveness for her past misdeeds through religion: "God is merciful. Little by little, He guided me away from my despair and made me want to live again. I came to understand that bitterness and animosity would eat my soul like a cancer. Only forgiveness would set me free" (p. 208).

Ferszt, Salgado, DeFedele, and Leveillee (2009) adapted a Houses of Healing program for a sample of 36 women in a prison in the Northeast. Ethnically, most of the women were Latina or European American; multiple losses were identified by just under half of the group members. This 12-week facilitated course was designed to promote healing in women from a lifetime of losses that have occurred in their journey from childhood to prison. Participants were taught techniques of meditation and relaxation and healthy ways of dealing with negative emotions such as resentment and guilt. To accomplish these goals, group facilitators conducted sessions on reading, writing, group discussions, and special exercises. In follow-up interviews, the participants reported improved psychological functioning, increased self-esteem, and better coping skills for dealing with stress.

Healing from Trauma

Posttraumatic stress disorder (PTSD), as discussed in Chapter 5, is a chronic, debilitating psychiatric disorder that can follow exposure to extreme stressful experiences. It is characterized by hyperarousal and increased startle responses, reexperiencing of the traumatic event, withdrawal or avoidance behavior, and emotional numbing (Stam, 2007). During avoidance, a victim's psychological defense mechanisms help repress overwhelming emotions and thoughts related to the trauma. This is a normal response to an abnormal situation. Avoidance may last for many years.

Because the unconscious knows even when the memory does not, flashbacks may occur, characterized by the confusion and intensity of feelings. Such compulsive reexperiencing of pain may be regarded as unconscious attempts to integrate and heal the past. Fewer than 7% of the victims of child sexual abuse, in fact, disclose the abuse during childhood (Dziegielewski & Resnick, 1996). According to Morgan, Rigaud, and Taylor (1990), astonishingly, the average length of time between sexual trauma and addressing the trauma in adulthood is 17 years.

The irony of ironies is that child molesters often feel no guilt at all while their victims are left with a sense of uncleanness and even self-disgust. The guilt feelings internalized by the child victim that may remain with her until adulthood seem to make little sense on the surface. A public acknowledgment of the victimization such as through courtroom prosecution of the perpetrator may induce feelings of shame in the survivor.

Related to these reactions to the victimization are compulsive/addictive behaviors that commonly accompany traumatic stress disorders of a sexual nature. The client may get stuck in the avoidance phase of PTSD if compulsive behaviors are not addressed (Morgan et al., 1990). It is generally known that persons who use drugs as a means of escape fail to develop effective coping skills. Numbing their senses at the time of a crisis, they do not grow. To "be present" in mind as well as in body for the therapy sessions, sobriety is an absolute necessity. For survivors of childhood abuse, there is an entire spectrum of feelings to be worked through: grief over losses that may have accompanied the trauma, anger surrounding betrayal and lack of protection, acceptance, letting go, and making peace with the past (Dziegielewski & Resnick, 1996).

Whether a woman is subjected to one-time rape by a stranger or to a pattern of incest by a family member, the emotional scars may be with her always. Because the unconscious has no sense of time, past and present are interlocked in the mind, and exposure to terrifying events can leave permanent scars on the brain and central nervous system; exposure to trauma in vulnerable persons is associated with depression and can even alter the immune system (Stam, 2007). Breslau, Peterson, and Schultz (2008), in their empirically based study in a large sample of medical patients. found that it was not exposure to trauma itself but the susceptibility to PTSD that determines one's vulnerability to developing symptoms in later potentially traumatic situations (for example, military combat). To reduce the vulnerability to PTSD, which Breslau et al. estimate to be around 23 percent of persons exposed to the worst kind of trauma, treatment as soon as possible after the immediate horrifying event is over is desirable. Encouragement to talk about what happened will help the victim deal with the crisis with her conscious mind in order to prevent the kind of unhealthy repression that can be associated with nightmares and neuroses 20 and 30 years later.

Witness the case of Denise, a 31-year-old prison inmate, whose story is related by Mary Gilfus (1998):

> Without drugs Denise cannot have sex with her husband, she cannot go out in public or socialize with people, she has trouble sleeping, feels depressed, and "hates" herself. With drugs she feels confident and happy, able to meet people, and be sexual with her husband. Once again, her description of her experiences suggest that she may still suffer symptoms of post-traumatic stress disorder (PTSD). (p. 18)

To have any impact on recidivism, rehabilitation programs must help these women understand how victimization has affected their social and psychological functioning (Sorbello et al., 2002). In order to effectively work with a female offender who is a victim of herself and of society, knowledge of the basic skills of strengths-based counseling is essential. Sometimes just contact with one person who believes in her—for example, a prison chaplain, teacher, or Alcoholics Anonymous sponsor—is all it takes to help her find her way out of a life of crime. Gender-sensitive intervention at the right moment, even within prison or training school walls, can help offenders become motivated to prepare to take advantage of educational and vocational offerings that might be available down the road. An excellent resource for counselors working with survivors of child sexual abuse is Bass and Davis's (2003) *Beginning to Heal*. Written in the second person to address the survivor, this book takes the reader through the key stages of the healing process, from crisis times to breaking the silence, grief, and anger, to resolution and moving on. Past and present are intertwined in marvelous ways in this book. *The PTSD Workbook* by Williams and Poijula (2002) similarly offers a wealth of exercises in a low-priced format that would be very useful in a therapy group of women who need to deal with flashbacks, memories, and stress. Sample exercises are constructing a trauma inventory, my positive traits, safety assessment, and creating a safe space.

Because exposure to sexual violation is associated with low self-esteem and mistrust, group therapy can be invaluable in helping survivors sort things out, develop trust with other group participants, and let go of their self-blaming thoughts and feelings of hurt. As group members come to share each other's stories of brutalization, a revelation may take place. In conjunction with an emerging sense of "we" instead of "I," the revelation may become something like "We did not deserve these things to happen to us." Group therapy gives survivors the opportunity to share their stories in a safe environment among others who have been through it as well; consequently, their sense of isolation and stigmatization can be dramatically reduced. The impact on one individual is revealed in the letter she wrote to me from the women's federal prison in Danbury, Connecticut, describing her appreciation for treatment she received in a well-run but underfunded program. In her words:

> Currently at the prison, there is a program that assists female offenders who have a history of physical, emotional, or sexual abuse. This program is called "The Bridge." In the counseling group, I speak about these issues. Within the trauma unit, there is a remarkable support system which we render to anyone that happens to be going through a crisis. The confidentiality is a must, as the topics that many of us disclose are painful. The trauma unit is the only support network that is offered to abuse survivors in the entire Bureau of Prisons. Hopefully, programs such as this one will crop up in every federal prison....

> The psychologist, through his hours of counseling, has shown me that I am a strong capable woman.... Without him, I firmly believe that I would have ended my own life. I can reclaim all the pieces of myself that had been stolen by stronger, cruel people who did whatever they wanted. (quoted in van Wormer, 2001, p. 286)

Working on trauma issues within a prison setting, the therapist needs to instill a sense of psychological safety in the client. Otherwise, according to Bloom, Owen, and Covington (2003), there is little likelihood of a positive outcome. Central to the therapeutic culture is a focus on a sense of belonging, safety, openness, participation, and empowerment.

A major task of trauma work is to help clients understand the experience and move through it in a purposeful and therapeutic manner (Behrman &

Reid, 2006). The kind of self-understanding that develops in talking to a knowledgeable therapist can be a tremendous relief to the survivor of a disturbing event or series of events. "I thought I was just going crazy" is a typical response. Therapists who are themselves survivors of abuse can be excellent role models in helping clients cope with the legacy of a painful past. Discussion of typical symptoms of PTSD—denial, numbing, flashbacks, intrusive thoughts, guilt feelings, sleep disturbances, jumpiness, and preoccupation (as listed by the American Psychiatric Association, 2000)—can help the survivor see that her seeming abnormal behavior is an abnormal response to an abnormal situation. Addictive and criminal behavior, such as compulsive shoplifting, similarly may be found to have deep psychological roots.

In recovery, survivors can be taught as a cognitive strategy to examine their self-talk; to write down their destructive, negative, self-blaming thoughts (e.g., "I should have told my teachers about the incest; I should have fought harder against the rapist; I should never have taken a ride with that man who was drunk at the party"); and to relinquish them in favor of positive self-talk (e.g., "I did not deserve what happened to me; it could have happened to anyone; I can live with this; my life is valuable"). In a group setting, clients can help other group members catch and check their self-destructive thinking. With practice, the nurturant, collective voice of the group can become their own.

From the strengths perspective, an effective strategy is to affirm the resourcefulness of women who managed to use all the wiles at their disposal to survive and who have survived ever since. In recovery, the survivor will review a situation in which she seemed to have been completely overtaken yet in which she in fact used many creative maneuvers for her own protection. In this way, a new meaning can be given to the trauma of rape or childhood sexual abuse. Some individuals, as they discard their sense of a damaged self, will embrace instead the belief that the misfortune they endured made them stronger and more compassionate toward human suffering.

To help women get in touch with their feelings of anger and underlying emotions such as guilt and loss, one strategy is to have clients write their sexual assault experiences on worksheets. The therapeutic task for the survivor is to rewrite her memories and thereby reauthor an important part of her life. The idea is not to change the past, which is not possible in any case, but to change the way one perceives the past. Detailed accounts of the rape serve to provoke sensory responses—what was seen, heard, smelled—as well as thoughts and feelings during the incident. Intense reactions are commonly experienced at this assignment. Anger, rage, horror, and disgust are among the emotions felt. The therapist helps the woman get through mental blocks that are areas of major difficulty. Therapist and client work together to find patterns or themes in the essay that reflect unhealthy thoughts or beliefs in a joint effort to replace them with healthy, affirming statements.

Because research indicates a high percentage of sexual and relationship problems following sexual trauma, fear of intimacy and conflict about sexuality are appropriate topics for short-term groups. Since the therapy we are talking about takes place, typically, a long time after the rape or incest, women are encouraged to refer to themselves as survivors rather than as victims. The idea is to reject the passive connotation that pervades the victim label, not rejecting the reality of victimization and oppression.

Healing Powers of Forgiveness

The term *forgiveness* does not in anyway excuse the acts of wrongdoing by the perpetrator but refers instead to letting go of the pain caused by these acts. The burgeoning interest in the healing potential of victim forgiveness has catapulted the field of restorative justice into the limelight because of its ability to achieve emotional repair for crime victims (Armour & Umbreit, 2006). When harmful emotions such as anger, bitterness, and anxiety are reduced, major health benefits often result. Through professionally mediated restorative justice dialogue, victims may be able to free themselves from the negative power of the offense: This is what forgiveness is all about. From the offender's perspective, the experience of being forgiven is associated with feeling accepted by the community. Making amends to the person or people who were wronged can constitute a first step for a girl or young woman in "finding her voice" and developing empathy for others at the same time. Counseling that builds on her strengths can further facilitate the transition from a state of lawbreaker to wholeness. Through this healing process, in short, the girl or woman can improve her relational competency, and both victim and offender are empowered in restoring the balance of a community wronged.

Archbishop Desmond Tutu, who was instrumental in establishing South Africa's Truth and Reconciliation Commission hearings to help his nation heal from a century or so of human rights abuses, spoke eloquently on this aspect of human nature: "There's something in all of us that hungers after the good and true, and when we glimpse it in people, we applaud them for it. We long to be just a little like them. Restorative justice is focused on restoring the personhood that is damaged or lost" (quoted by Green, 1998, pp. 5–6).

Forgiveness fosters healing, and healing, in turn, hastens forgiveness. The person who stands to benefit the most from forgiving, or letting go of the hurt and the hatred, is the one who does the forgiving. Forgiveness can be viewed as an unfolding process, a journey that involves working through many issues.

And who or what do women violators of the law have to forgive? In each case, the source of the woundedness is different. The source could stem from the woman's family of origin (for acts of neglect or mistreatment), from an abusive relationship in adult life, or from oppression within the social or criminal justice system (for its racism and lack of mercy provided).

In the feminist book *Women Who Run with Wolves*, Clarissa Pinkola Estés (1992) perceives in forgiveness an act of creation; you can forgive a person, a community, a nation for an offense; you can forgive for now or for all time; you can forgive part, all, or half of the offense. And how does a person know if she has forgiven? As Estés tells us, and as we can tell our clients: "You tend to feel sorrow over the circumstances instead of rage. You understand the suffering that drove the offense to begin with. You are not waiting for anything. You are not wanting for anything" (pp. 372–373).

But healing does not imply passivity in the face of injustice. In *Sisters of the Yam*, hooks (1993) writes poignantly of an African American midwife Miss Onnie who shared memories passed down in her family history of the pain of slavery. Miss Onnie names the sorrows while evoking the need for Black people to let go of bitterness. In their historical role as caretakers, Black women, as hooks notes, practiced the art of compassion and knew that forgiveness not only eased the pain of the heart but made love possible. "When we feel like martyrs," hooks (p. 168) observes, "we cannot develop compassion." Moving from the micro to macro realm, hooks leads us into the highest level of empowerment. If we genuinely desire to change our world by cultivating compassion and the will to forgive, hooks states, we should be able to resist oppression and exploitation, "to joyfully engage in oppositional struggle" (p. 172).

Healing can be regarded as a kind of journey. It is a journey from isolation to intimacy, from alienation to meaning, and from running away to reaching toward. In other words, it is an achievement of serenity and of spiritual health.

Spiritual Healing

Defined as "a capacity to relate to the infinite," *spirituality*, according to Royce and Scatchley (1996), is the number-one means of coping with stress. Citing two research studies, Royce notes that an overwhelming majority of alcoholism patients complained that their spiritual needs were not met in treatment programs. Few would deny that alcoholism is a spiritual as well as a physical and emotional illness.

Maria Carroll (1993) conceptualizes the spiritual journey in terms of breaking the bonds to earthly attachments and achieving a mastery of oneself through strengthened virtues. For the recovering alcoholic, for example, an earthly attachment is to the substance alcohol. Only when the bond to their addiction is broken can alcoholics move to higher things and embark on "a journey home." To Carroll, the journey home entails constructing a personal reality, becoming disillusioned with this reality, letting the ego-self disintegrate, surrendering, reframing the old reality, and then allowing a new reality to develop as the transformed state. Through surrendering to the reality of the present, the recovering alcoholic moves through a spiritual awakening process toward wholeness and a larger humanity. Fulfillment of the spiritual dimension is important in providing a sense of meaning in life.

The tremendous impact that prison chaplains can have on inmates turning their lives around is often neglected in the correctional literature. Church volunteers who spend a great deal of time working with inmates can have a tremendous impact as well. At the Iowa Correctional Institute for Women, the volunteer program is extensive. Approximately 10 churches come out for worship services on a rotating basis. Chaplain Kay Kopatich, herself a Catholic, offers two Protestant services and one Catholic service every Sunday. There is a Native American Sacred Circle and a sweat lodge. An imam provides traditional Muslim instruction. A Bible study group is popular. An article in the *Catholic Mirror* (Stanton, 2005) provides an interview with a chaplain at the women's prison at Mitchellville, Iowa:

> Overseeing the women's religious lives is Catholic Chaplain Kay Kopatich, the statewide religious coordinator for the Iowa Department of Corrections. "I got into prison ministry by default," said Kopatich. "I thought it would be a lot of sorrow and grief and I'd give it five years. But it ended up being a good fit for me. I find it very rewarding and I've been there 13 years now."

> Kopatich describes her role in terms of nurturing all faith traditions that are held by the mix of inmates. "I do not push Catholicism," she said. "I see the mosaic, all of the faith traditions working together among the inmates.

> "Be they Catholic, Jew, Protestant, Muslim, whatever, our chapel here serves everyone. My main goal is to work with the women. The gospel's good news is lived out in terms of the inmates, watching them work through the difficulties of coming to prison," she added. (p. 8)

Working through an ethnic lens, social workers should recognize that the values of individualism and self-determination are mainstream values that may be in conflict with the people we serve. This is why programs such as the Native healing programs have such power when offered as communal undertakings. Developing group consciousness is a key aspect of empowerment.

The Canadian correctional system provides for gender-sensitive and culture-specific healing programs for women as an active part of the treatment (Hayman, 2006), The Aboriginal Healing Lodge programs focus on the effects of cultural and self-esteem loss through contact with the industrialized world and deals with personal as well as community grief and loss. Spiritual ceremonies consist of drumming, smudging, sweats, and singing.

Not only is the Native influence strongly felt in the Canadian prisons, but the restorative system of justice (which stresses restitution and reconciliation over retribution) is widely used by Canadian tribes as an alternative to the adversarial system of settling disputes (van Wormer & Bartollas, 2007). The focus is on healing rather than punishing. Offender and victim join others in a circle. The offender accepts responsibility for the wrongs done and the resolution process begins. Prayers to the Creator guide the healing process.

For an example of the use of restorative justice in a U.S. women's prison, I want to share the next case example, which took place between a woman who was serving time for murder and the mother of the murder victim. This summary is derived from my personal correspondence with Cindy Rathjen, the mother of the homicide victim, on November 10, 2005.

Case Example from Cedar Rapids, Iowa

When first contacted by the Iowa Administrator of Victim and Restorative Justice Programs to participate in a meeting with the murderer of her daughter who was in prison serving out her sentence, Cindy refused the meeting. Her daughter had been killed by another woman, Tara, after a dispute over a man. The crime had been horribly brutal; Tara had run over the victim with her car, dragging the body for several blocks. Cindy refused this meeting as she felt that Tara was using the fact that she had been drinking as an excuse. However, when she read Tara's letter requesting the meeting, she was impressed that the inmate was taking responsibility for the crime. Both women received counseling to prepare them for the encounter. At the prison, the women met for three and a half hours, each expressing her feelings about the crime. In the end, Cindy told Tara that she wished the best for her, that her daughter would have wanted that for her, that she live a good life and avoid the bad company she had been in before. Since Tara was soon to be paroled, the meeting took on a special significance for both of the participants and resolved a number of difficult issues.

GENERATIVITY

Now we come to the fifth and final stage of the empowerment framework. *Generativity* refers to the act of generating or bringing into existence, procreating. Erik Erikson (1963), the psychoanalyst most closely associated with this term, defines generativity as what the mature generation imparts to the young and what it leaves behind—the legacy of life from generation to generation. In Erikson's scheme, the opposite of generativity is stagnation. Erikson's son, Kai, took the concept of generativity into the realm of social deviance. The road to a new self-image for the offender as one who has been publicly stigmatized is a process through which he or she makes a personal commitment to help others (K. Erikson, 1964).

At the personal level, care for the young is a major part of generativity. There is much we can do to strengthen mother-child interactions during and following a period of incarceration. Parenting programming as described in Chapter 4 provides a context for women to explore and manage their experiences as mothers (Sorbello et al., 2002). Such groups can help reduce the stress stemming from lengthy periods of incarceration or loss of custody of children (Wallace, 2005). The self-help group for mothers at the Bedford Hills Correctional Facility as described by former inmate Kathy Boudin (1998) provided a process that, as Boudin explained, would set loose the capacity of women to be active participants in their own process of growth. Group participants would share their life stories and work on their relationships with their children and on their children's needs.

The Girl Scouts' program of prison visitation, described in Chapter 5, offers another example of an effort toward giving across the generations. Work with the children of offenders, a seriously neglected group, is only in its infancy. We need to recognize that when mothers are punished, their children are punished as well. Psychological parent-child bonds are broken; years later, with the abrupt return of the mother to the community, the children's lives are disrupted once again. About-to-be-released offenders require a tremendous amount of help to prepare them to resume their parenting roles yet such help is rarely provided.

Drawing on Kai Erikson's formulation, restorative justice proponents Bazemore and Boba (2007) embrace the idea of helping others as a way of ensuring one's own recovery and a transformation in self-identity. Bazemore and Boba speak of making good by *doing good*. Such a process, they maintain, is consistent with the restorative principle of relationship building. This principle, as they further indicate, is also incorporated into the well-known 12 Step recovery program.

In working the Steps of Alcoholics Anonymous and the other 12 Step groups, people have derived a great deal of meaning and solace. Nancy Birkla (2003), an inmate of York Correctional Institution, shares how she came to find hope and a sense of purpose through working the program:

> Having come the long way around to a belief that a Power greater than myself could restore me to sanity, I had just completed the unfinished second step of my recovery and was approaching the third. I was on the verge of turning my will and my life over to the care of God. (p. 136)

Step 12 of Alcoholics Anonymous is the step of reaching out to help others. The Steps, although subject to much criticism by some feminist and minority groups, have been instrumental in the healing process for millions of people across the world. To read a version of the Steps as adapted to apply to all addictions, see www.12step.org. For a strengths-based adaptation for work with women with addictions problems, I have further adapted them, as presented next. My aim was to retain much of the original meaning and language while infusing the Steps with more positive words, such as wholeness and connectedness.

The Nine Steps
1. We acknowledge we had lost control over (the source of the addiction) — that our lives had become unmanageable.
2. We came to believe that a Power greater than ourselves could restore us to wholeness.
3. We made a decision to turn our will and our lives over to the care of a Higher Power as we understood him, her, or it.
4. We made a searching and fearless moral inventory of ourselves, our relationships, and our manner of living.
5. We acknowledged to the Higher Power, to ourselves, and to another human being the exact nature of our addiction.
6. We made a list of all persons whose suffering was connected to our own.
7. We made every effort to restore, physically and spiritually, to ourselves and others, those things that were lost.
8. We sought through prayer and/or meditation to enrich our sense of connectedness to nature and to one another.
9. Having had a personal and spiritual awakening as the result of these steps, we tried to carry this message to others in need and to practice these principles in all our affairs.

Generativity, as in this last step, involves taking our message of healing and recovery to others. To social activists such as bell hooks, this concept moves us from the personal into the political realm. "No level of individual self-actualization alive can sustain the marginalized and oppressed," she declares (1993, p. 162). "We must be linked to collective struggle."

We are closing this discussion on generativity with an appeal for more programming related to women's most creative function: childbearing and child raising. The journey toward a woman's empowerment can go only so far without an acknowledgment of her family roles.

SUMMARY

This, the final chapter in this book, was the third of the direct practice chapters for counseling girls and women in the criminal justice system. The first of these three chapters described gender-specific programming; the second was concerned with the development of a working relationship and the dynamics of motivational enhancement; and this chapter provided guidelines for direct strengths-based practice. Identification of feelings, the thinking/feeling nexus, use of self-talk, management of stress and expression of anger, and handling feelings of grief, guilt, and loss were among the topics discussed. Guidelines were provided for helping women understand the origins of their strong emotions and to express them in healthy and productive ways. That gender differences are pronounced in what triggers the various emotions and how these emotions are expressed, or if they are even expressed at all, is a basic assumption of this chapter. That a cognitive approach is an essential therapy tool in the change process—moving from a negative view of the world toward a more hopeful, positive one—is a second major assumption of this chapter and this book. This assumption is based on the scientific truth that in controlling your thinking, you can control your feelings.

In light of the heavy victimization in the backgrounds of so many girls and women who have gotten into trouble with the law, and the secondary victimization caused by the criminal justice system, work toward healing the woundedness is essential. Healing can be bolstered in a number of ways, through religion, in "working the steps," through restorative strategies that may encourage forgiveness or letting go, through generativity by caring for others, and through engaging in social advocacy for other victims. The road from victim to survivor can be encouraged in all these ways.

EPILOGUE

We need to make the kind of society where it is easier for people to be good.

— Dorothy Day, *The Long Loneliness*

The theme of restorative justice — *crime wounds ... justice heals* — sums up in a nutshell the basic thesis of this book. That justice for girls and women must take into account not the offense or crime alone, but the context in which that act occurred is a secondary theme. Treatment of the female offender in the courtroom and in correctional institutions, as in the therapy session, must be tailored to the individual within the full biological, psychological, and social sense of her being. If the woman is a psychopathic killer, one course of treatment can be provided; for the drug abuser who drove the getaway car during a robbery, another course of therapy would be appropriate. And just as the law, in the interests of fairness, would differentiate among individual girls and women who have committed the same crime but for different motives, so equitable justice would differentiate between male and female roles in crime assuming there were differences. Sameness of treatment as embodied in state law often leads to injustice in the name of equality. For justice to be equitable, biological, psychological, and social differences among individuals must be taken into account.

In an effort to integrate gendered theory and practice, *Working with Female Offenders: A Gender-Sensitive Approach* is informed by insights about growing up female, enhancing motivation, and the thinking/feeling dyad (from psychology); the strengths perspective (from social work); the philosophy of restorative justice (from criminal justice). Throughout the United States and to a larger extent in Canada, gender-sensitive initiatives are proliferating. A major challenge to progressive workers within the system, including administrators, is these initiatives, which we might conceive of as niches of empowerment, exist within a structure that is punitive and designed for hardened male convicts. Within this context, behaviors associated with disease

257

and early life trauma are treated by the courts not as mental health problems but as criminal justice problems. And correctional counselors sometimes find themselves dealing as much with the trauma caused by the system as the trauma in the backgrounds of their clients related to their offending and addictive behavior. There is a growing recognition in many circles that sometimes the crimes committed against female offenders are every bit as heinous as the crimes committed by the offenders themselves.

In the interests of rehabilitation, gender and cultural sensitivity must be manifested at every level of the criminal justice system. A continuity of philosophy must parallel the continuity of care. We cannot superimpose a sensitive, gendered approach on a harsh, militaristic-style framework. Concerning women's prisons, the cold and forbidding architecture and the physical isolation from the community speak volumes. And yet, as we have seen, correctional counselors are doing invaluable work with the girls and women who come to their attention. Providing addiction treatment, mental health counseling, and parenting classes as needed, many counselors using a gender and culturally sensitive approach help their clients negotiate a difficult system and in many cases to exit from that system. Such treatment providers in juvenile and adult facilities or court-based departments realize that the antisocial behaviors and mind-set targeted in much of the cognitive-behavioral programs are more characteristic of male offenders and are of limited value to their charges. They rely on a strengths-based, empowering approach to bring out the best in the girls and women and to help them develop a sense of self-worth that is essential for them to get a new start in life once they are out on their own.

Looking back over this volume, surveying the work as a whole, I am mindful of the amazing contradictions in a system that seems at times more set-up to bring out the bad in people than the good. Many of these incongruities no doubt are a product of the attempt by society to blend two seemingly disparate elements: criminal justice with its law enforcement focus and social work with its people-changing and societal-changing focus. Among the paradoxes that emerged in the writing of this book and that come most readily to mind are:

- The contradiction between the steadily declining crime rates and the swelling incarceration rate
- The rhetoric of family values matched by punitive corrections policies (and welfare restrictions) that tear families apart
- The absurdity in women who were led by their (often abusive) partners into (usually drug-related) crime sometimes serving longer sentences than their partners who turned them in

- The near-constant offender/victim overlap
- Society's siphoning off vast amounts of money from social services and public education that could prevent crime while investing it in law enforcement and prison construction efforts
- The fact that the very equality that is a boon to some women is being used as a weapon against other women who never stood to benefit from equal opportunity in the first place
- The fact that the war on drugs is being played out as a war on poor women of color
- The incarceration of women in male-model prisons where they are, in turn, sexually objectified by male officers who respond to them as the women they are
- The use of the death penalty to send a message that human life is sacred
- The statistics that show that domestic violence services seem to be doing more to save men's lives from the women who might otherwise kill them than to prevent the murder of women whose lives they were built to save
- The reality that the oldest form of justice—restorative justice—is also the newest form
- The irony that an approach that is more nurturant and on the feminine side of the continuum (restorative-strengths) is an approach with much to offer male as well as female offenders
- And finally, the revelation that the same process geared toward the needs of the victim and community—to right the wrong—can be equally beneficial to the offender, in many instances, providing a kind of catharsis for both offender and victim simultaneously

Given the many contradictions in the system, most of which stem from the prioritizing of punishment over rehabilitation, the journey from a legal system built on retribution to one built on restoration and hope is a long one. For individuals in trouble with the law, the path from offender, to being motivated to change, to healing from their experiences is a long one as well. These paths to recovery and rehabilitation can merge in a gender-sensitive, restorative model for corrections centered on eliciting strengths.

At the personal level, correctional counselors need to impart encouragement and hope. At the policy level, the society needs to look past the masculine war on drugs and adversarial ways of meting out justice (which so often victimize rather than protect women) and toward reform strategies built on the principles of restoration, equitable justice, and truth. If we truly want to create a society in which it is easier for girls and women to stay out of trouble in the first place, we need to invest in relevant economic and treatment resources. And if we want to help ex-offenders achieve their potential, we must reconsider policies that exclude them from subsidized housing, federal educational grants, licensing for certain jobs, and welfare benefits.

Today, nationally, we are at a crossroads; some of us still seeking after just deserts and punishment and others of us looking in new directions. One path, the one we have been following blindly, stubbornly, up until now, leads further down into the mire of fear and darkness. The other trail, almost obscured by the weeds, leads uphill toward the light. This trail we need to follow: The way may not be clearly marked, and it may be steep in places, rocky, and, at times, circuitous. And no doubt there will be a sense of backtracking. Transition is never easy, especially when it involves not only a slight shift in vision but also a repudiation of what went before.

Grassroots organizations, judges, and politicians are currently looking to alternative forms of justice to incarceration and isolation. The Second Class Act, which was signed into federal law in the United States in 2008, established rehabilitation as a key priority of the federal criminal justice system and provided extensive funding for reentry programming (Spjeldnes & Goodkind, 2009). Initiatives to give victims a voice are merging with initiatives to help offenders maintain their family ties and make amends to their victims and the community.

While restorative justice is making inroads in the correctional arena, the strengths perspective is rapidly becoming the predominant theoretical framework of social work practitioners. Within prison walls, even in the most mainstream of settings, gender-specific and ethnic-sensitive programming are coming into their own. And the federal government is actively endorsing gender-specific correctional programming for juvenile and adult females. We may be on the threshold of a new paradigm of justice, an emphasis on treatment rather than on punishment. These treatment innovations must cope with the backdrop of an antifeminist backlash chorus and a political war on drugs that has seen the incarceration of women in prison increase eightfold over the past decade and a half.

Even as the incarceration rate in the United States passes well beyond the 2 million mark, we can find beacons of hope in the form of healing circles, Native family conferencing, victim/offender mediation, extensive mass media attention to forgiveness and restorative justice projects, and a groundswell of grassroots activity for prison reform. Drug courts and other alternatives to prison are proliferating in a society tired of endless wars on crime. Whether on a small or a large scale, a paradigm shift is in the wind. My prediction is based on these three facts:

1. There is a growing recognition that, as a society we are failing victims and failing offenders and the children of offenders.
2. Some people are beginning to realize that a denial of male/female differences is not always in the best interests of women.
3. There is a steady realization that offenders too are victims.

Sweeping change is happening in Canada, in New Zealand, and in Vermont and Minnesota. People are beginning to echo the words of Sister Helen Prejean (2000), who said simply, "Maybe there is another way."

REFERENCES

Abbott, A. A. (2003). Meeting the challenges of substance misuse: Making inroads one step at a time. *Health and Social Work, 28*(2), 83–88.

Abrahams, N. (1996). Negotiating power, identity, family, and community: Women's community participation. *Gender and Society, 10*(6), 768–796.

Acoca, L. (1998, January). Defusing the time bomb: Understanding and meeting the growing health care needs of incarcerated women in America. *Crime and Delinquency, 44*(1), 49–69.

Acoca, L. (2004). Outside/inside. The violation of American girls at home, on the streets, and in the juvenile justice system. In M. Chesney-Lind & L. Pasko (Eds.), *Girls, women, and crime: Selected readings* (pp. 77–96). Thousand Oaks, CA: Sage.

Acoca, L., & Dedel, K. (1998). *No place to hide: Understanding and meeting the needs of girls in the California juvenile justice system.* San Francisco: National Council on Crime and Delinquency.

Acosta, B. (2005, March 11) The redeemers: Ellen Spiro and "Troop 1500." *Austin Chronicle.* Retrieved May 2009, from http://www.mobilusmedia.com/press5.html

Adler, F. (1975). *Sisters in crime: The rise of the new female criminal.* New York: McGraw-Hill.

Alejos, M. (2005, March). *Babies and small children residing in prisons.* Geneva, Switzerland: Quaker United Nations Office.

Alexander, R. (2000). *Counseling, treatment, and intervention methods with juvenile and adult offenders.* Belmont, CA: Wadsworth.

Allport, G. (1954). *The nature of prejudice.* Reading, MA: Addison-Wesley.

American Association of University Women. (1995). *How schools shortchange girls: A study of major findings on girls and education.* New York: Marlow & Company.

American Bar Association. (2009, April 6). *Criminal justice improvements: The Juvenile Justice Delinquency Prevention Act. ABA Practice Essentials.* Retrieved May 2009, from https://www.abanet.org/poladv/priorities/juvjustice/.

American Bar Association and National Bar Association. (2001). *Justice by gender: The lack of appropriate prevention, diversion and treatment alternatives for girls in the justice system.* Retrieved October 2007, from www.abanet.org/crimjust/juvjus/pubs.html.

American Civil Liberties Union. (2005, May 17). *Caught in the net: The impact of drug policies on women and families.* ACLU. Retrieved from www.civilrights.org.

American Psychiatric Association. (2000). *Diagnostic and statistical manual of mental disorders* (4th ed.) text revision (*DSM-IV-TR*). Washington, DC: Author.

American Psychological Association (2002, August). *Guidelines on multicultural education, training, research, practice.* Washington, DC: Author. Retrieved from http://www.apa.org/pi/multiculturalguidelines.pdf.

American Psychological Association. (2007, December 3). Mental illness and drug addiction may co-occur due to disturbance in part of the brain. *ScienceDaily.* Retrieved June 2008, from http://www.scincedaily.com/releases/2007/12/071203090143htm.

Amnesty International. (1999). *Not part of my sentence: Violations of the human rights of women in custody.* New York: Author.

Amnesty International. (2007). *Stop violence against women.* Retrieved January 2008, from http://www.amnestyusa.org/Abuse_of_Women_in_Custody.

Anderson, G. S. (2007). *Biological influences on criminal behavior.* Boca Raton, FL: Taylor and Francis.

Andreasen, N. (2001). *Brave new brain: Conquering mental illness in the era of the genome.* New York: Oxford University.

Andreasen, N. (2006, July). Interviewed by P. Tyre and J. Scelfo in "Why girls will be girls," *Newsweek, 148*(5), 46.

Archer, L., & Grascia, A. (2005, March/April). Girls, gangs, and crime: Profile of the young female offender. *Social Work Today,* 38–41.

Armour, M. P. (2002). Experiences of co-victims of homicide: Implications for research and practice. *Trauma, Violence, and Abuse, 3*(2), 109–124.

Armour, M. P., & Umbreit, M. S. (2006).Victim forgiveness in restorative justice dialogue. *Victims and Offenders, 1,* 123–140.

Arnold, E. M., McNeece, C. A., & Stewart, J. C. (1999). *A community-based intervention for female prostitutes.* Paper presented at the Criminal and Juvenile Justice Symposium. Council on Social Work Education, March 10–13, San Francisco, California.

Aronson, E. (2007). *The social animal.* New York: Worth.

Ashford, J., Sales, B., & LeCroy, C. (2006). Aftercare and recidivism prevention. In D. W. Springer & A. R. Roberts (Eds.), *Handbook of forensic mental health with victims and offenders* (pp. 491–516). New York: Springer.

Australia Bureau of Statistics. (2004). *Prisoners in Australia 2003.* Canberra, Australia. Retrieved December 2007, from http://www.aic.gov.au/stats/cjs/corrections/females.

Babooram, A. (2008, December). The changing profile of adults in custody. *Statistics Canada, 28*(10). Retrieved from http://www.statcan.gc.ca/pub/85-002-x/2008010/article/10732-eng.pdf.

Bacon, V. (2007). What potential might narrative therapy have to assist indigenous Australians reduce substance misuse? *Australian Aboriginal Studies, 1,* 71–82.

Baker, D. V. (2007). Systemic white racism and the brutalization of executed black women in the United States. In R. Muraskin (Ed.), *It's a crime: Women and justice* (4th ed., pp. 394–443). Upper Saddle River, NJ: Prentice Hall.

Baletka, D., & Shearer, R. (2005). Assessing program needs of female offenders who abuse substances. In B. Sims (Ed.), *Substance abuse treatment with correctional clients* (pp. 227–242). New York: Haworth.

Barker, R. (2003). *The social work dictionary* (5th ed.). Washington, DC: NASW Press.

Baron-Cohen, S. (2003). *The essential difference: The truth about the male and female brain.* New York: Basic Books.

Barovick, H. (1999, December 27). Bad to the bone. *Time,* 130–131.

Barrionuevo, A. (2007, December 12). Rape of girl, 15, exposes abuse in Brazil prison system. *New York Times International.*

Basham, K., & Miehls, D. (2004). *Transforming the legacy: Couple therapy with survivors of childhood trauma.* New York: Columbia University.

Bass, E., & Davis, L. (2003). *Beginning to heal (revised ed.): A first book for men and women who were sexually abused as children.* New York: Collins.

Bayse, D. (1996). Teaching inmates to achieve true freedom: The foundation of successful inmate rehabilitation programs. In *Creative therapies and programs in corrections.* American Correctional Association, 5–20.

Bazemore, G., & Boba, R. (2007). "Doing good" to "make good": Community theory for practice in a restorative justice civic engagement reentry model. *Journal of Offender Rehabilitation, 46*(1/2), 25–56.

Beaucar, K. O. (1999, October). Feeling a client's pain too sharply. *NASW News,* 5.

Beck, A. (1991). Cognitive therapy: A 30-year retrospective. *American Psychologist, 46*(4), 368–375.

Beck, A., & Hughes, T. (2005). *Sexual violence reported by correctional authorities, 2004.* U.S. Department of Justice: Bureau of Justice Statistics.

Beck, A. J., & Harrison, P. (2008, April 9). *Sexual victimization in state and federal prisons.* Washington, DC: U.S. Department of Justice, Bureau of Justice Statistics.

Beck, A. J., Harrison, P., & Adams, D. B. (2007, August). *Sexual violence reported by correctional authorities, 2006.* Washington, DC: U.S. Department of Justice, Bureau of Justice Statistics.

Beck, A. T., Rush, J. A., Shaw, B. F., & Emory, G. (1979). *Cognitive theory of depression.* New York: Guilford.

Behnke, S. (1999, June 20). Program aims to break chain of imprisonment. *Waterloo-Cedar Falls Courier* (Iowa).

Behrman, G., & Reid, W. H. (2006). Posttrauma intervention basic tasks. In D. W. Springer & A. R. Roberts (Eds.), *Handbook of forensic mental health with victims and offenders* (pp. 563–572). New York: Springer.

Belenko, S., Patapis, N., & French, M. (2005, February). *Economic benefits of drug treatment: A critical review of the evidence for policy makers.* Philadelphia: Treatment Research Institute at the University of Pennsylvania.

Belknap, J. (2007). *The invisible woman: Gender, crime, and justice* (3rd ed.). Belmont, CA: Thomson.

Bender, K., Kim, J., & Springer, D. W. (2007). Treatment effectiveness with dually diagnosed adolescents: Implications for juvenile offenders. In D. W. Springer & A. R. Roberts (Eds.), *Handbook of forensic mental health with victims and offenders* (pp. 173–203). New York: Springer.

Berg, I. K. (1994). *Family based services: A solution-focused approach.* New York: Norton.

Bhatti-Sinclair, K. (1994). *Developing an anti-racist social work curriculum.* Paper presented at the 27th Congress of the International Schools of Social Work. Amsterdam, the Netherlands.

Bianco, R. (2000, January 18). USA movie tells shocking tale of Letourneau surprisingly well. *USA Today,* p. 10D.

Birkla, N. (2003). Three steps past the monkeys. In W. Lamb (Ed.), *Couldn't keep it to myself: Wally Lamb and the women of York Correctional Institution* (pp. 133–141). New York: Regan Books.

Blake, W. (1793/1967). "A poison tree." *English romantic poets* (p. 61). New York: Harcourt, Brace & World.

Blanchette, K., & Brown, S. L. (2006). *The assessment and treatment of women offenders: An integrative perspective.* West Sussex, UK: John Wiley & Sons.

Block, D. (2008, Winter). More suicides—Whose responsiblilty? *The Fire Inside, 36.* Retrieved May 2008 from http://www.womenprisoners.org/fire/000705.html.

Bloom, B., & Chesney-Lind, M. (2007). Women in prison: Vengeful equity. In R. Muraskin (Ed.), *It's a crime: Women and justice* (pp. 542–563). Upper Saddle River, NJ: Prentice-Hall.

Bloom, B., & Covington, S. (2001, November 7–10). Effective gender-responsive interventions in juvenile justice: Addressing the lives of delinquent girls. Paper presented at the Annual Meeting of the American Society of Criminology. Atlanta, Georgia.

Bloom, B., Owen, B., & Covington, S. (2003). *Gender-responsive strategies: Research, practice, and guiding principles for women offenders.* Washington, DC: U.S. Department of Justice, National Institute of Corrections. Retrieved June 2009, from www.nicic.org.

Bloom, B., Owen, B., & Covington, S. (2004). Women offenders and the gendered effects of public policy. *Review of Policy Research, 21*(1), 31–48.

Boudin, K. (1998). Lessons from a mother's program in prison: A psychosocial approach supports women and their children. *Women and Therapy, 21*(1), 103–125.

Boudin, K. (2007). The resilience of the written off: Women in prison as women of change. *Women's Rights Law Reporter—Rutgers, 29,* 15–27.

The boy crisis: At every level of education, they're falling behind (2006, January 30). *Newsweek.* Front Cover.

Breslau, N., Peterson, E., & Schultz, L. (2008). A second look at prior trauma and the posttraumatic effects of subsequent trauma. *Archives of General Psychiatry, 65*(4), 431–437.

Bricking, T. (1998, June 17). Girls' crimes start to match boys'. *Cincinnati Enquirer,* p. 17.

Brimeyer, L. (2003). Iowa implements mental health re-entry program. *Corrections Today, 65,* 38–39.

British Broadcasting Company. (2001, November 20). Mothers in prison. *Woman's Hour.* Retrieved from www.bbc.co.uk/radio4.

British Broadcasting Company. (2007, January 30). *Jail system in "serious crisis."* Retrieved from http://news.bbc.co.uk/2/hi/6311629.stm.

Brizendine, L. (2007). *The female brain.* New York: Broadway.

Brooker, D. (2007). The reentry programs for women. In R. Muraskin (Ed.), *It's a crime: Women and justice* (pp. 564–571). Upper Saddle River, NJ: Pearson.

Brown, C. (2007). Situating knowledge and power in the therapeutic alliance. In C. Brown & T. Augusta (Eds.), *Narrative therapy: Making meaning, making lives* (pp. 3–22). Thousand Oaks, CA: Sage.

Burdge, B. (2007). Bending gender, ending gender: Theoretical foundations for social work practice with the transgender community. *Social Work, 52*(3), 243–250.

Bureau of Justice Statistics. (1980). *Uniform Crime Report.* Washington, DC: U.S. Department of Justice.

Bureau of Justice Statistics. (2000, October). *Women offenders.* Washington, DC: U.S. Department of Justice. Retrieved December 2007, from www.ojp.usdoj.gov/bjs/pub/pdf/wo.pdf+bjs+1999+female+offenders.

Bureau of Justice Statistics. (2002). Recidivism of prisoners released in 1994. *Federal Sentencing Reporter, 15*(1), 58–65.

Bureau of Justice Statistics. (2006). *Mental health problems of prison and jail inmates.* Washington, DC: U.S. Department of Justice. Retrieved June 2008, from www.ojp.usdoj.gov/bjs/pub/pdf/mhppji.pdf.

Bureau of Justice Statistics. (2007, July). *Homicide trends in the U.S.: Intimate homicide.* Washington, DC: U.S. Department of Justice.

Bureau of Justice Statistics. (2008, August). *Criminal victimization in the United States—Statistical tables.* Table 38. Washington, DC: U.S. Department of Justice. Retrieved July 2009, from www.ojp.usdoj.gov/bjs/abstract/cvus/single_offender_victimizations298.htm.

Bureau of Justice Statistics. (2009a). *Capital punishment statistics.* Washington, DC: U.S. Department of Justice.

Bureau of Justice Statistics. (2009b, May). *Probation and parole statistics.* Retrieved July 2009 from www.ojp.usdoj.gov/bjs/pandp.htm.

Burrell, I., & Wallis, L. (1999, February 22). New unit to treat female paedophiles. *The Independent* (UK).

Bush-Baskette, S. R. (1998). The war on drugs as a war against black women. In S. L. Miller (Ed.), *Crime control and women: Feminist implications of criminal justice police* (pp. 113–129). Thousand Oaks, CA: Sage.

Butterfield, F. (2003, December 29). Women find a new arena for equality: Prison. *New York Times.* Retrieved November 2007, from http://query.nytimes.com/gst/fullpage.html?res=9A05E5D6123EF93AA15751C1A9659C8B63.

Buying sex can yield jail term: News from Norway. (2007, July 4). *Aftenposten.* Retrieved January 2008, from www.aftenposten.no/english/local/article1870915.ece.

Cabeza, R. (2002). Hemispheric asymmetry reduction in older adults: The HAROLD model. *Psychology & Aging, 17,* 85–100.

Cahill, L. (2006). Why sex matters for neuroscience. *Nature Reviews Neuroscience, 7,* 477–484.

Canadian Association of Elizabeth Fry Societies. (2007). *Criminalized and imprisoned women.* Retrieved January 2008, from http:// www.elizabethfry.ca/eweek07/pdf/crmwomen.pdf.

Carmody, M. (1997). Submerged voices: Coordinators of sexual assault services peak of their experiences. *Affilia, 12*(4), 452–470.

Carroll, M. (1993). *Spiritual growth of recovering alcoholic children of alcoholics.* Unpublished doctoral dissertation, University of Maryland, Baltimore.

Catalano, S., Smith, E., Snyder, H., & Rand, M. (2009, October 23). *Female victims of violence.* Washington, DC: U.S. Department of Justice. Retrieved from http://www.ojp.usdoj.gov/bjs/pub/pdf/fvv.pdf.

Cauffman, E. (2008). Understanding the female offender. *Future of Children, 18*(2), 119–143.

Cela-Conde, C., et al. (2009). Sex- related similarities and differences in the neural correlates of beauty. *Proceedings of the National Academy of Sciences of the United States of America, 106*(10), 3847–3852.

Center for Substance Abuse Treatment. (2004). *Substance abuse treatment and family therapy.* Treatment Improvement Protocol (TIP) Series 39. Rockville, MD: Substance Abuse and Mental Health Services Administration.

Center for Substance Abuse Treatment. (2005). *Substance abuse treatment for persons with co-occurring disorders.* Treatment Improvement Protocol (TIP) Series 42. DHHS Publication No. (SMA) 05-3922. Rockville, MD: Substance Abuse and Mental Health Services Administration.

Centers for Disease Control and Prevention. (2006). *Youth risk behavior surveillance—United States, 2005.* Washington, DC: Author. Retrieved October 2007, from www.cdc.gov/mmwR/preview/mmwrhtml/ss5302a1.htm.

Centers for Disease Control and Prevention. (2007, January 27). *Victimization of persons with traumatic brain disorder.* Retrieved June 2009, from www.cdc.gov/ncipc/tbi/FactSheets/VictimizationTBI_FactSheet4Professionals.htm-42k.

Chesney-Lind, M., Morash, M., & Stevens, T. (2008). Girls' troubles, girls' delinquency, and gender responsive programming: A review. *Australian and New Zealand Journal of Criminology, 41*(1), 162–190.

Chesney-Lind, M., & Pasko, L. (2004). *The female offender: Girls, women, and crime.* Thousand Oaks, CA: Sage.

Chesney-Lind, M., & Pollock, J. (1994). Women's prisons: Equality with a vengeance. In A. Merlo & J. Pollock (Eds.), *Women, law and social control* (pp. 155–177). Boston: Allyn & Bacon.

Chesney-Lind, M., & Shelden, R. (2004). *Girls, delinquency, and juvenile justice.* Belmont, CA: Thomson.

Chestnut Health Systems. (2002). *Project Safe overview.* Lighthouse Institute. Retrieved May 2008 from http://www.chestnut.org/LI/projectsafe/Overview.html.

Colon, E. (2007). A multidiversity perspective on Latinos: Issues of oppression and social functioning. In G. A. Appleby, E. Colon, & J. Hamilton (Eds.), *Diversity, oppression, and social functioning: Person-in-environment assessment and intervention* (2nd ed., pp. 115–134). Boston: Allyn & Bacon.

Comack, E., & Brickey, S. (2007). Constituting the violence of criminalized women. *Canadian Journal of Criminology and Criminal Justice, 49*, 1–37.

Corcoran, J. (2005). *Building strengths and skills: A collaborative approach to working with clients.* New York: Oxford University.

Correctional Association of New York. (2006, May). *Bedford Hills Correctional Facility.* Retrieved July 2009, from http://www.correctionalassociation.org/publications/ download/wipp/facility_reports/bedford_2005.pdf.

Correctional Association of New York. (2007). *Report on mental health programs and services at Bedford Hills Correctional Facility.* Retrieved June 2008, from http://www. correctionalassociation.org/WIPP/prison_monitoring/Bedford_MentalHealth_2007 .pdf.

Correctional Association of New York. (2009, April). *Fact sheet: Incarcerated women and HIV/Hepatitis C. Women in Prison Project.* Retrieved July 2009, from http:// www.correctionalassociation.org/publications/download/wipp/factsheets/HIV_ Hep_C_Fact_Sheet_2009_FINAL.pdf.

Correctional Service of Canada. (1990/2007). *Creating choices: The report of the task force on federally sentenced women.* Retrieved July 2009, from http://www.csc-scc .gc.ca/text/prgrm/fsw/choices/choice1e-eng.shtml.

Corston, J. (2007, March). *The Corston report: Executive summary.* London: Crown Publishers.

Cournoyer, B. (2008). *The social work skills workbook* (5th ed.). Belmont, CA: Brooks/ Cole.

Cowger, C., Anderson, K., & Snively, C. (2006). Assessing strengths: The political context of individual, family, and community empowerment. In D. Saleebey, *The strengths perspective in social work practice* (4th ed., pp. 93–115). Boston: Allyn & Bacon.

Crites, L. (1976). Women offenders: Myth vs. reality. In Laura Crites (Ed.), *The female offender* (pp. 36–39). Lexington, MA: Lexington Books.

Curley, B. (2004, September 2). *Recovery advocates, drug courts seek common ground at conference.* Join Together Online. Retrieved June 2006, from http://www .jointogether.org/sa/news/features.

Curley, B. (2009, February 6). *New Hazelden survey finds strong support for treatment, recovery.* Join Together Online. Retrieved May 2009, from http://www.jointogether .org/news/features/2009/new-hazelden-survey.html.

Curran, N. (2000). Blue hairs in the bighouse: The rise in the elderly inmate population. *New England Journal on Criminal and Civil Confinement, 26*(2), 225–264.

Cusack, K. J., Morrissey, J. P., & Ellis, A. R. (2008). Targeting trauma-related interventions and improving outcomes for women with co-occurring disorders. *Administration and Policy in Mental Health and Mental Health Services Research, 35*(3), 147–158.

Dabbs, J. M. Jr. (1998). Testosterone and the concept of dominance. *Behavioral and Brain Sciences, 21,* 370–371.

Daily suicide battle at prison. (2006, February 27). BBC. Retrieved July 2009, from http://news.bbc.co.uk/2/hi/uk_news/england/manchester/4753178.stm.

Daly, K. (1994). *Gender, crime, and punishment.* New Haven, CT: Yale University.

Day, D. (1952). *The long loneliness.* New York: Harper & Row.

Defeis, M. (1996, May 18). Women and children—hidden casualties in the drug war. *America, 174*(17), 6–9.

De Jong, P., & Berg, I. K. (2002). *Interviewing for solutions* (2nd ed.). Belmont, CA: Wadsworth.

De Jong, P., & Berg, I. K. (2007). *Interviewing for solutions* (3rd ed.). Belmont, CA: Brooks/Cole.

Dell, C., Fillmore, C., & Kilty, J. (2009). Looking back 10 years after the Arbour inquiry. *The Prison Journal, 89* (3), 206–308.

Demaree, H. A., Harrison, D. W., & Rhodes, R. D. (2000). Quantitative electroencephalographic analyses of cardiovascular regulation in low- and high-hostile men. *Psychobiology, 28*(3), 420–431.

De Santis, M. (2007). *Sweden's prostitution solution: Why hasn't anyone tried this before?* Women's Justice Center. Retrieved December 2007, from http://www.justicewomen.com/cj_sweden.html.

Deschenes, E., Ireland, C., & Kleinpeter, C. (2009). Enhancing drug court success. *Journal of Offender Rehabilitation, 48,* 19–36.

Dolgoff, R., Loewenberg, F. M., & Harrington, D. (2005). *Ethical issues for social work practice* (7th ed.). Belmont, CA: Brooks/Cole.

Downs, W. R., Capshew, T., & Rindels, B. (2004). Relationships between adult men's alcohol problems and their childhood experiences of parental violence and psychological aggression. *Journal of Studies on Alcohol, 65*(3), 336–345.

Drug Policy Alliance. (2007). *Drugs, police, and the law.* Retrieved December 2007, from http://www.drugpolicy.org/law/publicbenefi/index.cfm.

Drug Prevention Networks of the Americas. (2002, April). *The changing face of European drug policy.* Retrieved November 2007, from http://www.dpna.org/resources/trends/changingface.htm.

Dziegielewski, S. F., & Resnick, C. (1996). Assessment and intervention: Abused women in the shelter setting. In A. R. Roberts (Ed.), *Crisis management and brief treatment: Theory, technique and application* (pp. 123–141). Edinburgh: University of Edinburgh.

Edwards, T. M. (1998, February 16). Mad about the boy. *Time,* 103.

Egan, T. (1999, February 28). The war on crack retreats, still taking prisoners. *New York Times.*

Eghigian, M., & Kirby, K. (2006, April). Girls in gangs: On the rise in America. *Corrections Today, 68*(2), 48–51.

Egley, A., & Ritz, C. (2006, April). *Highlights of the 2004 National Youth Gang Survey.* Washington, DC: U.S. Department of Justice.

Eleven-plus to be abolished. (2004, January 26). BBC News. Retrieved July 2009, from http://news.bbc.co.uk/2/hi/uk_news/northern_ireland/3429541.stm.

Elliott, W. (2006). Power and control tactics employed by prison inmates—a case study. *Federal Probation, 70*(1), 45–48.

Ellis, A. (2001). *Overcoming destructive beliefs, feelings, and behaviors: New directions for rational emotive behavior therapy.* Amherst, NY: Prometheus Books.

Elsner, A. (2006). *Gates of injustice: The crisis in America's prisons* (2nd ed.) Boston: Pearson.

Erez, E. (1988). The myth of the new female offender: Some evidence from attitudes toward law and justice. *Journal of Criminal Justice, 16*(6), 499–509.

Erikson, E. (1963). *Childhood and society* (2nd ed.). New York: Norton.

Erikson, K. (1964). Notes on the sociology of deviance. In H. S. Becker (Ed.), *The other side* (pp. 9–22). New York: Free Press.

Erikson, K. (1966). *Wayward Puritans: A study in the sociology of deviance.* New York: John Wiley & Sons.

Estés, C. P. (1992). *Women who run with the wolves: Myths and stories of the wild woman archetype.* New York: Ballantine.

Eurochips. (2007, September). *News: Sweden.* Retrieved from http://www.eurochips.org/uk_news.html

Ex-teacher, rapist has second child. (1998, October 18). *Des Moines Register* (Iowa). From Tacoma, Washington, Associated Press.

Fadem, P. (2006, Fall). A medical assistant stands up for human rights. *The Fire Inside, 34.* Retrieved May 2008, from http://www.womenprisoners.org/fire/000651.html.

Failinger, M. (2006). Lessons unlearned: Women offenders, the ethics of care, and the promise of restorative justice. *Fordham Urban Law Journal, 33*(2), 487–527.

Faith, K. (1993). *Unruly women: The politics of confinement and resistance.* Vancouver: Press Gang.

Faith, K. (2004). Progressive rhetoric, regressive policies: Canadian prisons for women. In B. Price and N. Sokoloff (Eds.), *The criminal justice system and women: Offenders, victims, and workers* (pp. 281–288). New York: McGraw-Hill.

Families Against Mandatory Minimums (1997, December 19). Press statement. In M. Owens (Ed.), *Testimony on behalf of the National Center for Women in Prison.* Washington DC: Report to the U.S. Congress.

Farley, M., & Barkan, H. (1998). Prostitution, violence, and post-traumatic stress disorder. *Women and Health, 27*(3), 37–50.

Farr, K. A. (2004). Defeminizing and dehumanizing female murderers: Depictions of lesbians on death row. In B. Price & N. Sokoloff (Eds.), *The criminal justice system and women* (pp. 249–260). Boston: McGraw-Hill.

Farrell, A. (1998). Mothers offending against their role: An Australian experience. *Women and Criminal Justice, 9*(4), 47–67.

Federal Bureau of Investigation. (1998, September). *Uniform Crime Reports. Persons arrested.* Washington, DC: U.S. Department of Justice. Retrieved June 2009, from http://www.fbi.gov/ucr/Cius_97/97crime/97crime4.pdf.

Federal Bureau of Investigation. (2009, September). *Uniform Crime Reports.* Washington, DC: U.S. Department of Justice. Retrieved from http://www.fbi.gov/ucr/cius2008/data/table_42.html.

Feinman, C. (1980). *Women in the criminal justice system.* New York: Praeger.

Feinman, C. (1994). *Women in the criminal justice system* (3rd ed.). Westport, CT: Praeger.

Ferszt, G., Salgado, D., DeFedele, S., & Leveillee, M. (2009). Houses of healing: A group intervention for grieving women in prison. *Prison Journal, 89*(1), 46–64.

Fisher, A. (2004). *If I knew then.* Lincoln, Nebraska: iUniverse.

Ford, H. (2006). *Women who sexually abuse children.* West Sussex, UK: John Wiley & Sons.

Fordham, S. (1993). "Those loud black girls": (Black) women, silence, and gender "passing" in the academy. *Anthropology and Education Quarterly, 24*(1), 3–32.

Foreshaw, B. (2003). Family, power, and pants. In W. Lamb (Ed.), *Couldn't keep it to myself: Wally Lamb and the women of York correctional institution* (pp. 245–265). New York: Regan Books.

Fraerman, A. (2007, March). *Gypsies account for one in four female inmates.* One World Net. Retrieved from www.oneworld.net.

Franklin, C., & Lutze, F. (2007). Home confinement and intensive supervision as unsafe havens: The unintended consequences for women. In R. Muraskin (Ed.), *It's a crime: Women and justice* (4th ed., pp. 608–623). Upper Saddle River, NJ: Prentice Hall.

Fredrickson, C., & McCurdy, J. (2008, February 12). *Federal cocaine sentencing laws. Reforming the 100-to-1 crack/powder disparity.* Washington, DC: American Civil Liberties Union. Retrieved June 2009, from http://www.aclu.org/images/asset_upload_file4_34081.pdf.

Friedman S. H., Horwitz, S. M., & Resnick, P. J. (2005). Child murder by mothers: A critical analysis of the current state of knowledge and a research agenda. *American Journal of Psychiatry, 162,* 1578–1587.

Fromm, E. (1956). *The art of loving.* New York: Harper & Brothers.

Furst, G. (2006). Prison-based animal programs: A national survey. *Prison Journal, 86,* 407–430.

Gaarder, E., & Belknap, J. (2004). Tenuous borders: Girls transferred to adult court. In B. Price & N. Sokoloff (Eds.), *The criminal justice system and women: Offenders, prisoners, victims and workers* (pp. 69–93). New York: McGraw-Hill.

Garcia, C., & Lane, J. (2009). What a girl wants, what a girl needs: Findings from a gender-specific focus group study. *Crime and Delinquency.* doi:10.1177/0011128709331790.

Garcia, E. (2008, April 18). A painful choice for moms in prison. *Mercury News,* San Jose, CA. Retrieved April 2008, from http://www.mercurynews.com/ci_8969528?source=most_viewed.

Gaskins, S. (2004). "Women of circumstance"—the effects of mandatory minimum sentencing on women minimally involved in drug crimes. *American Criminal Law Review, 41*(4), 1533–1554.

Gendreau, P., & Ross, R. (1980). *Effective correctional treatment.* Toronto: Butterworth.

General Accounting Office (1999). *Women in prison: Issues and challenges confronting U.S. correctional systems.* Washington, DC: U.S. Department of Justice.

Giallombardo, R. (1966). *Society of women.* New York: John Wiley & Sons.

Gibbens, T. C. N. (1971). Female offenders. *British Journal of Hospital Medicine, 6,* 279–286.

Gilfus, M. E. (1998, March 4–8). *Trauma and ethical dilemmas in the narrative voices of incarcerated women.* Paper presented at the Council on Social Work Education, Orlando, FL.

Gilfus, M. E. (2002). *Women's experiences of abuse as a risk factor for incarceration.* Applied Research Forum. National Electronic Network on Violence against Women. Retrieved September 2007, from www.vawnet.org.

Gilligan, C. (1979). Woman's place in a man's life cycle. *Harvard Educational Review,* 49(4), 431–446.

Gilligan, C. (1982). *In a different voice: Psychological theory and women's development.* Cambridge, MA: Harvard University.

Gilligan, C. (2002). *The birth of pleasure.* New York: Knopf.

Gilligan, C. (2003). Sisterhood is pleasurable: A quiet revolution in psychology. In R. Morgan (Ed.), *Sisterhood is forever: The women's anthology for a new millennium* (pp. 94–102). New York: Washington Square.

Gilligan, C. (2009, January). Interviewed by Mechthild Kiegelmann. Making oneself vulnerable to discovery. *Forum: Qualitative Social Research,* 10(2), article 3. Retrieved May 2009, from http://www.qualitativeresearch.net/index.php/fqs/article/view/1178/2718.

GlenMaye, L. (1997). Empowerment for women. In Guitérrez, L. Parsons, R. J., & Cox, E. O. (Eds.), *Empowerment in social work practice: A sourcebook* (pp. 29–51). Pacific Grove, CA: Brooks/Cole.

Goff, C. (1999). *Corrections in Canada.* Cincinnati, OH: Anderson.

Goodkind, S. (2005). Gender-specific services in the juvenile justice system: A critical examination. *Affilia, 20,* 52–70.

Goodkind, S., Ng, I., & Sarri, R. (2006). At risk of involvement with the juvenile justice system or the impact of sexual abuse in the lives of young women involved. *Violence against Women, 12,* 456–477.

Gordon, K. G. (2004, January). *From corrections to connections: A report on the AMICUS girls' restorative program.* Unpublished paper. Retrieved October 2007, from http://www.amicususa.org/Girls%20Final%20Report%20-%20Jan%2004.pdf.

Gordon, R. (2008, May 20). Settlement plan offers prison alternatives. *San Francisco Chronicle.* Retrieved June 2008, from http://www.sfgate.com/cgibin/article.cgi?file=/c/a/2008/05/20/BAOK10PBM1.DTL.

Gormley, M. (2007, October 20). *Records: Seduction, manipulation by teachers lead to affairs.* Retrieved December 2007, from http://www.ap.org/foi/foi_102107a.html.

Green, C. (1998, January 11). Without memory, there is not healing: Without forgiveness, there is no future. *Parade,* 5–7.

Greene, J., & Pranis, K. (2006). *Treatment instead of prisons.* Drug Policy Alliance. Retrieved January 2007, from http://drugpolicy.org.

Gundersen, K., & Svartdal, F. (2006). Aggression replacement training in Norway: Outcome evaluation of 11 Norwegian student projects. *Scandinavian Journal of Educational Research, 50*(1), 63–81.

Gur, R. C., Gunning-Dixon, F., Bilker, W., & Gur, R. E. (2002). Sex differences in temporo-limbic and frontal brain volumes of healthy adults. *Journal of Cerebral Cortex, 12*(9), 998–1003.

Gutiérrez, L., Parsons, R. J., & Cox, E. O. (Eds.). (1997). *Empowerment in social work practice: A sourcebook.* Pacific Grove, CA: Brooks/Cole.

Gutiérrez, L., & Suarez, Z. (1999). Empowerment with Latinas. In L. A. Gutiérrez & E. A. Lewis (Eds.), *Empowerment of women of color* (pp. 167–186). New York: Columbia University.

Hamilton, G., & Sutterfield, T. (1998). Comparison study of women who have and have not murdered their abusive partners. *Women & Therapy, 20*(4), 45–55.

Hannah-Moffat, K., & Shaw, M. (2003). The meaning of "risk" in women's prisons: A critique. In B. E. Bloom (Ed.), *Gendered justice: Addressing female offenders* (pp. 45–68). Durham, NC: Carolina Academic Press.

Hargrove, M., & Dabbs, J. M. (1997). Age, testosterone, and behavior among female prison inmates. *Psychosomatic Medicine, 59*(5), 477–480.

Harper Index. (2007, December 17). *Privatization—Harper conservatives quietly eye options.* Retrieved July 2009, from http://www.harperindex.ca/ViewArticle. cfm?Ref=0067.

Harris, J. (1988). *They called us ladies.* New York: Zebra Books.

Hartman, A., & Laird, J. (1983). *Family-centered social work practice.* New York: Free Press.

Hayman, S. (2006). *Imprisoning our sisters: The new federal women's prisons in Canada.* Montreal: McGill-Queen's University.

Healey, K. (1999, February). *Case management in the criminal justice system.* National Institute of Justice. Retrieved from http://www.ncjrs.gov/pdffiles1/173409 .pdf.

Heim, C., et al. (2000). Pituitary-adrenal and autonomic responses to stress in women after sexual and physical abuse in childhood. *Journal of the American Medical Association, 284,* 592–597.

Hemenway-Forbes, M. (2001, April 30). Comfort in love. *Waterloo-Cedar Falls Courier.*

Hensley, C., Castle, T., & Tewksbury, R. (2003). Inmate-to-inmate sexual coercion in a prison for women. *Journal of Offender Rehabilitation, 37*(2), 77–87.

Hensley, C., Tewksbury, R., & Koscheski, M. (2002). Wardens' perceptions of prison sex. *Women and Criminal Justice, 13*(2/3), 125–139.

Hess-Biber, S. (2007). *The cult of thinness.* New York: Oxford University.

Holsinger, K., & Holsinger, A. (2005). Differential pathways to violence and self-injurious behavior: African American and white girls in the juvenile justice system. *Journal of Research in Crime and Delinquency, 42,* 211–242.

Holtfreter, K., & Cupp, R. (2007). *Gender and risk assessment: The empirical status of the LSI-R for women.* Annual meeting of the American Society of Criminology, Atlanta, GA.

Hooks, B. (1993). *Sisters of the yam: Black women and self-recovery.* Boston: South End.

Hosser, D., Windzio, M., & Greve, W. (2008). Guilt and shame as predictors of recidivism: A longitudinal study with young prisoners. *Criminal Justice and Behavior*, 35(1), 138–152.

Hubbard, D., & Matthews, B. (2008). Reconciling the differences between the "gender-responsive" and the "what works" literatures to improve services for girls. *Crime and Delinquency*, 54, 225–258.

Human Rights Watch. (2003). *Ill equipped: U.S. prisons and offenders with mental illness.* New York: Author. Retrieved December 2007, from http://www.hrw.org/reports/2003.

Human Rights Watch. (2006, September). *Girls abused in New York's juvenile prisons: Violent restraints, sexual abuse must stop.* New York: Author. Retrieved October 2007, from http://hrw.org.

Human Rights Watch. (2007, December 16). *New report by Justice Department underscores need for zero tolerance.* Retrieved July 2009, from http://www.hrw.org/en/news/2007/12/15/us-federal-statistics-show-widespread-prison-rape.

Human Rights Watch Women's Rights Project (1996). *All too familiar: Sexual abuse of women in U.S. state prisons.* New York: Human Rights Watch.

Jackson, M., & Banks, C. (2007). Fatal attraction in Arizona, In R. Muraskin (Ed.), *It's a crime: Women and criminal justice* (4th ed., pp. 160–180). Upper Saddle River, NJ: Pearson.

Jacobs, M. S. (2006). Loyalty's reward—a felony conviction: Recent prosecutions of high-status female offenders. *Fordham Urban Law Journal*, 33(3), 843–876.

Jessamy, M. (2003). Mother love. In W. Lamb (Ed.), *Couldn't keep it to myself: Wally Lamb and the women of York correctional institution* (pp. 245–265). New York: Regan Books.

Johnson, C. (2009, October 16). Bill targets sentencing rules for crack and powder cocaine. *Washington Post.* Retrieved from http://www.washingtonpost.com/wp-dyn/content/article/2009/10/15/AR2009101501992.html.

Johnson, H. (2004). *Psyche and synapse expanding worlds: The role of neurobiology in emotions, behavior, thinking, and addiction for non-scientists* (2nd ed.). Greenfield, MA: Deerfield Valley.

Jones, A. (1980). *Women who kill.* New York: Holt, Rinehart & Winston.

Joo Lin, T. (2008, September 8). Jailbabes. *The Straits Times.* Asiaone: Just women. Retrieved from http://www.asiaone.com/Just%2BWoman/Motherhood/Stories/Story/A1Story20080904-85886.html.

Kantrowitz, B. (1997, July 7). Cradles to coffins. *Newsweek*, 52–54.

Kasinsky, R. (1994). Child neglect and "unfit" mothers: Childsavers in the progressive era and today. *Women and Criminal Justice*, 6, 97–129.

Kassebaum, P. (1999). *Substance abuse treatment for women offenders: Guide to promising practice.* Rockford, MD: U.S. Department of Health and Human Services.

Katz, R. (2000). Explaining girls' and women's crime and desistance in the context of their victimization experiences: A developmental test of revised strain theory and the life course perspective. *Violence Against Women*, 6, 633–660.

Kendall, K., & Pollack, S. (2003). Cognitive behavioralism in women's prisons: A critical analysis of therapeutic assumptions and practices. In B. E. Bloom (Ed.), *Gendered justice: Addressing female offenders* (pp. 69–96). Durham, NC: Carolina Academic Press.

Killeen, T., Hien, D., Campbell, A., Brown, C., Hansen, C., Jiang, H., et al. (2008). Adverse events in an integrated trauma-focused intervention for women in community substance abuse treatment. *Journal of Substance Abuse Treatment, 35*(3), 304–312.

Kimmel, M. (November 2000). A war against boys? *Tikkun, 15*(6), 57.

King, N. (2003). *Providing a promising future for Nevada's girls: A statement gender-specific services plan.* Carson City, NV: Juvenile Justice Program Office.

Klar, A. (2004). Excess of counterclockwise scalp hair-whorl rotation in homosexual men. *Indian Academy of Sciences Journal of Genetics, 83*(3), 251–255.

Kopala, M., & Keitel, M. (Eds.) (2003). *Handbook of counseling women.* Thousand Oaks, CA: Sage.

Kress, V., & Hoffman, R. (2008). Non-suicidal self-injury and motivational interviewing: Enhancing readiness for change. *Journal of Mental Health Counseling, 30*(4), 311–329.

Kruttschnitt, C., & Vuolo, M. (2007). The cultural context of women prisoners' mental health: A comparison of two prison systems. *Punishment & Society, 9*, 115–150.

Kubiak, S. (2009). Assessing the therapeutic environment in hybrid models of treatment: Prisoner perceptions of staff. *Journal of Offender Rehabilitation, 48*, 85–100.

Kubiak, S., & Arfken, C. (2006). Beyond gender responsivity: Considering differences among community-dwelling women involved in the criminal justice system and those involved in treatment. *Women and Criminal Justice, 17*(2/3), 75–94.

Kubiak, S., & Rose, I. (2007). Trauma and posttraumatic stress disorder in inmates with histories of substance use. In D. W. Springer & A. R. Roberts (Eds.), *Handbook of forensic mental health with victims and offenders* (pp. 445–466). New York: Springer.

Lake, J. (2007). Nonconventional and integrative treatments of alcohol and substance abuse, *Psychiatric Times, 24*(6). Retrieved June 2008, from http://www.psychiatrictimes.com/substanceabuse/article/10168/53926?pageNumber=3.

Lamb, W. (2003). *Couldn't keep it to myself: Wally Lamb and the women of York Correctional Institution.* New York: Regan Books.

Landsberg, G., & Rees, J. (2007). Forensic practices and serving dually diagnosed youth involved with the juvenile justice system. In D. W. Springer & A. R. Roberts (Eds.), *Handbook of forensic mental health with victims and offenders* (pp. 205–223). New York: Springer.

Lane, B. (2003). Puzzle pieces. In W. Lamb (Ed.), *Couldn't keep it to myself: Wally Lamb and the women of York Correctional Institution* (pp. 211–243). New York: Regan Books.

Lederman, C. S., Dakof, G. A., Larreal, M. A., & Hua, L. (2004). Characteristics of adolescent females in juvenile detention. *International Journal of Law and Psychiatry, 27*, 321–337.

Leinwand, D. (2009, May 20). U.S new drug czar targets prescription abuse as priority. *USA Today*.

Lemieux, C. (2008). *Offenders and substance abuse: Bringing the family into focus.* Alexandria, VA: American Correctional Association.

Lerner, R. (2007). *The good teen: Rescuing adolescents from the myths of the storm and stress years.* New York: Crown.

Leukefeld, C., et al. (2009). Drug abuse treatment beyond prison walls. *Addiction Science and Clinical Practice, 5*(1), 24–30.

Leverentz, A. (2006). The love of a good man? Romantic relationships as a source of support or hindrance for female ex-offenders. *Journal of Research in Crime and Delinquency, 43,* 459–488.

Levin, J. (1999, February). Uncle Tom's cell: Prison labor gives a market fact to an old idea—slavery. *Perspective Magazine.* Retrieved from www.digitas.harvard.edu/~perspy/issues/1999/feb/uneleton.shtml.

Levine, K. L (2006). No penis, no problem. *Fordham Urban Law Journal.* Emory Public Law Research Paper No. 05-37. Available at SSRN: http://ssrn.com/abstract=869028.

Levine, S. (2007, August 2). Female inmates show high rate of HIV. *Washington Post.*

Listwan, S., Shaffer, D., & Hartman, J. (2008). Combating methamphetamine use in the community: The efficacy of the drug court model. *Crime & Delinquency, 20*(10), 627–644.

Lithwick, D. (2009, April 20). Women: The fairer sex. *Newsweek,* 13.

Lombroso, C., & Ferrero, W. (1895). *The female offender.* London: T. Fisher Unwin.

Lovins, L., Lowenkamp, C., Latessa, E., & Smith, P. (2007). Application of the risk principle to female offenders. *Journal of Contemporary Criminal Justice, 23*(4), 383–398.

Luke, K. (2008). Are girls really becoming more violent? A critical analysis. *Affilia, 23*(1), 38–50.

Luxenburg, J., & Guild, T. E. (2007). Women, AIDS, and the criminal justice system. In R. Muraskin, (Ed.), *It's a crime: Women and justice* (4th ed., pp. 379–391). Upper Saddle River, NJ: Pearson.

Mabin, C. (2007, February 25). Corrections, agency pay closer attention to aging inmates. *Journal Star* (Lincoln, Nebraska). Retrieved June 2008, from www.journalstar.com/articles/2007/02/25/news/local.

MacDonald, J., & Chesney-Lind, M. (2004). Gender bias and juvenile justice revisited. In M. Chesney-Lind & L. Pasko (Eds.), *Girls, women and crime* (pp. 128–143). Thousand Oaks, CA: Sage.

Maidment, M. (2006). "We're not all that criminal": Getting beyond the pathologizing and individualizing of women's crime. *Women & Therapy, 29*(3/4), 35–56.

Maison, S. R., & Larson, N. R. (1995). Psychosexual treatment program for women sex offenders in a prison setting. *Nordisk Sexology, 13,* 149–162.

Marks, A. (2003, March 7). For more black girls, a violent cycle. *Christian Science Monitor,* 2.

Martin, A. D., Epstein, L., & Boyd, C. (2007, July 25). *Untangling the causal effects of sex on judging.* Paper presented at the annual meeting of the Law and Society Association, Berlin, Germany. Retrieved June 2009, from http://epstein.law .northwestern.edu/research/genderjudging.pdf.

Maruschak, L. (2008). *HIV in prisons, 2006.* Washington, DC: U.S. Department of Justice, Bureau of Justice Statistics.

Matthews, B., & Hubbard, D. J. (2008). Moving ahead: Five essential elements for working effectively with girls. *Journal of Criminal Justice, 36,* 494–502.

McCurley, C. (2006). *Self-reported law-violating behavior from adolescence in a modern cohort.* Rockville, MD: National Institute of Justice. Retrieved October 2007, from http://www.ncjrs.gov/pdffiles1/nij/grants/217588.pdf.

McGoldrick, M., Giordano, J., & Garcia-Petro, N. (Eds.). (2005). *Ethnicity and family therapy* (pp. 1–40). New York: Guilford.

McKee, G. (2006). *Why mothers kill: A forensic psychologist's casebook.* New York: Oxford University.

McQuaide, S., & Ehrenreich, J.H. (1998). Women in prison: Approaches to understanding the lives of a forgotten population. *Affilia, 13*(2), 233–246.

Men are from Mars: Neuroscientists find the men and women respond differently to stress. (2008, April 1). *Science Daily.* Retrieved June 2009, from http://www .sciencedaily.com/videos/2008/0403-men_are_from_mars.htm.

Men are more likely than women to be victims in dating violence.(2006, May 19). *UNH Media.* Interview with Murray Straus. Retrieved July 2009, from http://www .unh.edu/news/cj_nr/2006/may/em_060519male.cfm?type=n.

Messerschmidt, J. (2005). Men, masculinities, and crime. In M. Kimmel, J. Hearn, & R. Connell (Eds.), *Handbook of studies on men and masculinities* (pp. 196–212). Thousand Oaks, CA: Sage.

Miazad, O. (2002). Legislative focus. *Human Rights Brief.. 10*(1), 37. Washington College of Law. Retrieved October 2007, from http://www.wcl.american.edu/ hrbrief/10/1gender.cfm.

Middle school girls catching up to boys in delinquency (2005, October 5). Research news. *University of Florida News.* Retrieved September 2007, from http://news.ufl .edu/2005/10/05/middle-school/.

Miley, K. K., O'Melia, M., DuBois, B. (2006). *Generalist social work practice: An empowering approach* (5th ed.). Boston: Allyn & Bacon.

Miller, B. (1998, December). Different not more difficult: Gender-specific training helps bridge the gap. *Corrections Today,* 142–144.

Miller, J. (2001). *One of the guys: Girls, gangs, and gender.* New York: Oxford University.

Miller, J. (2008). *Getting played: African American girls, urban inequality and gendered violence.* New York: New York University.

Miller, J. B. (1976). *Toward a new psychology of women.* Boston: Beacon Press.

Miller, W. R., & Carroll, K. M. (2006). Drawing the science together: Ten principles, ten recommendations. In W. R. Miller & K. M. Carroll (Eds.), *Rethinking substance abuse: What the science shows* (pp. 293–312). New York: Guilford.

Miller, W. R., & Rollnick, S. (2002). *Motivational interviewing: Preparing people for change* (2nd ed.). New York: Guilford.

Miller, W. R., Rollnick, S., & Moyers, T. (1998). *Motivational interviewing: Professional training series*. Albuquerque, NM: University of New Mexico.

Mills, C. W. (1959). *The sociological imagination*. New York: Oxford University.

Minnesota Department of Corrections. (2007, June 30). Restorative justice activities. Retrieved May 2008, from http://www.corr.state.mn.us/rj/documents/RJactivities2007.pdf.

Moe, A., and Ferraro, K. (2003). Malign neglect or benign respect: Women's health care in a carceral setting. *Women and Criminal Justice, 14*(4), 53–80.

Mohr, H. (2008, March 2). 13,000 abuse claims in juvie centers. *Macleans*. Retrieved April 2008 from http://www.macleans.ca/article.jsp?content=w030386A.

Morgan, C., Rigaud, J., & Taylor, S. (1990). Treatment for sexual trauma. *The Professional Counselor, 1*, 31–35.

Morris, N. (2007, March 14). The big question: Should women's prisons be closed? *The Independent* (UK). Retrieved January 2008, from http://news.independent.co.uk.uk/crime/article.

Morris, N. (2009, November 2). Record numbers of women imprisoned. *The Independent* (UK). Retrieved from http://www.independent.co.uk/news/uk/home-news/record-numbers-of-women-imprisoned-1813174.html.

Morrissey, J., & Meyer, P. (2005, July). Extending assertive community treatment to criminal justice settings. *The National GAINS Center*. Retrieved from http://www.naco.org/Content/ContentGroups/Programs_and_Projects/Criminal_Justice/FINALACTfactSheet606.pdf.

Mothers in prison. *Woman's hour*. (2001, November 20). Retrieved July 2009, from http://www.bbc.co.uk/radio4/womanshour/2001_47_tue_03.shtml.

Mueser, K., Noordsy, D., Drake, R., & Fox, L. (2003). *Integrated treatment for dual disorders: A guide to effective practice*. New York: Guilford.

Mullins, C. W., Wright, W. R., & Jacobs, B. A. (2004). Gender, street life and criminal retaliation. *Criminology, 42*, 911–940.

Mummert, M. (2007, November 1). The war on drugs' war on families. *Unitarian Universalist, 11*(1). Retrieved from http://www.uuworld.org/ideas/articles/50586.shtml.

Mumola, C., & Karlberg, J. (2006, October). *Drug use and dependence, state and federal prisoners, 2004*. Washington, DC: U.S. Department of Justice, Bureau of Justice Statistics.

National Center on Addiction and Substance Abuse at Columbia University (CASA) (2003, September 16). *Reducing teen smoking can cut marijuana use significantly*. Retrieved November 2003, from www.casacolumbia.org/newsletter1457.

National Institute of Corrections. (2006, September). *Women offender case management model*. Prepared by Orbis Partners, Ottawa, Canada. Retrieved June 2009, from http://nicic.org/Downloads/PDF/Library/021814.pdf.

National Institute of Corrections. (2008, May). *Technical assistance and training to implement a case management model for women offenders.* Retrieved June 2009, from http://community.nicic.org/blogs/nic/2008_28_5_WOCMM_RFA.pdf.

National Institute of Health. (2009, May 7). *Director's page: Nora Volkow.* Washington, DC: National Institute on Drug Abuse. Retrieved June 2009, from http://www.nida.nih.gov/about/welcome/volkowpage.html.

National Institute of Justice. (1999). *Adolescent girls: The role of depression in the development of delinquency.* Washington, DC: U.S. Department of Justice. Retrieved October 2007, from http://www.ncjrs.gov/pdffiles1/fs000244.pdf.

National Institute of Justice. (2006, June). *Drug courts: The second decade.* Retrieved May 2008, from.http://www.ncjrs.gov/pdffiles1/nij/211081.pdf.

National Institute of Justice. (2008, February). *Drug courts.* U.S. Department of Justice. Retrieved May 2009, from http://www.ojp.usdoj.gov/nij/topics/courts/drug-courts/welcome.htm.

National Institute on Drug Abuse. (2006). *Principles of drug abuse treatment for criminal justice populations: A research-based guide.* NIH Publication No. 06–5316. Rockville, MD: Author.

National Institute on Drug Abuse. (2007, August 22). NIDA addiction research news. *NIDA News Scan.* Retrieved June 2009, from http://www.nih.gov/news/pr/aug2007/nidanews_08222007.pdf.

National Institute on Drug Abuse. (2008, July 22). *A cognitive-behavioral approach: Treating cocaine addiction.* Washington, DC: Author. Retrieved June 2009, from http://www.nida.nih.gov/TXManuals/CBT/CBT5.html.

National Juvenile Justice Networking Forum. (2007, June 14). *Girls study group.* Research Triangle Institute, Washington, DC: Retrieved October 2007, from http://girlsstudygroup.rti.org/docs/GSG_NJJNC_June_2007.pdf.

National Youth Gang Center. (2007). *National youth gang survey analysis.* Retrieved November 2007, from http://www.iir.com/nygc/nygsa/.

Nelson, V. (1993). Prostitution: Where racism and sexism intersect. *Michigan Journal of Gender and Law, 1,* 81–89.

Newman, B., & Newman, P. (2008). *Development through life: A psychosocial approach.* Belmont, CA: Wadsworth.

Niebuhr, R. (1934, 1987). *The essential Reinhold Niebuhr: Selected essays and addresses,* R. M. Brown (Ed.), p. 251. New Haven, CT: Yale University.

Nolan, P. (2009, July 27). *Justice fellowship: Combating prison rape.* Correspondence sent to the Prison Fellowship listserv including K. van Wormer.

Obeidallah, D., & Earls, F. (1999). *Adolescent girls: The role of depression in the development of delinquency* (FS000244). Washington, DC: U.S. Government Printing Office, National Institute of Justice.

O'Brien, P., & Young, D. (2006). Challenges for formerly incarcerated women: A holistic approach to assessment. *Families in Society, 87*(3), 359–366.

Office of Juvenile Justice and Delinquency Prevention. (2009, April). *Juvenile arrests 2007.* Washington, DC: U.S. Department of Justice.

Office of Performance Evaluations. (2003, February). *Programs for incarcerated mothers*. State of Idaho Legislature. Retrieved December 2006, from www.legislature .idaho.gov/ope.

O'Hanlon, B., & Rowan, T. (2003). *Solution oriented therapy for chronic and severe mental illness*. New York: Norton.

Ohio Department of Rehabilitation and Correction. (2006, November). *Best practices tool-kit: Gender-responsive strategies*. Columbus, OH: Department of Rehabilitation and Correction.

Okamoto, S., & Chesney-Lind, M. (2003). What do we do with girls? In A. Roberts (Ed.), *Critical issues in crime and justice* (2nd ed., pp. 244–252). Thousand Oaks, CA: Sage.

Olson, D., Olson-Sigg, A., & Larson, P. (2008). *The couple checkup*. Nashville, TN: Thomas Nelson.

O'Neill, J. V. (2000, March). Drugs: Pregnancy brief filed. *NASW News*, p. 7.

Orenstein, P. (1994). *Schoolgirls*. New York: Doubleday.

Owen, B. (1998). *In the mix: Struggle and survival in a women's prison*. New York: State University of New York.

Oxford Dictionary. (2007). *The shorter Oxford English dictionary*. New York: Oxford University.

Pace, P. (2006, March). Breaking the mom/daughter prison cycle. *National Association of Social Workers News, 51*(3), 4. Retrieved June 2008, from http://www.utexas .edu/ugs/uls/pdf/nasw_article.pdf.

Pagnozzi, A. (1999, June 15). Prison rape too severe a penalty. *Hartford Courant*.

Palmer, J. (2008, April 14). Traders' raging hormones cause stock market swings. *New Scientist*. Retrieved from http://www.newscientist.com/article/dn13664-traders-raging-hormones-cause-stock-market-swings.html?feedId=online-news_rss20.

Paltrow, L. M. (2004, April 5). The pregnancy police. *AlterNet*. Retrieved August 2007, from www.alternet.org.

Parsons, L., & Osherson, D. (2001). New evidence for distinct right and left brain systems for deductive versus probabilistic reasoning. *Cerebral Cortex, 11*(10), 954–965.

Patton, P., & Morgan, M. (2002, July). *How to implement Oregon's guidelines for effective gender-responsive programming for girls* (pp. 7–10). Retrieved June 2008, from http://www.oregon.gov/OCCF/Documents/JCP/GenderSpecific.pdf.

Peele, S. (1976). *Love and addiction*. New York: Signet.

Petersilia, J. (2003). *When prisoners come home: Parole and prisoner reentry*. New York: Oxford University.

Pettway, C. (2006, November). *Best practices tool-kit: Gender responsive strategies*. Columbus: Ohio Department of Rehabilitation and Correction.

Pfeiffer, M. B. (2007). *Crazy in America: The hidden tragedy of our criminal mentally ill*. New York: Carroll & Graf.

Pipher, M. (1994). *Reviving Ophelia: Saving the selves of adolescent girls*. New York: Ballantine.

Pollack, S. (2004). Anti-oppressive social work practice with women in prison: Discursive reconstructions and alternative practices. *British Journal of Social Work, 34*, 693–707.

Pollack, S. (2005). Taming the shrew: Regulating prisoners through women-centered mental health programming. *Critical Criminology, 13*, 71–87.

Pollock, J. M. (1998). *Counseling women in prison.* Thousand Oaks, CA: Sage

Pollock, J. M. (1999). *Criminal women.* Cincinnati, OH: Anderson.

Pollock, J. M., & Davis, S. M. (2005). The continuing myth of the violent female offender. *Criminal Justice Review, 30*(1), 5–29.

Pomeroy, E., Rountree, M., & Parrish, D. (2006). Best practices with HIV infected/affected incarcerated women. In D. W. Springer & A. R. Roberts (Eds.), *Handbook of forensic mental health with victims and offenders* (pp. 467–490). New York: Springer.

Prejean, H. (1994). *Dead man walking.* New York: Vintage.

Prejean, H. (2000, March 17). Speech before the Catholic Peace Mission, Des Moines, Iowa.

Prendergast, M. (2009, April). Interventions to promote successful re-entry among drug-abusing parolees. *Addiction Science and Clinical Practice*, 4–13.

Prochaska, J., & DiClemente, C. C. (1983). Stages and processes of self-change of smoking: Toward an integrative model of change. *Journal of Consulting and Clinical Psychology, 51*, 390–395.

Prochaska, J., & Norcross, J. (2007). *Systems of psychotherapy: A transtheoretical analysis* (6th ed.). Belmont, CA: Wadsworth.

Project MATCH Research Group. (1993). Project MATCH: Rationale and methods for a multisite clinical trial matching patients to alcoholism treatment. *Alcoholism: Clinical and Experimental Research, 17*, 1130–1145.

Pugh-Lilly, A., Neville, H., & Poulin, K. (2001). In protection of ourselves: Black girls' perceptions of self-reported delinquent behaviors. *Psychology of Women Quarterly, 25*, 145–154.

Puzzanchera, C. (2009, April). Juvenile arrests, 2007. Office of Juvenile Justice and Delinquency Prevention (OJJDP). *Juvenile Justice Bulletin* (Washington, DC: Office of Juvenile Justice and Delinquency Prevention.) Retrieved from www.ncjrs.gov/pdffiles1/ojjdp/225344.pdf.

Quaker Council on European Affairs. (2007). *Women in prison.* Retrieved May 2008, from http://qcea.quaker.org/prison/Final%20Report%20Part1.pdf.

Raeder, M. (2005, Spring). A primer on gender-related issues that affect female offenders. *Criminal Justice, 20*(1), 5–21.

Rahman, Q., & Wilson, G. D. (2003). Large sexual-orientation differences in performance on mental notation and judgment of line orientation tasks. *Neuropsychology, 17*(1), 25–31.

Rand, M. (2008). *Criminal victimization, 2007.* Washington, DC: Bureau of Justice Statistics. Retrieved from http://www.prisonandjail.org/bjs/pub/pdf/cv07.pdf.

Rasche, C. (2003). Cross-sex supervision of incarcerated women and the dynamics of staff sexual misconduct. In B. Bloom (Ed.), *Gendered justice: Addressing female offenders* (pp. 141–172). Durham, NC: Academic.

Rasche, C. (2007). The dislike of female offenders among correctional officers: Need for specialized training. In R. Muraskin (Ed.), *It's a crime: Women and justice* (4th ed., pp. 689–706). Upper Saddle River, NJ: Prentice-Hall.

Ratey, J. (May/June, 1997). Out of the shadows. *Psychology Today*, 46–80.

Rathbone, C. (2005). *A world apart: Women, prison and life behind bars.* New York: Random House.

Rauch, L. (2006, July 14). Vegas sex workers demand rights, respect. *USA Today*.

Rawls, J. (1971). *A theory of justice.* Cambridge, MA: Harvard University.

Reinitz, J. (2006, May 8). *Drug court.* Waterloo/Cedar Falls Courier (Iowa). Retrieved from http://www.wcfcourier.com/news/metro/article_72658b24-ae0b-5ce1-9fec-c63997d7e2ce.html.

Rekart, M. (2005, December 17). Sex-work harm reduction. *The Lancet, 366,* 2123–2135.

Reuter, P., & Bushway, S. (2007). Revisiting incapacitation: Can we generate new estimates? *Journal of Qualitative Criminology, 23*(4), 259–265.

Rice, S., & Associates (2003). *Providing a promising future for Nevada's girls: A statewide gender specific services plan.* Nevada Juvenile Justice Program Office. Retrieved July 2009, from http://www.dcfs.state.nv.us/Juvenile/GenderBook.pdf.

Richie, B. E. (1996). *Compelled to crime: The gender entrapment of battered black women.* New York: Routledge.

Ringrose, J. (2006). A new universal mean girl: Examining the social regulation of a new feminine pathology. *Feminism & Psychology, 16,* 405.

Robbins, S. P., Chatterjee, P., & Canda, E. (2006). *Contemporary human behavior theory* (2nd ed.). Boston: Allyn & Bacon.

Roberts, A. R. (2007). Domestic violence continuum, forensic assessment and crisis intervention. *Families in Society, 88*(1), 42–54.

Roderick, L. (1988). *If you see a dream.* Song retrieved December 2007, from http://www.libbyroderick.com/Lyrics. Reprinted with permission.

Rodriguez, N., & Griffin, M. (2005, November). *Gender differences in drug market activities.* Unpublished federally funded grant final report. Retrieved July 2009, from http://www.ncjrs.gov/App/Publications/abstract.aspx?ID=233440.

Rogers, C.R. (1951). *Client-centered therapy.* Boston: Houghton Mifflin.

Ross, S. (2006, February). Why meth? Why here? The story of meth in the Ozarks. *Ozarks Magazine,* 17.

Rowe, C. (2004, May 13). Violence among girls on the rise. *Seattle Post-Intelligencer Reporter.* Retrieved June 2009, from http://www.seattlepi.com/local/173133_girlfights13.html.

Rowley, T. (2003). Hair chronicles. In W. Lamb (Ed.), *Couldn't keep it to myself: Wally Lamb and the women of York correctional institution* (pp. 95–111). New York: Regan Books.

Royce, J. E., & Scatchley, D. (1996). *Alcoholism and other drugs* (2nd ed). New York: Free Press.

Sagatun-Edwards, I. (2007). Legal and social welfare response to substance abuse during pregnancy. In R. Muraskin (Ed.), *It's a crime: Women and justice* (4th ed., pp. 346–362). Upper Saddle River, N.J.: Prentice Hall.

Saleebey, D. (2001). *Human behavior and social environments: A biopsychosocial approach.* New York: Columbia University.

Saleebey, D. (2006). Introduction: Power in the people. In D. Saleebey (Ed.), *The strengths perspective in social work practice* (pp. 1–24). Boston: Allyn & Bacon.

Saleebey, D. (2009). *The strengths perspective in social work practice* (5th ed.). Boston: Allyn & Bacon.

Salina, D., Lesondak, L., Razzano, L. & Weilbaecher, A. (2008). Co-occurring mental disorders among incarcerated women. *Journal of Offender Rehabilitation, 45* (1/2), 207–225.

Samenow, S. (1984). *Inside the criminal mind.* Bethel, CT: Crown.

Samenow, S. (2004). *Inside the criminal mind, revised and updated.* Bethel, CT: Crown.

Sanville, J. (Ed.) (2003). *Therapies with women in transition.* Madison, CT: International Universities Press.

Sarnikar, S., Sorensen, T., & Oaxaca, R. (2007, June). *Do you receive a lighter prison sentence because you are a woman? An economic analysis of federal criminal sentencing guidelines.* IZA Discussion Paper No. 2870. Retrieved July 2009, from http://ssrn.com/abstract=999358.

Schaffner, L. (2006). *Girls in trouble with the law.* New Brunswick, NJ: Rutgers University.

Schanzenbach, M. (2005). Racial and sex disparities in prison sentences. *Journal of Legal Studies, 34,* 57–92.

Schulberg, D. (2007). Dying to get out: The execution of females in the post-Furman era of the death penalty in the United States. In R. Muraskin (Ed.), *It's a crime: Women and justice* (pp. 572–591). Upper Saddle River, NJ: Prentice Hall.

Schulz, M. L. (2005). *The new feminine brain: How women can develop their inner strengths, genius, and intuition.* New York: Free Press.

Schwartz, I., Steketee, M., & Schneider, V. (2004). Federal juvenile justice policy and the incarceration of girls. In M. Chesney-Lind & L. Pasko (Eds.), *Girls, women and crime* (pp. 115–127).Thousand Oaks, CA: Sage.

Schwartz, J. M., & Begley, S. (2003). *The mind and the brain: Neuroplasticity and the power of mental force.* New York: Regan Books.

Severance, T. (2004). The prison lesbian revisited. *Journal of Gay and Lesbian Social Services, 17*(3), 39–57.

Sharry, J., Darmody, M., & Madden, B. (2002). A solution-focused approach to working with clients who are suicidal. *British Journal of Guidance & Counselling, 30,* 383–399.

Shaw, M. (1996). Is there a feminist future for women's prisons? In R. Matthews and P. F. Francis (Eds.), *Prisons 2000: An international perspective on the current state and future of imprisonment* (pp. 179–200). New York: St. Martin's.

Shaywitz, B., & Shaywitz, S. (1995). Sex differences in the functional organization of the brain for language. *Nature, 373*, 607–609.

Shaywitz, S. (2003). *Overcoming dyslexia.* New York: Knopf.

Sherman, F. T. (2005). *Pathways to juvenile detention reform—Detention reform and girls.* Vol. 13. Baltimore, MD: Annie E. Casey Foundation. Retrieved July 2009, from http://www.ojjdp.ncjrs.gov/ojstatbb/nr2006/downloads/chapter3.pdf.

Shrinking the prison population. (2009, May 10). *New York Times*, p. A22.

Siegal, N. (2004). Stopping abuse in prison. In B. R. Price & N. Sokoloff (Eds.), *The current justice and women* (pp. 275–279). Boston: McGraw-Hill.

Simpson, S., Yahner, J., & Dugan, L. (2008). Understanding women's pathways to jail: Analysing the lives of incarcerated women. *Australian and New Zealand Journal of Criminology, 41*(1), 84–109.

Skiffer, L. T. (2009). *How black female offenders explain their crime and describe their hopes: A case study of inmates in a California prison.* Lewiston, NY: Edwin Mellen Press.

Smith, B. (2006). Sexual abuse of women in United States prisons: A modern corollary of slavery. *Fordham Urban Law Journal, 33*(2), 571–607.

Smith, D., Leve, L., & Chamberlain, P. (2006). Adolescent girls' offending and health-risk sexual behavior: The predictive role of trauma. *Child Maltreatment, 11*(4), 346–353.

Snyder, H., & Sickmund, M. (2006). *Juvenile offenders and victims: 2006 national report.* Washington, DC: U.S. Department of Justice, Office of Justice Programs, Office of Juvenile Justice and Delinquency Prevention.

Sommers, C. H. (2000). *The war against boys: How misguided feminism is harming our young men.* New York: Simon & Schuster.

Sorbello, L., Eccleston, L., Ward, T., & Jones, R. (2002). Treatment needs of female offenders: A review. *Australian Psychologist, 37*(3), 198–205.

Spear, L. (2000). Modeling adolescent development and alcohol use in animals. *Alcohol Research & Health, 24*(2), 115–123.

Spjeldnes, S., & Goodkind, S. (2009). Gender differences and offender reentry: A review of the literature. *Journal of Offender Rehabilitation, 48*, 314–335.

Springer, D. W., McNeece, C. A., Arnold, A. (2003). *Substance abuse treatment for criminal offenders.* Washington, DC: American Psychological Association.

Springer, D. W., et al. (2007). *Transforming juvenile justice in Texas: A framework for action.* Blue Ribbon Task Force Report. Austin: University of Texas at Austin, School of Social Work.

Stam, R. (2007). PTSD and stress sensitization: A tale of brain and body: Part 1: Human studies. *Neuroscience & Biobehavioral Reviews, 31*(4), 530–557.

Stanton, S. (2005). Prison ministry rewarding opportunity. *The Catholic Mirror* (Des Moines, IA.). Retrieved from http://www.dmdiocese.org/files/documents/436_june,%202005%20for%20web2.pdf.

State considering prison nurseries (2007, February 27). *Charleston Gazette* (South Carolina). Retrieved January 2008, from http:www.wvgazettemail.com.

State won't pay for prisoner to have abortion. (1999, February 7). Waterloo-Cedar Falls *Courier Journal* (Iowa). Retrieved from www.courierjournal.com/localnnews/1999/9nordland43902/07.

Steele, R. (2008, May 1). Drug court reclaims lives. Waterloo, Iowa, KWWL Television. Retrieved May 2008, from KWWL.com.

Steffensmeier, D., & Schwartz, J. (2004). Trends in female criminality: Is crime still a man's world? In B. Price & N. Sokoloff (Eds.), *The criminal justice system and women* (3rd ed., pp. 95–111). Boston: McGraw-Hill.

Steffensmeier, D., Zhong, H., Ackerman, J., Schwartz, J., & Agha, S. (2006). Gender gap trends for violent crimes, 1980 to 2003: A UCR-NCVS comparison. *Feminist Criminology, 1,* 72–98.

Stein, B. (1996, July). Life in prison: Sexual abuse. *The Progressive,* 23–24.

Stolzenberg, L., & D'Alessio, S. J. (1997). Impact of prison crowding on male and female imprisonment rates in Minnesota: A research note. *Justice Quarterly, 14*(4), 793–809.

Stosny, S. (2008). *Love without hurt: Turning your resentful, angry or emotional abusive relationship into a compassionate loving one.* Cambridge, MA: De Capo.

Stout, K. D., & McPhail, B. (1998). *Confronting sexism and violence against women: A challenge for social work.* New York: Longman.

Strand, S., & Belfrage, H. (2005). Gender differences in psychopathy in a Swedish offender sample. *Behavioral Sciences and the Law, 23,* 837–850.

Strauss, V. (2008, May 20). No crisis for boys in schools, study says. *Washington Post.*

Strong, J. (2008, January 19). Sex with inmates gets former jailer 8 years in prison. *Des Moines Register* (Iowa).

Substance Abuse and Mental Health Services Administration. (1999). *TIP 35: Enhancing motivation for clients in substance abuse treatment.* Rockville, MD: Author. Retrieved May 2008, from http://www.ncbi.nlm.nih.gov/books/bv.fcgi?rid=hstat5.chapter.61302.

Substance Abuse and Mental Health Services Administration. (2005). *Substance abuse treatment for adults in the criminal justice system. A treatment improvement protocol (TIP) 44.* Washington, DC: U.S. Department of Health and Human Services.

Substance Abuse and Mental Health Services Administration. (2006). Incarceration vs. treatment: Drug courts help. *SAMHSA News, 14*(2). Retrieved August 2007, from www.samhsa.gov/samhsa_news.

Sudbury, J. (2004). Women of color, globalization, and the politics of incarceration. In B. Price & N. Sokoloff (Eds.), *The criminal justice system and women* (3rd ed., pp. 219–234). Boston: McGraw-Hill.

Sydney, L. (2005). *Gender-responsive strategies for women offenders.* U.S. Department of Justice, National Institute of Corrections. Retrieved December 2008, from http://nicic.org/pubs/2005/020419.pdf.

Talvi, S. (2007. *Women behind bars: The crisis of women in the U.S. prison system.* Emeryville, CA: Seal.

Tate, C. (2004, August 5). *LeTourneau, Mary Kay*. HistoryLink.org. Free online ency-
clopedia of Washington state history. Retrieved from http://www.historylink.org/
index.cfm?DisplayPage=output.cfm&file_id=5727.

Tavris, C. & Aronson, E. (2008). *Mistakes were made (but not by me): Why we justify foolish beliefs, bad decisions, and hurtful acts*. Orlando, FL: Harcourt
Books.

Taylor, T. (2001). *Treating female sex offenders and standards for educational training
in marriage and family therapy programs*. Unpublished research paper.

Teplin, L., Abram, K., McClelland, G., Mericle, A., Dulcan, M. & Washburn, J.
(2006). *Psychiatric disorders of youth in detention*. Washington, DC: U.S.
Department of Justice. Retrieved October 2007, from www.ojp.usdoj.gov/ojjdp.

Tyre, P. (2006, January 30). The trouble with boys. *Newsweek, 44*–53.

United Kingdom Parliament. (2004, October 28). Women in prison. Debate, House
of Lords, London. Retrieved July 2009, from http://www.publications.parliament
.uk/pa/ld200304/ldhansrd/vo041028/text/4102 8-16.htm.

Unruh, D., & Bullis, M. (2005). Female and male juvenile offenders with disabilities:
Differences in the barriers to their transition to the community. *Behavioral Disorders, 30*(2), 105–117.

University of Washington. Anti-social behavior in girls predicts adolescent depression
seven years later. (2009, February 18). *Science Daily*. Retrieved June 2009, from
http://www.sciencedaily.com/releases/2009/02/090217141538.

U.S. Department of Justice. (2005, May 13). *Sex abuse of federal inmates by guards;* "A
significant problem." Office of Inspector General. Retrieved December 2006, from
www.november.org.

U.S. Department of Justice. (2008, May). *Girls study group. Violence by teenage girls*.
Washington, DC: Office of Justice Programs. http://girlsstudygroup.rti.org/docs/
OJJDP_GSG_Violence_Bulletin.pdf.

U.S. Department of Justice. (2009). *Girls study group. Resilient girls: Factors that
protect against delinquency*. Office of Justice Programs. Retrieved May 2009, from
http://www.ncjrs.gov/pdffiles1/ojjdp/220124.pdf.

U.S. teacher sex epidemic spreading across planet. (2005, December 14). *WorldNet-
Daily*. Retrieved December 2007, from http://www.worldnetdaily.com/news/article
.asp?ARTICLE_ID=47895.

Valandra (2007). Reclaiming their lives and breaking free: An Afrocentric approach to
recovery from prostitution. *Affilia, 22*, 195–208.

Van Den Bergh, N. (Ed.). (1995). *Introduction: Feminist practice in the 21st century*.
Washington, DC: NASW Press.

Vandiver, D. M. (2006). Female sex offenders. In R. D. M. Anulty & M. M. Burnette
(Eds.), *Sex and sexuality* (Vol. 3, pp. 47–80). Westport, CT: Praeger.

Van Voorhis, P. (2005). Classification of women offenders: Gender-responsive approaches
to risk/needs assessment. *Community Corrections Report, 12*(2), 19–20, 26–27.

Van Voorhis, P., Braswell, M., & Lester, D. (2000). *Correctional counseling and rehabilitation* (4th ed.). Cincinnati, OH: Anderson.

van Wormer, K. (1979). *Sex-role behavior in a women's prison: An ethnological analysis*. San Francisco: R & E Research Associates.

van Wormer, K. (2001). *Counseling female offenders and victims: A strengths-restorative approach*. New York: Springer.

van Wormer, K. (2004). *Confronting oppression, restoring justice: From policy analysis to social action*. Alexandria, VA: Council of Social Work Education (CSWE).

van Wormer, K. (2007). *Human behavior and the social environment, micro level: Individuals and families*. New York: Oxford University.

van Wormer, K., and Bartollas, C. (2010). *Women and the criminal justice system* (3rd ed.). Boston: Allyn & Bacon.

van Wormer, K., & Davis, D. R. (2008). *Addiction treatment: A strengths perspective*. Belmont, CA: Thomson.

van Wormer, K., & Kaplan, L. (2006). Results of a national survey of wardens in women's prisons: The case for gender-specific treatment. *Women & Therapy, 29*(1/2), 133–151.

van Wormer, K., & Roberts, A. R. (2009). *Death by domestic violence: Preventing the murders and the murder-suicides*. Westport, CT: Praeger.

Vines, G. (1999, November 29). The gene in the bottle. *New Scientist*, 39–43.

Violence Policy Center. (2006). *American roulette: The untold story of murder-suicide in the United States*. Retrieved July 2007, from www.vpc.org/studyndx.htm.

Vito, G., Maahs, J., & Holmes, R. (2007). *Criminology: Theory, research and policy*. Boston: Jones & Bartlett.

Walker, L., Sakai, T., & Brady, K. (2006). Restorative circles—A reentry planning process for Hawaii inmates. *Federal Probation, 70*(1), 33–37.

Wallace, B. (2005). *Making mandated treatment work*. Lanham, MD: Jason Aronson.

Walmsley, R. (2007). *World prison population list* (6th ed.). London: International Centre for Prison Studies.

Walsh, T. C. (1999). Psychopathic and nonpsychopathic violence among alcoholic offenders. *International Journal of Offenders and Comparative Criminology, 43*(1), 34–48.

The war on crack retreats, still taking prisoners (1999, February 28). *New York Times*. Retrieved from http://www.nytimes.com/1999/02/28/us/war-on-crack-retreats-still-taking-prisoners.html.

Websdale, N., & Chesney-Lind, M. (2004). Doing violence to women: Research synthesis on the victimization of women. In B. Price & N. Sokoloff (Eds.), *The criminal justice system and women* (pp. 303–322). Boston: McGraw-Hill.

Webster, J. (1998, October 11). Spain fights crime with luxury prisons. *Electronic Telegraph* (UK). Retrieved from http://www.telegraph.co.uk.

Wells, D., & Bright, L. (2005). Drug treatment and reentry for incarcerated women. *Corrections Today, 67*, 1–2.

Wells, W., & DeLeon-Granados, W. (2004, June). The intimate partner homicide decline: Disaggregated trends, theoretical explanations, and policy implications. *Criminal Justice Policy Review, 15*(2), 229–246.

West, H. C., & Sabol, W. (2009, April). *Prison inmates at midyear 2008*. Bureau of Justice Statistics. Washington, DC: U.S. Department of Justice.

Williams, M. B., & Poijula, S. (2002). *The PTSD workbook: Simple, effective techniques for overcoming traumatic stress symptoms.* Oakland, CA: New Harbinger.

Williams, M. B., & Rikard, R. V. (2004). Marginality or neglect: An exploratory study of policies and programs for aging female inmates. *Women and Criminal Justice,* 15(3/4), 121–141.

Wilson, K., & Anderson, S. C. (1997). Empowering female offenders: Removing barriers to community-based practice. *Affilia: Journal of Women and Social Work,* 12(3), 342–359.

Wirpsa, L. (1998). Trying to make justice work for women. *National Catholic Reporter,* 34(30), 12–14.

Women in Prison. (2008, April). *Prison Reform International.* Retrieved from www .penalreform.org/women-in-prison.html.

Women just as violent as men: Survey: Australia. (2006, August, 20). *The Age.* Retrieved September 2007, from www.theage.com.au/news/National/Women-just-as-violent-as-men-survey/2006/08/20/1156012393952.html.

Woolfenden, J. (1997). Open space: A bereavement and loss group in a closed women's prison. *Psychodynamic Counseling,* 3(1), 77–82.

Wrangham, R., & Peterson, D. (1996). *Demonic males: Apes and the origins of human violence.* Boston: Houghton Mifflin.

Yochelson, S., & Samenow, S. E. (1976). *The criminal personality, Vol. I: A profile for change.* New York: Jason Aronson.

Zahn, M. (2007). The causes of girls' delinquency and their program implications. *Family Court Review,* 45(3), 456–465.

Zavlek, S., & Maniglia, R. (2007). Developing correctional facilities for female juvenile offenders: Design and programmatic considerations. *Corrections Today,* 69(4), 58–63.

Zehr, H. (2002). *The little book of restorative justice.* Intercourse, PA: Good Books.

INDEX